THE
ONLY GIRL
IN THE CAR

THE
ONLY GIRL
IN THE CAR

A Memoir

Kathy Dobie

The Dial Press

THE ONLY GIRL IN THE CAR
A Dial Press Book / March 2003

Published by The Dial Press
A division of Random House, Inc.
New York, New York

Book design by Virginia Norey

The Dial Press® is a registered trademark of Random House, Inc.,
and the colophon is a trademark of Random House, Inc.

Library of Congress Cataloging in Publication Data
Dobie, Kathy.
The only girl in the car / Kathy Dobie.
p. cm.
ISBN 0-385-31880-4
1. Hamden (Conn.)—Memoir. 2. Teenage girls—Memoir. I. Title.

PS3604.O25 O55 2003
813'.6—dc21   2002029928

Manufactured in the United States of America
Published simultaneously in Canada

10 9 8 7 6 5 4 3 2 1

*To James, who from the moment he heard this story
said that one day I must write it down*

All the names have been changed,
except for Roscoe, Craig, Linda, Leslie, Mrs. Colasanto,
Chris, and the members of the DeAngelis family and my own.

THE
ONLY GIRL
IN THE CAR

Prologue

IN THE SPRING OF MY FOURTEENTH YEAR, THE EARTH BLOSSOMED with men and boys, staggered under the weight and richness of their profusion. They were everywhere. Driving cranes alongside the highway, bagging groceries in the supermarket, mowing lawns, filling up our station wagon with gas, taking my father's money, giving him directions. They wore bandannas and their chests shone with sweat; they wore suits and their thighs were thick under the soft, hot cloth.

In the supermarket, my eye found the restless son; at the picnic grounds, the sullen brother hanging back, slouching in all that sunshine. From the backseat of my father's car, I scanned I-95. Under the signs that said "New York" and "New Haven," an endless river of men in trucks and cars. Men at the wheel. A man with his face in shadow, revealing only an arm and a slice of downy T-shirt. The arm was tanned with a strand of leather tied around the wrist. The hand beat out a tune on the van door. The cigarette was thrown sharp and hard, like a spear, down into the speeding pavement. Sparks flew. Every boy was an orphan; every man, unfulfilled.

One Saturday that following September, I put on my candy-striped halter top, bell-bottom jeans, and platform shoes, went out the front door of my parents' house, and sat myself down in the middle of the green, green lawn. I'd made a decision. I was going to lose my virginity.

Our front lawn faced the intersection of Treadwell and Clifford. There was a traffic light by then and enough cars to make things interesting. The grass looked silky, but it was sharp and sticky against my skin. Our dog was at my side, clumsy, faithful Sebastian, named after the butler in the TV show *Family Affair*. He was a miniature Shetland sheepdog with a round, friendly-looking rump and an orange and white coat, like a Creamsicle. His feathery tail swished back and forth across the grass. I stroked and knotted his fur, and waited.

Cars sped by, honking. Boys hissed, whistled, blew kisses, yelled. If they had to wait at a red light, they grew shy, though one boy wagged his tongue at me like a pendulum and then ran it, slowly, up the window.

It was a full-grown man who finally stopped. He did a U-turn, parked in front of the house, and got out. He made his way over to me, long hair swinging. He had a pockmarked face and eyes that pretended friendliness.

Brian was thirty-three. I remember that, because it impressed me that he was the same age as Jesus was when he died on the cross. It seemed right that there should be something so significant about him. It didn't matter that I wasn't attracted to him. He was what other girls would call "sleazy," a loser. He still lived with his mother; he had bad skin; he was picking up fourteen-year-olds. But to see that man's form, tight-jeaned, T-shirted, gliding through the grass, intent on me, and already mine in ways I didn't yet fully understand . . .

He smiled cagily, nodded at the house. "You live here?" And then, "Are your parents home?" He crouched down in the grass and picked at a blade. "Uh . . . so you're just hanging out with your dog?" He circled me with questions, patronizing, nervous as a thief. A jewel out in the open—was there really no one looking? No cop behind a tree, no string attached?

"So, uh, what's your dog's name?"

Slowly, carefully, he reeled me in—or so he thought. He was so sure that was the way it went, he'd missed the obvious: A minute ago he'd been sailing down Treadwell Street, as free as you please, and yet here he was, flung up on the lawn. I hadn't moved an inch.

"So . . . you want to go to the movies sometime?"

"Okay."

"Oh. Uh, good. When?"

That night, he picked me up at my parents' house.

I like to think of myself as having sprung fully formed from that green lawn, coming into the world at fourteen wearing a halter top and platform shoes, like a boy I once saw wearing a python at an outdoor fair, an everyday boy who volunteered from the audience when the man with the python asked if anyone wanted to come up and hold it. The boy jumped right up onto the stage before anyone else had even raised their hand. The snake was thicker than the boy's torso and easily twice his length, but as the man draped it carefully over him, the boy just grinned and widened his stance to take the weight, as if he had always known what to do if a python were set on his shoulders.

Immediately the snake began to wind itself around the boy's body, creeping under his arm and around his waist. When it slipped, the boy hitched it back up over his hip, and then helped it stay there by curling his arm under it. His chin was lifted high, his brown eyes blazing with glory and pride. Not once did he scan the crowd, as children will, looking for someone's approval, an echo to his joy. He seemed motherless, fatherless, a boy out of Mark Twain, a boy who joins circuses or travels west with a pistol and a dog; a boy born to wear a python. That's how I felt at fourteen.

1

A House for Children

LET ME SHOW YOU THE HOUSE OF MY CHILDHOOD. A GRAY HOUSE, oyster gray with white trim, sitting on the intersection of Treadwell and Clifford streets in Hamden, Connecticut, neither grand nor mean, just a solid-looking house with a small backyard, a one-car garage with an orange basketball hoop set above the doors, and tiger lilies languid along the driveway. In the backyard, there's a red-and-green jungle gym and swing set that my parents bought at Sears and my father put together himself, kneeling down in the grass in his shirtsleeves, the instructions spread out in front of him, holding a metal rod in each hand, sweat pouring down his face.

The front yard is moon-shaped and open to the street, giving it a wild and friendly feeling like you might get running down a hill or holding your arms out to someone else running down. On the right side of the house, there's a sunporch with a red-and-green striped awning, which faces Clifford, a fence and a privet hedge. Between the fence and the hedge, a dirt path has been worn through by my brothers, sisters, and me, a shortcut, a children's way to go from front yard to back. The adults must go up the driveway that runs along the other side of the house. There, our blue station wagon is parked under the basketball net.

A white picket fence runs between our house and the house of the family next door, the Wrights, who have a girl named Terry who is my age—eight on the day I'm picturing—and a tomboy. Terry takes trumpet lessons and so does my older brother Bill, and sometimes they take their trumpets and play out of the attic windows to each other, leaning out over the driveway below.

Terry also takes dance classes with me at Miss Marie's Dance Studio on Whitney Avenue. I like ballet, she hates it. Only tap is rough and noisy enough for her. Tap, tap, tap, jump and bang away on the wood floor. Once in ballet class, we had our legs up on the bar and Terry fell over backward. She stayed in the same pose, flat on her back but with one leg up and her toes pointed prettily in the air, did it because she thought it was funny to see Miss Marie and Miss Vera—who didn't give a damn about her—fuss and fuss because they thought she might be hurt, a hopeless dancer but still a tuition-paying daughter of somebody. When I want to play with Terry, I don't ring the doorbell, I stand at the back fence and yell, "Ohhhhh, Terr-eeeeee!" And sometimes to make her laugh I say, "When you're wright, you're wright."

Here's the attic of our house with its slanted, wood-paneled ceilings and the windows tucked under them. There are two bedrooms up here, my sister Cindy's and mine, and our older brothers' room, Michael and Bill's.

In my brothers' room, two of the three windows look out over the intersection of Treadwell and Clifford. It's not much of a view, I suppose, gray and white houses going up along the block, smallish yards, telephone wires looping above the trees like a pencil sketching, a solitary traffic light bobbing above the intersection like a boat on a breeze; but to a child of the suburbs, the view from an attic window is like the view from a castle or a hilltop. Only three floors up but you're as high as almost any high suburban thing, up there with the treetops, the gray roofs and chimneys, the crows, the sparrows, the rain when it's coming down fast before it hits anything.

Michael and Bill have a nubby red carpet in their room, red-and-tan bedspreads, and twin beds that are always made up—we can't go downstairs in the morning without first making our beds. Their desks are already boys' desks, the ink blotters covered with graffiti, the shelves above lined with basketball trophies and not much more, none of the pretty little knickknacks that my sister Cindy and I have collected. Michael's the oldest in the family, a redhead like me, wiry and energetic, and that's his bed by the two windows overlooking the intersection, and his desk next to the third window in the room, the one that looks down onto the backyard with its swing set and jungle gym. Michael's ten and already confident of his place in the world. Or so it seems to me.

After we come home from church on Sunday, Michael makes the rest of us kids play Mass in the dining room—he is the priest and we are the parishioners, standing and kneeling and standing and sitting and kneeling all over again. We call him Captain Catfish because he's the firstborn and because we have a catfish in the tank downstairs that is the same coloring as Michael, an orangy red, like a flame.

Michael gets the window views but Bill, one year younger, blond and blue-eyed, the family wit, if you can be a wit at nine, gets the bigger desk and dresser. My parents try hard to keep things balanced between us.

"I love all of my children equally!" my mother says, so fervently and so often that I feel it should be inscribed in the house somewhere, above the kitchen doorway perhaps.

Here's the bedroom I share with my sister Cindy, who's one year younger than I—our twin beds with their white blankets, our blue-painted desks, hers covered with statues and pictures of owls and mine with bells and dolls. We have only two little windows, and they look out over the driveway and into the attic of Terry Wright's house, so close it seems like the houses might be secretly talking to each other.

A real live hamster lives in a cage on the shelf above Cindy's desk. His name is Mr. H., and when he's not hurrying and snuffling along the sawdust on the cage floor, he's running on the wheel, running and running and running, his long claws clicking on the wheel and the wheel making a rattling, whirring sound. Between his running and the fact that he ate his mate after she ate all her babies, Cindy and I don't like him much, but what can we do? We have to live with this murderer, this monster, feed him pellets and water in the morning, clean his cage on Saturdays, and watch him exercise all day.

The four of us older kids are only one year apart from each other—ten, nine, eight, and seven. We make up a little tribe of our own, a merry band, the Four Musketeers, and the attic is our domain and hideaway.

Up until this year, we all slept together in the boys' bedroom, but then my father and my great-uncle Lance built another room and we were divided, the boys and the girls, a division I think of as not unlike one of God's acts of creation in Genesis, which seem to me to be about making distinctions, separating the day from the night, the land from the sea, sending birds up, fish down.

We're very close, the four of us, and we manage that without really knowing one another. We don't talk about our feelings. We don't know the exact shape of each other's fears and joys, but we know the scent of each other when we sleep, the sharp, sweet smell and rushing sound of one of us peeing in the toilet bowl in the morning, the feel of Michael's stiff curly hair, springy on the palm of my hand, the shape of the whitish scar on Billy's knee where a long sliver of wood pierced it when he went sliding across a wooden floor one day, the sound of Cindy's dreams at night, the murmurs and quickened breath and sudden shouts of "Help! He's getting away! The frog's on the bridge!"

Our closeness is mute and sensual. We're like a pack of wild animals, eating, drinking, running, always running together until we rest together, running up and down the stairs, through all the rooms of the house, out the back door and over the green, green lawn like lions or birds or floods.

In the weeks after our parents separated us, the girls in one room, the boys in the other, we slept with our doors open, not wanting to shut one another out. Michael and Bill sang Cindy and me to sleep at night, or tried to. Mostly they sang church songs, rousing and mournful and not in any particular order, so their dirgelike rendition of

"Swing Low, Sweet Chariot" might be followed with their shouting out, "When the Saints Go Marching In." Cindy and I were so appreciative, and so worried that they wouldn't know how appreciative, that we felt obliged to applaud after each song and call out, "Encore! Encore!" It became what you call a vicious cycle—we couldn't sleep and they couldn't stop singing, and so after a while they gave it up. One night, the bedroom doors seemed to close of their own accord.

Down the stairs we go, to the second floor, where my parents sleep, and little Beth, and where the baby will sleep, too, when he arrives. Beth Ann has a tribe of stuffed animals in her bedroom. She needs a tribe of them, I think, for she is a few years apart from the rest of us and so just a little outside of our merry band. I don't know if she's lonely. I know she's solitary, telling her secrets to her animals and her Mrs. Beasley doll. It makes me feel odd that she has an old lady for a doll, a blue and-white polka-dotted lady, but old nonetheless with an apron and granny spectacles. Who is taking care of who here?

She's four and she will become Mommy's helper once I stop—the oldest girl and then the youngest, each stepping up in her own time to pound the cutlets, peel the carrots, measure the flour, run down to the basement and put the laundry in the dryer.

Beth Ann's real name is Elizabeth Ann. Our parents named her after the newest saint to be canonized, Elizabeth Ann Seton, but from the start they simply called her Beth Ann.

Beth Ann has long blond hair, which my mother or I brush back into a ponytail. The tail makes a corkscrew and bounces up and down just like a spring when she walks. She has tiny features, pink cheeks, blue eyes. This fifth child was born with arthritis in one leg, and before she even turned two, they made her wear a cast and then a brace for a year. So Beth Ann didn't stand and then walk the way other toddlers do. She got as far as standing, and then they put her in a brace and she had to go back down on the ground, pulling herself along with her arms. My father called her a "trouper." When she looked up at me from the floor, all wide blue eyes and pink cheeks, her little lips in a Cupid sort of bow, she looked like a cheerful storybook caterpillar.

Stephen isn't born yet. He's in my mother's belly. It's fall and he won't arrive until the middle of winter.

Let's take a morning, any morning, a school morning in the fall of that year. The second-floor hallway smells of Irish Spring soap and shaving cream. The bathroom door is open and the steam from my father's shower is still tunneling out and filling the cold autumn hallway with moist heat and prickly scent, like the tracks a big animal might leave, for my father has just finished his shower and left to begin dressing. From my parents' bedroom, I can hear bureau drawers being pulled out and slammed shut, their brass pulls clanking with each motion, closet doors opening and closing, the sharp, swift sounds of my father getting ready to go to work, his feet, in shoes now, tapping briskly across the wood floor, a readiness and an energy that puts my sleepiness to shame and thrusts me down the stairs—late, late, I can't be late! I'm always late, it seems, always one step behind where I'm supposed to be.

The hallway stairs lead into the living room, and both are covered in a blue and green shag carpet, an ocean of a carpet, all waving tendrils, lovely on the feet and the source of many games for us children, games I'm beginning to grow out of, like "shark," in which we must hop from one piece of the furniture to the other, never letting our feet touch the sharky sea of the carpet, lest we be eaten alive.

In the kitchen, the light is fluorescent bright on the white linoleum floor and the gray Formica table, and my brothers and sisters are already seated and bent into their cereal bowls, tucked in behind boxes of Cheerios and Kix and Lucky Charms, Michael and Bill and Cindy reading the backs of theirs while they eat, Beth Ann pretending to.

"Hi, honey," my mother says. "Did you have a good sleep?"

She is in her lacy pink nightgown, her green furry robe, her satiny slippers and white athletic socks, and still she shivers. The end of her nose is pink. She has hazel eyes, and her short hair, a brownish blond, is tousled. Her face is young, though varicose veins wind themselves around her slender legs, pushing out knots here and there as if a beautiful blue vine were putting out hard buds.

My mother spends her days in the kingdom of children. There, she is our queen, and also our most lowly servant. She was only nineteen when she married my father, dropping out of college against her mother's wishes, twenty when Michael was born, twenty-one when Bill came along, twenty-three and -four for me and Cindy. Her childhood was the exact opposite of ours; it's as if she was born in another country altogether. She was an only child, and fatherless, too, for her parents separated when she was two years old. Her mother had left her husband and driven halfway across the country from Oklahoma to Connecticut, where her sister Bert was living, and my mother never saw her father again. When she was a girl, she prayed to God for a brother or a sister just so she would have some company. Now, with five of us and another one snuggled inside, she's never alone, but she's shy around other adults, and when we are out among strangers I feel that we, her children, serve to cloak and protect her.

She's allergic to something in the morning air, and while she fixes our lunches and tells us to take our elbows off the table or get our pajama sleeves out of the milk, she furiously rubs the end of her nose and sneezes, always in groups of three, achoo achoo achoo. From behind his cereal box, my brother Bill says, "God bless, God bless, God bless you." And no matter how many times he has said that, and this must be the seven hundredth, my siblings and I marvel at his wit.

We're a grim lot most weekday mornings, though; silent, bleary-eyed, hanging over our cereal bowls like dogs, milk dripping from our mouths. We grip our spoons in our fists like laborers with shovels, digging our way into the day ahead.

For long moments there's no talk, just the sound of the sugar bowl skating back and forth between us like a busy waiter. Michael's knee keeps up a steady beat against the underside of the table. He never stops moving; he's not even aware of it. The table shakes slightly, continuously, jiggling the milk in my bowl until my mother pulls him into consciousness, saying only, "Michael!" For a minute, the table is still and I can hear all their spoons clicking like clocks.

The refrigerator door opening and closing, Michael's knee moving faster and faster, the slurping of milk and ticking of spoons, the faces of my brothers and sisters growing more animated, sharper and brighter as the day outside the window takes its shape—these are the conveyor belts pulling me toward yet another school day.

Is there any way I can stop it? Slow the morning down enough to jump off and stay here at home with *her*? A stomachache, a sore throat, something that I can use like a brake on the hour that is moving me swiftly and surely away from her?

And then in the middle of my anxious deliberations, my father comes shooting into the kitchen in his sharp dark suit, his high forehead lit like a lantern, jaw freshly shaved, calling for his glasses, every day the same question: "Kay! Did you see my glasses?"

In his breast pocket is a monogrammed white handkerchief that Cindy or I would have ironed. He bears the spicy, cold scent of cologne but he's warm, his lips are a schoolboy red, slightly wet when he leans over and kisses me on the top of my forehead. Auburn hair, blue eyes, freckles. He kisses my mother on the mouth and calls out to us, "You guys have a good day at school!" and sails out the back door with a smoking mug of coffee in one hand, an attaché case in the other. The station wagon gives a kick, and then we watch the plume of exhaust smoke sail by the kitchen window, backward down the drive.

It's only a fifteen-minute drive to New Haven and his job at Yale, where he runs the dining halls and food service; he'll get there in ten. He likes to drive fast.

How does he do it? Leave us every day so easily, so, you have to say, triumphantly. It is unimaginable to me that I will ever feel the way he does, so cold, so sure, so hot, so ready.

His leaving is a signal to us kids—now or never. If one of us is going to fake being sick and try to stay home, this is the time to tell my mother about the sore throat or upset stomach. If not, it's time to run upstairs and shower and dress.

I push my cereal bowl away and hold my stomach, but like a waitress who has been given too many tables to serve, my mother cleverly avoids making eye contact. She begins to pack up the cereal boxes, says to the air, "Kids, you're going to be late."

In our attic bedroom, Cindy and I pull on our St. Rita's school uniforms—white blouses and red-and-green plaid jumpers, green knee socks, red ties, and fat, rubber-soled shoes that look like closemouthed bugs when you lace them up.

Cindy's blond hair is cut short, pixie-style, and because of her widow's peak she has half a bang hanging out over her forehead like the brim of a rakishly set hat. Cindy's a tomboy. Almost every girl I know at this point of my life is, though I am not.

My parents and teachers say that I'm a dreamer, a girl with her head in the clouds. "Earth to Kathy! Come in, please!" my father often calls out to me, because I'm a girl who loses hats and mittens and forgets to turn off lights and gets so lost in her imagination that once she even forgot she had the bathwater running until it overflowed. "You'd forget your head altogether if it wasn't attached to your body by its neck," he'll say to me, joking in that fierce way he has sometimes, his blue eyes lit and boring into me. Even my brothers join in the fun. They call me the Absentminded Professor, making me sorry that we went to see that movie, though I liked it when we did.

On the shelf above Cindy's desk, Mr. H. begins his morning run on the wheel, around and around, the whole cage rattling. Cindy and I move in a rush that is by turns nervous and eager, but even with the clock ticking and the hamster racing, we stop for a moment to play a private game of ours, not a game so much as the setting up of a tableau. We call it the Mad Family Band and arrange ourselves side by side in front of the bedroom door, scowling and strumming air guitars and tapping our feet angrily. We twist our heads from side to side, Cindy's bangs flying out each time, and we hum a dark music louder and louder, as we imagine The Family waiting for us downstairs, mad as hell because we're late. "Late, late! For a very important date!" we shriek, and tumble out the door.

Perhaps every child born to a big family feels the same—that the family itself has a personality. To me, The Family was an entity, a being with needs and desires, an appetite all its own. Often those needs and desires were quite different from mine. The Family had to have clean rooms, for instance, and order at the dinner table. It needed our children's prayers at night and our cooperation all day. It had a great appetite for activity, for cheerfulness and busyness, and it would never let me sleep late in the morning or disappear into an afternoon nap. The Family got up early and went off to school and work; it had dinner at six sharp. It did its chores on Saturday, and on Sunday after church it went into action when the call went out—"Saddle up! Grab your towels and sunglasses! We're off to the lake! Last one in the car is a rotten egg!"

"Your family's like the Army!" my best friend in high school, Sylvia, would exclaim. She was impressed by the order, the prescribed chores, the routines that seemed to be written in stone, but she missed the act of devotion involved. For whenever I picked up a dust cloth, or Cindy and I trundled the vacuum cleaner upstairs, singing, "Whistle while you work," I knew I was in service to something much bigger than myself.

And when I would hear someone say our name aloud back then, or even see it printed on an envelope, *The Dobie Family*, a strange and fevered jumble of things would come to my mind—the red and green jungle gym in the backyard and my mother's tiger lilies; my grandfather's gray hat and his nickname for me, Old Bricktop; the mean old man neighbor with his rake; the red stop sign on our corner; the squeaking birds in the trees; the bloodworms in the ground and my brothers dragging them out. In short, everything. It seemed we had only to look at a thing and it became a part of us, a part of who we were. My family astonished me.

2

Chain of Desire

THEY CAME IN THROUGH THE FRONT DOOR TOGETHER, ALL THREE OF them, on a sunny winter's day, my father's large face beaming over my mother's shoulder, my mother returned to us from the hospital, not only alive but wearing a glamorous cherry-colored car coat with bright lipstick to match, and expertly, tenderly cradling a brand-new baby in a blue blanket, the tiniest human being I'd ever seen. A gust of snow swirled up from the steps, showering my mother's stockinged ankles and glittering in the brief seconds before the door was closed. My brothers and sisters were up on their toes trying to get a better look.

"You can all take turns holding him," my mother told us, a smile in her voice. I waited for mine and then I sat down in the living room rocking chair, my brothers and sisters crowded around, as she carefully handed our new little brother to me. I looked down at his sleeping face—his eyelids were purplish and paper-thin, his nose barely more than nostrils, his lips, poked into the air, smaller than a creamer spout. He squirmed once, scrunched his face into a red ball—was he going to cry? what should I do?—and then his face relaxed and he fell back into sleep, his breath not even a whisper. I leaned down and sniffed the top of his head; he smelled like milk and sugar. His hair was so fine and soft it looked like a puff of wind might blow it away, but his fingers were long and skinny and red, a monkey's wrinkled fingers. . . .

"Look at his fingernails!" I cried, and my brothers and sisters leaned in close while my parents smiled.

"You were all that small once," my mother said. Impossible.

When the Baby Stephen was born, the *Hamden Chronicle* reported, "The Dobie household is bursting at the seams with the arrival of . . ." Grandma Dobie, my father's mother, had called the item in. I was nine and I thought I detected a sneer at our fecundity.

I commemorated his birth with a poem, my first: "Now that we have Stephen / The boys and girls are even." When I recited it to my brothers and sisters, Billy looked halfway astonished and then he rubbed my hair, saying roughly, "You're a poet and don't even know it." He was only ten, but the look on his face was that of a proud father.

I was so delighted with that poem, and the fact that my brothers and sisters went around the house loudly repeating it, that I sat down and wrote a letter to God, promising Him I would be a writer when I grew up. I signed it *Your Most Loving and Adoring Servant* and then hid it in the bottom drawer of my dresser with the seashells and plastic saints. This was my secret chapel, a rendezvous point for me and God. At night, I prayed with my head bowed into my chapel drawer.

You would have thought that when the new baby was born I'd feel crowded and pushed aside. Instead, I fell in love.

The day he arrived we would all compete to hold him, but in the weeks and months to come, as his novelty wore off for the others, my own enthusiasm for the Baby Stephen never lessened. Every afternoon, I would rush home from school to be with him and he would crow like a rooster when I came in the door. Sometimes Stephen sucked my thumb instead of his own; sometimes, when I held him on my hip, he hid his soft face inside my hair. *I will be your nest*, I thought. *I'll be your hideaway*. He made me regret every bony part of my little girl's body.

What a relief it was to love physically and with abandon. To touch someone I cared for. To sing him to sleep while rubbing his back and patting his diapered behind. To feel his arms wrapped tightly around my neck and his low giggle in my ear. Extravagant feelings need to be expressed physically, but I hadn't found a way to love like that until Stephen. Just to hold him was a revelation.

"There is no love without exaggeration," Oscar Wilde wrote. I loved my youngest brother without any carefulness. I loved him the way I was taught to love God—with all my heart and soul. And I loved him with my body, too.

I would have liked to pet my mother's face, I think, as I've watched my sister Cindy's children touch and pet and trace hers. But we didn't have that kind of physical intimacy. I never "owned" my mother the way I've seen Cindy's little girls own her, examining her teeth and pulling at her nose like curious monkeys, burrowing their heads into her belly, climbing her legs as if they were a steep hill, the youngest one making Cindy's hand into her "baby," cradling it and singing to it. My sister bathes with her daughters, something we never would've done with our mother. Once when I was a child, I walked into my parents' bedroom when my mother was changing and she turned away abruptly, blushing, covering her bare breasts with her arms "Kathy, you're supposed to knock!" she said in a voice both angry and embarrassed, and I felt confused; it was as if someone had thrown a veil over my eyes, for the room went dark and hazy; her breasts, in that one glimpse, had looked blue.

Sometimes it seemed that the women in my family wore signs that read, "Approach with Caution. Handle with Care." There was something electric and bristling inside each one, and I didn't know when I would set it off. I had to be careful with my mother. That's the way I felt as a child. My love for her felt too aggressive, too bold and clumsy, like a big enthusiastic dog chasing a butterfly. She was delicate, tricky; a puzzle to me. Sometimes she disappeared inside of herself, into a place I didn't know, but thinking she was sad or lonely, I stuck close by her.

At those moments my presence, what I thought of as my affection but was actually my need, was an intrusion—I could feel her tense up, though I didn't know why. It never occurred to me that she needed a break from us children.

And so I became cautious, clever, even devious in my loving of her. Early in the morning, I would take the valentines I'd made for her and hide them in the laundry basket, the frying pan, the broom closet, for her to find after I'd left for school. My love, a kind of haunting. I thought of myself as a giving child, not a hungry one. My mother and I were very much alike. I don't think she liked to see that part of herself in me.

Once, when I was around seven or eight, I remember waking from a nap at the home of my great-aunt Bert and walking down the hall from her bedroom to the kitchen, drawn by the sound of women's voices. I paused in the doorway. There she was, my mother, up on a footstool wearing a sleeveless black-and-white polka-dotted dress my grandmother had bought for her, turning slowly, like a ballerina in a music box, while Bert, who was a professional seamstress, knelt in front of her, sticking pins into the hem. Bert tapped and my mother turned. A pin went in. A tap. A turn.

"What do you think, Elsie?" Bert asked her sister, my grandma Callahan, who lived upstairs in the duplex they'd recently bought together. "A half-inch shorter?"

And Grandma warned, "You don't want it too short or it won't hang right!" Tap, turn. This is how they loved my mother, these two women who together had raised this fatherless child—not with embraces, words, a rush of affection, but with clothes shopping, tapping and turning, making sure she looked just right.

"Hi, honey! Did you sleep?" Mommy asked when she noticed me standing at the door. (The girl on the footstool, the daughter in the new spring dress holding her breath to make her stomach flat, was also my mother; the combined effect was mesmerizing.)

I thought I knew exactly what my mother was feeling up there on the kitchen stool, Grandma watching her as she smoked her Pall Malls, Bert's fingers tapping at her calf and then stroking my mother's thighs as she smoothed down the dress—*What do you think, Elsie?*

How mute and still my mother was as she soaked up their attention, taking in their love secretly, slyly, almost like a thief who was stealing it. She didn't want to ruin the moment.

From a young age, I had learned the unpredictable and sensual joys of passivity. When my mother combed my hair, I sat very still, my scalp rippling with pleasure, warmth moving down my body. The sensation reached a peak when my mother combed my hair absentmindedly, perhaps while answering one of my sisters' questions about her homework or explaining a Cub Scout merit badge to Michael or Bill.

When I was touched without really being noticed, I swooned with pleasure. Sixteen-year-old boys were my destiny.

But in the meantime, I had only these women, my mother's preoccupied attention to my hair or unbuttoned coat, the inadvertent touch of Bert and Grandma fixing my collar, yanking down the hem of my skirt, the secret thrill of being treated like an object, tugged and yanked at and talked about as if I weren't there. "It fits her well around the hips," Bert would say to Grandma as they eyed me in one of the outfits they had bought for me. "What about the shoulders?" Grandma would ask. "It seems a little tight across there." And then they would tell me to lift my arms while they plucked at the dress.

I wouldn't have dreamed of cuddling up to them. Grandma actually squirmed if I hugged her too close or for a few seconds too long. She was not a physical woman and she knew it. Many times she told me that she didn't think she was a very good mother to mine.

"I think your mother needed someone who was more physically affectionate," she would say. And then her watery blue eyes would go bright, her flat, emphatic voice suddenly arch upward. "Do you know my mother never kissed me, Kathy? Not a once!"

She wasn't feeling sorry for herself, not Elsie Callahan. She was an adult in the gratifying grip of a revelation.

"So you could say I *just didn't have the practice*!" she said, rapping the words out in her excitement. "I just didn't know how to be that way with your mother! I never had the knack."

I never got to really touch my grandmother until many years later when she was in her eighties and very sick. Then, one day in the hospital, I massaged her feet and hands with cream and carefully combed her baby-soft hair. She closed her eyes and sighed—never kissed by her mother!—and then, like a small child, drifted off to sleep.

I think when I was a child I felt ashamed of my extravagant feelings and ashamed of my physical nature—can a body have inclinations?—my desire not for sports or climbing trees or wrestling about on the carpet with my brothers and sisters but for acts of devotion and tenderness. Even now, when I love a man, I want to wash his feet.

After we buried my grandmother, the mourners came over to my parents' house for food. There was the usual air of unreality, the half-light, the full plates, the conversation drifting on to other things . . . a family unmoored. By nine o'clock everyone had left but my sisters and me. We had all moved away by then but had come back for the funeral.

My mother and I were alone, cleaning up in the kitchen, when she stopped, a dish towel in her hand, her back against the refrigerator, and asked, "Did she love me?"

She started to cry, her face screwed up, and tears smearing her mascara. All the while she was appealing to me with her eyes. She looked like someone had nailed her to the refrigerator door.

"I feel like I never measured up," she sobbed. Grandma had wanted her to be a college-educated career woman; Grandma had wanted her to lose weight. "I feel like I always disappointed her."

There she was again, the thin-skinned, beseeching little girl my mother could never shake. She was as visible to me when I was a child as the woman who taught me how to read and tucked me into bed each night.

When I was very young, I thought I could make my mother strong and secure. I wanted her happiness, of course, but being a child what I wanted most of all was her loving approval, just as she wanted her mother's. We seemed to make up a chain of desire, my mother, grandmother, and I, tied to one another quite hopelessly.

I didn't strive for freedom as a small child—that only came later. While other children were testing their independence, I was binding myself more tightly to my mother, as if I didn't trust her hold on me. "Kathy," she said to me once in a moment of exasperation at my clinginess, "you're too tied to my apron strings!" I was, and no less tightly for having tied the knots myself.

3

A Girl So Good

I WOULD BE KIND; I WOULD BE GOOD. WHEN MY MOTHER TOLD ME TO walk to school with the fat girl in my class, I jumped at the assignment. And I wouldn't step on a single line or crack in the sidewalk on the way. I wouldn't even *think* the words of that horrible rhyme. I would help old ladies cross the street and smile at the mentally retarded boy if I ever saw him again. (*Oh please, God, let me see him again!*) I would befriend all the lonely children, find the strays, feed the hungry, clothe the naked if the hungry and the naked ever crossed my path—they were hard to come by in Hamden.

No doubt these lessons about kindness and goodness were important to my mother, but she could hardly have imagined how feverishly I took them in. I wanted to be special, but that was a sin. You might call that my Original Dilemma, the first really difficult problem I had to solve for myself, for I was the oldest girl in a Catholic family and I was supposed to be generous and self-effacing—to give and give way, step aside and let the younger ones go first. But I could hardly just step aside and let my brothers and sisters take center stage. In a family of six small children, all clamoring for our mother's attention, I would have risked disappearing altogether.

Well, I thought I had found a solution to my dilemma. I would become special through selflessness, but a complete and astonishing selflessness. In short, I would become a saint.

There was no Saint Kathleen. I had found that out when I went looking through a book of saints to pick my confirmation name. I was disappointed at first, surprised, even shocked, that my parents, my churchgoing Catholic parents, hadn't thought to name me after a saint. But in the middle of my disappointment, I suddenly had a glimpse of God. He didn't say anything—I could hardly let Him open His mouth, His coming to me was already far too grand. He merely looked sideways at me, all-knowing and even a bit bug-eyed, like he was trying to point out something to me with his eyeballs alone. Didn't I see? No Saint Kathleen; a blank space where a saint could be.

Eagerly, I began throwing myself into the middle of my brothers' and sisters' fights, holding my arms out in a gesture of peace. "The little martyr," Bill sneered, but instead of feeling crushed I swelled with pride.

They gave me a nickname. "Peacemaker, peacemaker," they chanted. I wore a sorrowful look on my face. I was tied to the stake, in the middle of the screaming mob, craning my neck, looking to see if *she* was watching.

I vacuumed excessively, I dusted the venetian blinds, I sang religious songs as I worked: "Holy, holy, holy, Lord God Almighty!" I let Cindy and Beth Ann go first and second and third. "Forget me, I'm okay, you go ahead!" I called out softly while Cindy snorted and rolled her eyes. My devotion—and ambition—knew no bounds. It was all very Catholic. I was racing fast to be last, meekly trying to inherit the earth.

When Advent arrived that year, it was as if someone had taken a whip to an already galloping horse, for this was a holy season and I was a saint-in-the-making. Every afternoon I could be found kneeling and praying in front of the Nativity scene we had set up on an end table in the dining room. My brothers and sisters and I had covered the table with fake snow, placed the stable on top of that snowy field,

and then, lovingly, arranged the figures of Mary and Joseph, the shep-
herds and the farm animals, around the empty manger where the
baby Jesus would lie on Christmas morning. It was like a dollhouse,
only much more beautiful and serious, for the figures were painted in
the rich and faded colors you find in museums.

My mother told us that for every good deed we performed, we
could put a straw in the manger—the better we were, the softer the
baby's bed would be when He arrived.

These were private good deeds. We weren't supposed to tell our
mother or brag about them. The only one who would know was God
and, I supposed, any angels who happened to be watching. But one
day I felt I'd been spectacularly good—a very busy, ten-straw kind of
day!—and I waited until early evening to put my straws in the
manger. By then, my mother was at the stove cooking dinner, and
from there she had a perfect view of me through the kitchen doors. I
knelt down in front of the stable, made the sign of the cross, bowed
my head and prayed as if I were at the altar in St. Rita's church. Then
I put my straws on the little wooden manger one at a time, a straw for
smiling at an old lady I'd seen on the way home from school, another
one for doing a load of laundry, a third for forgiving Beth Ann when
she broke the leg off my Barbie doll. . . . Between each straw, I
peeked up at my mother as she worked, hoping she would note how
long I was kneeling at the stable.

In my mind's eye, I could see her turning to my father at the end
of the day, when we were all in bed, and telling him how incredibly
selfless I was. He would shake his head in admiration. "Our daughter
sure is something," he would say.

It was in my search for goodness, guiltlessness, my mother's
approval—and a desire to impress God, too—that I arrived home one
afternoon without my blue coat.

I'd walked the mile and a half from St. Rita's alone, because Cindy
was out sick that day and Michael and Bill had gone ahead, racing or

fighting each other as they often did. There was snow on the ground and patches of ice that we used as mini–skating rinks most days, zipping across them on our rubber-soled shoes, twirling on one foot like fancy skaters.

A soft silence came off the lakes, frozen solid almost clear across, reflecting nothing but a watery, wintery light. I imagined the cold water on the bottoms of floating birds, the cold ice on their webbed feet, and shivered for them, though there were no birds in sight.

When I walked into the brightly lit kitchen, I was wearing only my plaid jumper, a sweater, knee socks, and shoes. My knuckles, nose, and knees were a scarlet red.

"Kathy, where is your coat?" my mother exclaimed.

I looked down at my body, shocked into silence, not because my coat was missing but because of her alarm. "I don't know," I said.

"You don't know? What do you mean? What did you do with it?"

No matter what she asked—did I leave school with it on, did I stop anywhere on the way home?—I couldn't bring myself to tell her. I knew I'd gone too far this time. The nuns were called, the classroom and coatroom searched, the janitor even looked in the school yard, but it was never found. Losing that coat cemented my reputation as a dreamer, as the girl who would forget her head if it weren't attached to her body.

It was a brand-new blue coat, I remember it still, with large, glassy buttons. Grandma Callahan had given it to me that Christmas. Halfway home from school, at the abandoned parking lot next to the Servoss Street woods, I'd taken it off and laid it on a rock for some poor, coatless child. I felt like I was opening up a conversation with God, He who saw all things. What would be His reply?

I had visions of birds swooping down from the sky in a bolt of light to carry away my coat in their beaks and drop it at the feet of a shivering street urchin. What joy then! I felt like the giver *and* the receiver, so vividly did I imagine the scene.

And wouldn't I arrive home as both? Giver of coats and coatless? Generous and pathetic? I'd been so taken by the beauty of my plan, the perfection of metaphor, that I hadn't exactly thought out what I'd say to my mother.

But when I stepped into the bright kitchen and her shocked question, I froze. It seemed like the worst idea I'd ever had, and impossible now to explain. I looked down at my coatless body, dumbfounded by my own self.

4

A Boy So Bad

ST. RITA'S GRAMMAR SCHOOL, WHERE ALL THE DOBIE CHILDREN WERE
sent, each in his or her own turn, stood on top of a hill, a steep green
hill rising up from Whitney Avenue toward heaven. A silver cross
hung on the pinkish-red bricks, calling all Catholic boys and girls
inside.

It took me three years to get used to going to that school. I
couldn't understand the scratchy uniforms we all had to wear, the
way my knees were always cold (why were the adults letting us go
bare-legged in winter?), the black-winged nuns, the desks lined up
like soldiers, the closed door of the classroom, which became a cell
imprisoning me with a group of strange children. Where were my
brothers? Why were they kept in separate classrooms, away from me
and from each other? And where, above all, was Cindy, whom I slept
with every night and woke with every morning, so in tune with each
other that we never had to discuss whether we were waking up as
rabbits or horses, nuzzling each other with our cold rabbit noses or
galloping around the bedroom unable to get out because, as everyone
knows, horses can't turn door handles?

One morning during that first year at St. Rita's, I was standing
alone at the end of the long corridor, looking down at the ice-cold
moss-green linoleum and then up as a nun started making her way toward me from the other end. I watched as her black dress sailed out

wider and wider, her white face grew larger and larger, until I could see the gold crucifix swinging and banging on her chest like a bell clapper. Now, I thought, as I waited there for her, she was going to explain it all to me, meaning would be revealed, the pieces would fall into place.

"The cheese stands alone," she said briskly, almost merrily, as she stared down at me. "Has Little Bo Peep lost her sheep?"

And that's the way it went, for three long years, strangeness heaped upon strangeness, absurdity on absurdity.

The nuns clacked their handheld clickers—they looked like giant clothespins—and called us "wild Indians" or "children of God"; they hit the big blackboards with their long wooden pointers; and they spanked the boys when they were bad. When Bill was in first grade, Sister Joseph Mary spanked him, taking him completely by surprise. Down went Billy's pants in front of the classroom. Smack went her hand on his bottom. The same nun gave me a gold star for my reading test—it twinkled on the top of the page.

When boys were bad, they were badder than girls—that's what we were being taught at St. Rita's. And boys were sturdier, they could take more punishment, though Bill, six-year-old Billy, standing there in his underwear, was crushed.

The year I entered fourth grade, I became obsessed with Frank Lee—no one called him simply Frank—a boy so bad and crazy that the rest of us kids were dull, stupefied angels next to him. Frank Lee was in my class.

Perhaps his father had given him that crew cut, so close to the head he looked bald until he was right up in front of you. He had a big head, ash-blond hair. His glasses were broken and heavily taped, but he wore them like they were something dangerous. He had tattooed his arms with Nazi crosses, cutting the skin with a razor first and, once the skin had scarred over, drawing the lines in with a blue pen. He wore steel-toed boots and a trench coat over his school uniform.

Some evenings when the four of us kids were up in the attic playing and goofing around before bedtime, I would make a show of hugging and kissing my pillow and crooning, "Frank Lee, honey, baby!"

"Ecchhh, cut it out!"

"Shut up!"

"Kathy, you're disgusting!" I enjoyed making my brothers and sister squirm, it's true, but there was also something about Frank Lee that touched me. He was the first person I ever met who was "beyond the pale," a phrase the adults sometimes used that made me think confusedly of someone so white as to be almost ghostlike. All of the kids in St. Rita's hated Frank Lee, not just the kids in my class. He had not a single friend in the world and no clue, it seemed, as to how to go about getting one. Walking behind him after school I'd heard him sigh heavily to himself—little Nazi prince clumping home alone.

One day when Henry Brastberger was taking his seat in class, Frank Lee put a pencil under him, pointed side up. Henry was a big kid with womanly skin and a talent for science and math. Henry shrieked. The pencil had pierced the skin. He was rushed to the hospital with lead poisoning. It went straight to his spine. He almost died, they said. He was gone from school for weeks.

As for Frank Lee, he was never seen again. I couldn't get him out of my mind. Couldn't get over the fact that the first great sinner I ever met, in the flesh, not in the books, not Lucifer or Judas but someone alive and wearing glasses, was a boy my age.

I saw Frank Lee do it. I was seated next to him and watched him lean over his desk with his pencil and hold it, waiting for Henry to sit down, a look of great anticipation on his face I knew he wasn't thinking: lead poisoning, hospital, near death. I wondered how the adults could miss this, or worse, know and not care.

I should've learned from Frank Lee that you could be too lonely and too hungry. You might try too hard to connect. You might do something horrific and then be condemned to your solitude forever.

5

Spinster

EVEN WHEN I WAS A CHILD, GREAT-AUNT EMMA, PROPER AND STIFF-backed, wearing dresses made of a material as densely woven as upholstery, seemed to have come out of a storybook. Maybe not a very pleasant book, but something shivery that children would like.

Tall as a man and regal in bearing, Emma towered over us. Her wrists and fingers were thin and elegant and looked quite brittle. She kept a handkerchief tucked into the cuff of her sweater. Her head was smallish. Her metal-rimmed glasses and her hair were the same glinting gray. She lived with Grandma and Grandpa Dobie, as unmarried sisters were supposed to do at one time. That time had come and gone, but not for proper Emma, and so not for her sister, Betty, and her brother-in-law, Albert, either.

Every other Sunday we had dinner at Grandpa and Grandma Dobie's house, only three blocks from ours. And every time we arrived you would have thought they hadn't seen us in years. "Well, look who's here!" Aunt Barbara, my father's sister, would cry out, as if our presence was a complete surprise. Blue-eyed and auburn-haired, just like my father, she had a voice that was warm and rushing and sugary. "And in all of your springtime finery!" Then she'd look at my parents with a gleam in her eyes. "Hello, Mom and Dad," she'd say, and that gleam, the suddenly wry tone of her voice, were like secret codes. Adults were infinitely subtle. With one raised eyebrow they could call up years of shared experience, and that experience seemed to have led them to believe that life, at its heart, was comic.

We always got there at four in the afternoon, and by then the house was already filled with the rich smells of pork loin and boiled potatoes, canned green beans set to boiling on the stove until they were as dark and limp as something you might pull from the sea, Mott's applesauce, taken out of its jar and served ice-cold in a china bowl with a silver spoon. Grandma Dobie bustled in from the kitchen, her cheeks as pink as if she'd painted them, announcing with pride, "My family's arrived!" Grandpa came down the stairs, jiggling the change in his pocket and whistling five notes, always the same five, the beautiful beginning of an unnamed melody. First his big black shoes materialized, then his long legs in their gray pants, then his white shirt, the buttons dropping into view—my grandfather seemed to go on forever—and finally his long-jawed, high-browed face with the kind gray-blue eyes and the sparse gray hair swept back so his head seemed even larger, more horselike. When all of him had come into view, I'd feel his hand land on the top of my head, covering it like an overlarge hat: "Hello, ole bricktop, ole carrottop!" Great-aunt Emma hovered in the background, and after everyone else had greeted us, my brothers and sisters and I steeled ourselves for her touch. Her lips were liver-colored and very thin. She had to crank herself down low to kiss us; a quick, bony peck.

When it was time for the adults to have their cocktails, Emma was always very particular about hers: "Remember, don't make it too strong now, Barbara!" she would say. Then I could hear Aunt Barbara singing out the order in the kitchen—"And a not-too-strong whiskey sour for Miss Emma!"—and I knew the adults were signaling to each other again. Barbara always brought the cocktail into the living room with a towel thrown over her arm like a waiter, making a great flourish of bowing down and serving Emma, who was perched imperiously on the couch. "Queen Emma," Aunt Barbara called her.

Emma was big-breasted, and sometimes at dinner a crumb would fall and land on that broad expanse. As I watched, she would pick up her napkin and, pinching it between those bony, elegant fingers, use it to whisk the offending crumb away. Her hand never touched her breast; her lips were sucked in as if this close brush with her own body filled her with distaste.

There was no tenderness or sympathy to inform my picture of her, which is why so many childhood memories are so appalling. Emma reminded me of the dinosaur skeleton in the Peabody Museum in New Haven, the overlarge one in the central room with its tiny legs—how does it stay upright?

Though Emma was really only a guest in Grandpa and Grandma's house (a permanent guest, but still . . .), she insisted that the milk go into a pitcher before it was put on the big dining room table, the butter in a butter dish. If Grandma forgot the butter knife, Emma would remind her and Grandma would snort angrily and trot back into the kitchen to retrieve it.

When the meat platter was passed around, Emma carefully levered the serving fork under a slice, her pinky and index fingers pointed in the air like antennae. Around the table, eyes rolled and the next Dobie served would *stab* the meat. "Breast or thigh, Emma, what will it be?" Aunt Barbara would ask roughly, gaily, and Emma would suck in her lips and say, "White meat, please." I don't know when I realized that Emma was caught inside her spinsterhood, that when given a chance she was, in fact, curious and kind. It probably wasn't until my late twenties. I wasn't a kind, warmhearted child—I was highly sensitive, which isn't the same thing at all.

When I sat down next to her on the couch, Aunt Emma always asked the same question, "So how is school?" I didn't know what to say besides "Good," to which she would reply, "That's good," and then there was only silence tightening in the air between us like a screw. She had a smile on her face, a thin, close-lipped smile as she looked at me. Was she waiting for me, a child of eight or nine or ten, to pick up the conversation? First chance I got, I slid away—off to the sun parlor where my brothers and sisters were playing Mouse Trap or to the cheerful din of the kitchen where Aunt Barbara and Dad were teasing each other or arguing with Grandpa about his beloved Red Sox. If I looked back into the empty living room, there was Great-aunt Emma sitting stiffly on the couch, hands pinned to her lap, a smile frozen on her mouth.

Emma's bedroom was directly next to Grandma and Grandpa's, the door always open, as if the room were saying to unexpected company, "This is a bedroom, but everything is aboveboard!"

An armchair sat rigidly under the tasseled shade of a reading lamp. At the desk where she wrote letters and paid bills, the cubbyholes were neatly filled. There were letters from distant relatives in Germany whom none of us ever knew or cared to; stamps and stationery; rubber bands and paper clips kept in little boxes; figurines, music boxes, a Currier & Ives print of ice-skaters, and, everywhere, those pillows she embroidered with black-eyed daisies and purple clover, busy enough to attract bees.

The bed of a spinster aunt must, of course, be a modest-size bed, just big enough to sleep in. No spreading out for the spinster aunt, no hint of what beds are sometimes used for. Married people had big beds, as boastful and secure as ocean liners. The pillows were plumper, the bedspread seemed to go on forever before falling in luxurious folds to the floor. That big expanse of white seemed to be smiling mysteriously, testifying to the power of the married couple.

I couldn't stop myself from imagining Emma's chaste life in that bedroom. Thinking about no sex was not exactly like thinking about sex, but in its own way it was just as thrilling, and so I thought about it obsessively—Emma undressing for bed at night; Emma avoiding the sight of her body in the dresser mirror; Emma in her bed alone, long-legged, big-breasted Emma never making babies. Sometimes I would hold the figure of Great-aunt Emma and the figure of Frank Lee in my head at the same time until my skin prickled and my head swam.

Of course, it didn't occur to me then that Emma and Frank Lee had become objects of my obsession because they were both outsiders, each in their different ways. The tattooed misfit of a boy, the prim spinster aunt—both of them evidence that love had its limits, something I really didn't want to consider as a child. Frank Lee was too bad for the good nuns to keep around, too bad to be forgiven. And Great-aunt Emma was often only tolerated by the adults in our family, though she seemed impervious to their rolling eyes and quick retorts. No matter how many times she was teased, she went on tying plastic bags over her shoes whenever she went out in the rain. One afternoon, a few years after Grandpa had died, leaving the two sisters to live alone with each other, I watched Grandma chase Emma around the house, sweet little Grandma, brandishing Emma's umbrella and saying sarcastically, "Don't forget your umbrella, Emma, it might rain! Don't forget your galoshes!" There was nary a cloud in the sky.

Emma's carefulness around rain and children and food, that stiff posture and well-upholstered body, were anti-Dobie, for Dobies didn't fuss. They got down on the carpet and *played* with their children. They were quick with a joke, no-nonsense and plucky. When it rained on a picnic, they just laughed and said, "Typical Dobie weather." And you knew you had won their hearts if they called you "a real trouper."

When Great-aunt Emma fainted one night after just one pre-dinner cocktail, Aunt Barbara said, "Out like a light!" and Dad added, "Down for the count!" They laid her out on the couch, and having reached the consensus that Emma's girdle was probably too tight, everyone fled to the warm, noisy kitchen to have another drink, while Aunt Barbara, who was a nurse, was left to tend to her, and I stayed behind in the suddenly shadowy living room to watch.

There had been something deeply embarrassing about straight-backed Emma holding her cocktail glass with one bony finger pointed out and away and then saying with an apologetic chuckle, "I feel a little woozy." Something awful about watching Emma laid out in the dim light, proper Emma undone—all those straps and hooks!—undone roughly, while pots clattered and voices rang heartily in the other room. Emma's head was directly underneath a table lamp, and so it seemed she was about to be scientifically examined. Her cheeks were colorless and slack; her hair, a tinsely gray, though still black at the roots, sparkled in the light. Barbara unbuttoned her dress swiftly, as if she'd been called upon to do this many times before, and then began unsnapping her girdle, each snap going pop!, one small explosion of impatience after another.

"Well, at least you can breathe now, Emma," she said, though Emma couldn't hear her, and then she joined the others in the kitchen. "The patient's resting peacefully," I heard her announce. I stayed there in the dim living room, transfixed by Emma's solitude, her undone state. From the kitchen, I could hear Emma being discussed—my mother wondering softly if my father had made her drink too strong, my father protesting, and Barbara and Grandpa coming in fast and sure to say it wasn't the drink but the drinker. A screen door slammed and I heard Barbara greeting one of my brothers or sisters: "The sailor's home from the sea!" Grandma asked who was going to carve the roast, and everyone insisted that it must be my father—he was in food service, after all—and with that the conversation moved on to other things.

The kitchen doorway blazed with a sunny light, the roast was spilling its juice as my father carved, the sounds of laughter rang out. And yet I couldn't go in there. I was afraid. I imagined my mother trying to pretend she was as robust and stouthearted as her husband and in-laws. Suddenly it seemed that she and I had fallen in with a pretty rough crowd.

6

Julie the Slut

IN SIXTH GRADE, MY GIRLFRIENDS MAUREEN AND MARISA AND I, throwing caution to the winds, began writing dirty letters to the most popular boy in our class and signing them "Julie." That was the year that some of the girls began wearing bras and the boys started snickering, a brand-new sound from them. At recess, the boys did fly-by attacks, running up behind the girls and trying to unhook their bras, or at least yank them and make them snap like elastic bands. They began to "moo" at us, too, and at lunch they drank from their milk cartons with a sucking sound and a leer.

Suddenly, we girls were divided into two groups, the girls with bras and the girls without, the big-breasted and the no-breasted—because that is how all of us small-breasted girls felt. We would be freer than those girls with bras, not pushed around as much, but also irrelevant.

Under their desks, the boys' shoes looked bigger and sharper, more like our fathers' shoes. Their schoolboy uniforms began to resemble men's business suits—weren't they wearing belts, button-down shirts, and ties? Someday they would have to shave. They became more manly and much sillier that year. I could tell we weren't going to be friends anymore. Liking was no longer the currency. They were more like big brothers teasing and bullying us, only with more excitement all around.

We girls no longer wore our plaid jumpers to school. From sixth grade on, we had to wear skirts, and though no adult ever explained why, I was sure that it was because the front panels of the jumpers would accent our growing breasts. My imagination pictured those panels straining to contain two giant breasts, buoyant as balloons.

The adults tried to act like nothing was going on. When one of the boys asked a young, pretty nun to explain the story of "the burning bush," she must have known exactly what he was saying because she blushed tomato red, but then she just went on with the lesson, plunging into it with a nervous, reckless air. We understood. When it came to sex, we were on our own. The adults had left the scene, tiptoeing away, hoping, no doubt, that we would follow. Not a chance.

They had gone blind, but we could finally see—with our own eyes now, and not only what we were supposed to see. They went silent but we could talk, and we didn't bother to sound pleasing or nice, or even very sensible. Why should we? We understood each other perfectly—what was indecipherable about a "moo"?

At recess, Maureen, Marisa, and I huddled on the cement steps at the back of St. Rita's, keeping one eye out for the nun patrolling the school yard. I used my heavy geography book as a writing table.

Dear Danny, Hi, handsome! I wrote in that first letter.

"You don't know me but I know you," Marisa dictated, looking eagerly over my shoulder while I wrote it down. Marisa was a very freckled, light-skinned redhead; pale and bright, orange and white. She had a round face, a snub nose, a sturdy, farm girl's body.

I think about you all the time . . . I continued. *Especially when I'm in my bed at night.*

Maureen and Marisa giggled.

"I'm dying for you," Maureen added, her face suddenly serious. She reminded me of a beautiful monkey, all long limbs, sharp bones, and short, fluffy brown hair. Maureen was the first girlfriend I fell in love with. I thought the yoke of her collarbone and her jutting, deeply dimpled knees were like perfect pieces of architecture.

I want you to touch my titties, I wrote.

Danny Moore was good-natured and good-looking, with black

hair, dark, friendly eyes, and pink cheeks (though not too pink). His head was a little large for his body, so that part of him seemed to be a grown man. We could imagine Danny married; Danny in an office, sitting at a big desk on the phone; Danny fathering children. There was nothing sexier back then.

He blushed easily but he never tried to cover it up with bluster. He had a kind of grace to him, born simply of being good-hearted. We all loved Danny Moore, truant boys and nuns alike.

Danny had a girlfriend named Angela, the first girl in our grade to grow breasts, and it says something, says everything, that she was the only girl never to get into trouble for it. No boy ever mooed when she walked by. Or asked for some milk. No boy grabbed a squeeze, as Marty Egan did to me, walking behind my chair one day and quickly reaching over my shoulder and grabbing my right breast. He pumped it twice like it was a turkey baster. As soon as he squeezed, it seemed smaller.

When he lifted his hand, my chest felt blank, as though he'd taken the breast away and now it was lying there in his hand, warm and plump. It went with him when he went back to his seat, smirking. I was sorry it was so small; the word *titmouse* flew into my head, and *this little piggy*, and then *a bird in the hand is worth two* . . . Humiliation and titillation combined, and for the next few days whenever I was alone, I poked and prodded the moment mentally, like a boy with a stick.

But Danny and Angela were above all of this. He was our gentle prince and she was our little mother, our head cheerleader, the lilac-crowned May Queen that year. She had a woman's breasts, an improbable streak of gray in her black hair, and she was a foot taller than Danny. We would hand him a footstool so he could climb up on it and kiss her while we watched and cheered. They were our perfect bride and groom, mother and father shrunk down to size, and we were seriously invested in their romance.

Still, Maureen and Marisa and I wrote, *Baby, I'm here all alone. I wish you would sneak into my bedroom one night and squeeze my big titties.*

We closed with *Yours Forever*, tacked on some kisses and hugs. And then, after a quick discussion, signed the name "Julie," a pretty name and the name of no one we knew. Julie was free to become whatever we wanted her to become.

That afternoon, I handed Danny the letter, explaining that this girl named Julie had given it to me after school the day before. "She asked me to deliver it to you," I said solemnly, excitement twitching my toes.

When he read it, Danny blushed. The color streaked straight up his cheeks, red mercury rising. We told him that Julie was a girl we had met outside school and we didn't know how she knew him. "I guess she has a crush on you," Maureen said with remarkable non-chalance, revealing herself to be a pretty smooth liar and filling me with admiration.

Danny asked where this Julie lived, but we said we didn't know if she even *had* a home. "She just kind of hangs out in back of the school yard. That's where we met her."

Two days later—we could barely wait *that* long—we gave Danny another letter and he blushed again, but this time he asked us what she looked like.

"She's kind of fat," I said.

"Really?" His expression was impossible to pin down—pained, yes, but with what? Disappointment, pity, increased longing?

I went for broke. "Yeah, she's really fat. She doesn't have any friends, either, except us. . . ."

"Kind of us," Maureen said. "But we're not really her friends, we just see her sometimes."

He didn't ask why Julie was friendless; he wanted to know her last name. And the color of her hair, her eyes; did we find out where she lived yet? He began to sidle over to me at the beginning of each school day and ask if I had a letter from her. He was shy about it, but helplessly driven. We wrote him constantly.

I was becoming a different creature outside my family, outside of the gaze of adults; bolder, freer, a leader in many a strange expedition, more of a Dobie away from the Dobies, you might say. (Or away from my mother, at least, and my obsession with her every glance.) But the boldness of a dreamer is quite a different thing from the boldness of a tomboy; it can easily end in humiliation. An idea forms in your head, a marvelous idea—a blue coat sacrificed on a rock, perhaps—but act out that idea, let it take on flesh for all the world to see, and the idea is suddenly ridiculous.

But Julie wasn't my dream alone. Three of us had brought her into being, and as the weeks went by, she grew more and more real. She was fat. She was lonely. She was shameless.

My girlfriends and I never had to explain ourselves to one another; we seemed to share the same imagination, the way some friends share the same taste in movies or clothes. When we had sleep-overs at one another's houses, we conducted séances, circling around a flickering candle and calling Lizzie Borden back from the dead, terrifying ourselves. We rehearsed sultry voices and then made obscene calls to people picked randomly from the phone book, dialing the number for a John Anderson and asking the woman who answered the phone, "Is John home? He was supposed to meet me this afternoon." Maureen and I wrote love letters to each other under the names of Christopher Columbus and Queen Isabella; *My Nina, My Pinta, My Santa Maria!*

We were becoming enthralled with our Julie. We no longer giggled and snickered when writing her letters. I was so carried away by our project that I had begun writing some of them by myself in my room at night. She was as much a reply to my day at school as some other girl's diary might have been. Julie took everything the boys were throwing at us, the leering and mooing and grabbing at our breasts, and made it her own. If the boys made sucking sounds while drinking their milk, Julie listened and then wrote Danny, straight out, *I really want you to suck my tits.*

Even as I wrote the letters, I wondered what was going to come out of her mouth next. Sometimes she shocked me. I'd begun to like her, but I didn't think Julie had much use for girlfriends. It was too late for that. We may have created her, but now she was alive! Alive and dead-set on Danny Moore. I knew other girls couldn't cure her of her loneliness.

She had gotten under Danny's skin, too. Her isolation was the clincher. Who would've thought? The most popular boy in school, friend to all, enemy of none, and yet I could feel he had something private going with Julie, a mental pipeline that went direct to her, sitting alone in a room, waiting for him. And who would he be when he was with her, this straight-B student, this mother's son, this pride of nuns?

"She's got long brown hair, really long," I told him, pointing below my hips. He liked that. Julie wrote that she would come to him wearing only her hair, like Lady Godiva. Danny asked me who Lady Godiva was. "You know, on the candy boxes, the naked lady on the horse."

He seemed to trust me more than Maureen or Marisa, and he would wait till they weren't around and then ask me questions about Julie. It was as if he knew that I felt strongly about her, too.

Julie wrote that she wanted him to rest his head on her tits; they were as soft as pillows. She got fatter, and I had to tell Danny that people made fun of her. That hurt him. I said she had hazel eyes.

"Really beautiful eyes," I added casually, like a fact you couldn't argue with. Back and forth I went, making her grotesque in some small way (wasn't sex grotesque?) and then giving her something pretty (and tantalizing, too?), giving it to the both of them because I'd begun to want their relationship to work out.

On the day I told him that Julie was as big as a horse, he got a letter from her saying he could ride her bareback if he wanted. I picked that up from a boy in our class named Jerry.

Jerry had shiny blond hair, a suave demeanor. For an eleven-year-old, he was sleek and prosperous-looking, the only rich boy in our class and the only one whose parents had divorced. We didn't feel sorry for Jerry—he didn't appear the least bit crushed by his parents' separation. It only made him seem more sophisticated, especially when we learned that he got to read his father's *Playboys* and call his mother by her first name. He was always one step ahead of us. Marty Egan may have grabbed my breast but it was Jerry who one day decided that *bike* meant vagina. He went up to each girl and asked what color her bike was. And from innocent answers like "Blue," he reaped pleasure, or reaped it for the other boys. There was a certain joyless-ness to Jerry's corruption of us. It was as if he'd already seen and done everything, and he was only interested in giving the other boys a thrill.

I figured out what *bike* was, but then Jerry asked, "Do you have a fat bike or a skinny one?" There was so much to consider now.

Jerry changed euphemisms so fast that you always got caught say-ing something dirty. Once he got the boys thinking about cup size, you couldn't even get a grade on your test without feeling sticky and strange. When the nun read the grades aloud, you found yourself hop-ing you didn't get an A.

One morning when I walked into school, Jerry asked me if I had a pussycat—"Is she furry?" I'd just come from the breakfast table, from Sugar Pops and orange juice, my mother's and father's kisses good-bye. I blushed wildly and couldn't think of anything to say, but that night Julie sat down and wrote a letter. She signed it, *Love from YOUR PUSSYCAT.* Danny began to look haggard.

"How can I see her?" he asked again and again.

Finally, we arranged for them to meet at the ballpark after school.

When Danny arrived, Maureen and Marisa and I were standing at the edge of the baseball diamond, scraggly black woods and yellow brush behind us. We told Danny she was back there in the high brush and waiting for our signal.

We started singing, "Julie, Julie, Julie, do you love me? Julie, Julie, Julie, do you care?" We were corny girls, young for our age; we were wildly excited. "Julie, Julie, will you still be there!" And then we counted to ten and yelled like Ed McMahon, "Heeeeeere's *Julie!*"

We turned, arms spread, and I held my breath. For a split second I half-expected her to come striding out of those woods, huge, naked, hair tumbling, a bear of a girl, a girl beyond my imagination. I watched the brush, the high reeds, and waited for the rustle—any-thing could happen in God's world, so why not Julie? I had a power-ful desire to see her in the flesh, to see what she'd do next. But the woods revealed nothing.

We ran through the drumroll again but this time, after shouting, "Here's Julie!" we pointed at one another.

It took ten stop-and-go seconds for the meaning to reach Danny, and then he blushed.

"No. You? You're . . . ? No. You wrote . . . ?"

We confessed, doubled over with laughter, hiding our own reddening cheeks—what had we done? It never occurred to us until that moment that we'd be revealing ourselves. We were filled with confusion and embarrassment—*pussycat, big titties, please pet me, please, we wrote that!*—but Danny began laughing and shaking his head at our boldness. He was a good-natured boy, a heart like the sun.

When we left the park, we were quiet. Occasionally one of us giggled, and Danny would give a halfhearted shove to shove the giggler and we would all laugh loudly, but we were feeling kind of low.

"So, she doesn't . . . She's not real at all?" Danny asked one more time, embarrassed to bring her up again, but he had to. Maureen or Marisa started humming "Taps" and we all joined in.

I found myself missing Julie in the days and weeks ahead. Though I know that Danny and Maureen and Marisa felt the same way, none of us ever mentioned her again. Julie should have existed. That girl we created, lonely and bold, the composite of all the loathing and desire we had begun to feel in the air around us, that girl continued to take up space in my head. It was like a real person had died.

7

Mirror in the Window

"IN THE NEXT LIFE I'M COMING BACK AS LOUIS ARMSTRONG," MY FATHER always said, but in the meantime his horn, a saxophone, collected dust in the basement. Still, the wonderful world was on him; he brought it home the way other men bring home the bacon. When he walked in the door after work, sometimes he'd put a record on the turntable, loosen his tie, and dance across the living room in his black suit, fingers snapping, hips wagging, beckoning my mother to him while she stood watching in the kitchen doorway. He danced funky, then goofy, danced with his attaché case, danced with his tie, held his hand out to her. In her apron, she hesitated.

Ah, the leap to joy! Could she make it? Would she try? Each time I held my breath. It all depended. Dark day? Happy day? Longing flew out of her—to be that lovely in his eyes!—but her heels dug deeper into the linoleum. Where was her self? In that room, laughing, twirling, or in the long day behind her, housebound, nothing changing but the diapers? It was almost a moral battle. Could she, should she, would she snap out of her day, leave dishes, diapers, doubt, weariness behind, just because he was home, because he was happy? He withdrew his hand; my heart sank. But then he took his tie and roped her, pulling her from the doorway, from gloom to living room, to light, to him.

"Al!" She laughed, her white teeth flashing against the red, red lipstick. They danced.

And Louie went, *"Boo-bah-dah-dah."*

At night, under the bedcovers, I rode my barrette out to the high plains. Tall in the saddle, riding riding riding . . . I was Roy Rogers! Then Dale Evans! Sometimes both of them at once, astride my barrette, breaking into a gallop . . . Oh, married cowboy love!

My father had the swift gait and commanding, vigorous air of a man on a mission, but he also had Tom Sawyer freckles and dancing blue eyes. His lips would curl at the corners when he was up to some mischief—which was often. It was a very expressive face.

"It always gives me away," he would say to us kids, wagging his large head dolefully as if he were really upset, his eyes twinkling all the while, his lips tightening against the grin he could never quite repress. He loved to tell us stories, sometimes make-believe stories with ridiculously named characters like McGruff, McDuff, McWhosit, and McGillacutty, and sometimes real ones, but real or imaginary he always told them like they were stories written down in a book. Before he began, he would take a deep breath and then, following the rhythm of once-upon-a-time, he would say, "When I was just a boy . . ."

At St. Boniface in New Haven, where he went to grammar school, the nuns were not only strict, he told us, but vicious. "They would've been street thugs if they'd been born men." One winter afternoon at recess, young Albert and his friends had a snowball fight, and when they returned to class, the nun asked the boys who'd been playing in the snow to give themselves up. No one spoke, no one moved. But once again Albert's eyes gave him away. The nun ordered him out of his seat and handed him a bucket, telling him to go fill it with snow.

When he returned, she made him sink his hands in the snow and sit there like that for the rest of the hour. When the class was over, and his hands were swollen and red, she took a ruler and, using the sharp edge, struck the backs of his hands. At each strike, the frozen skin split.

When my father told us this story, he told it as an adventure, not a tale of woe. It was like a fairy tale, really, with hatchet-faced nuns who were wonderfully wicked and shrouded in black. They cackled as they stirred the cauldron and waited for little boys to come by so they could *eat*! But this boy was clever and brave; he would make it out of the woods alive.

And so I was given two opposing narratives as a child: My father's depicted life as filled with tests, danger, hard tasks, and adventure. Not only were these things interesting in and of themselves, but they made a rousing good story later. My mother, an only child whose memories were of a lonely childhood with no one but her mother, aunt, and uncle for company, spoke very rarely about her past, and when she did it wasn't a story so much as a keening complaint. Her narrative was mostly interior, about hurt feelings and unhappiness. There were never any happy endings, never any resolutions at all, really. My mother seemed to be struggling mightily against her past, even, you might say, against her own personality.

Nonetheless, for most of my childhood my mother's narrative was the one I identified and allied myself with. But as adolescence approached, my lovestruck gaze moved from my mother to my father. It felt like a betrayal, but of course I couldn't become myself while I was tied to her. One time she protested, "You all admire your father so much!" And how could we not? He came home each night with his chin up, forehead glowing, black shoes snapping on the linoleum, so at home in the world, so happy and energized there, it was as if he had a mistress. Sometimes he brought my mother red roses, and we would watch as her face softened and lit up. Often he delighted us by telling the story of meeting her. "As soon as I saw her standing on top of the stairs in that yellow dress, I was a goner," he would say, clutching his heart and slowly shaking his big, handsome head, a goner for all to see.

*   *   *

When my father came up the walk at the end of the day, we flew into his legs, his hips, his sharp dark suit, sniffing him like dogs. There, in the dense weave, was the faint smell of the rivers and continents he'd crossed.

After hugging and kissing us, he went into the kitchen and closed the folding doors. Then we heard the tinkle of ice in glasses and the murmur of voices. This was strictly grown-up time, treacherous and seductive. We gathered by the doors, like souls crowding the heavenly gates, listened hard but heard only tones—his spirited, hers murmuring. Trumpet and violin. And then their voices would almost disappear until finally the doors were flung open and we'd hear my father's shout, "Fee fie foe fum, I smell the blood of an Englishmun!" The giant emerged and we fled!

The best game was when Daddy was a bull, down on the living room floor, snorting and pawing the ground and wheeling angrily around as we attacked him in force, all four or five or six of us charging him and trying to knock him down, as we dodged his sharp horns and flaming eyes. Sometimes he fell with a groan and lay there, whimpering, and our hearts broke.

"Oh, don't hurt him!" we cried.

We petted his stiff auburn hair, cooing, "Poor little bull." Always a mistake, because he'd roar back to life, take a swipe, and then I'd be under him while he tickled my ribs ferociously.

"Help me! Save me!" I yelled. His belt buckle dug into my chest as he flailed about, grabbing at my brothers and sisters, who were now dashing in to try to pull me out from under him.

"Big ugly bull!" I grunted, trying to push him off of me.

He caught Cindy by the leg and pulled her down, her head clunking into mine, and she, too, started screaming: "Help! Save us!"

We always had to save one another, even if you really really didn't want to get caught by those octopus arms and tickled until it hurt and you had no breath left. The call of our siblings went straight to the heart. One cry for help and we had to throw ourselves into the battle. We were duty-bound, we were inflamed; we were positively patriotic about one another.

Sometimes the whole weight of his body would be pinning me down so that I could hardly breathe, or maybe I was wearing a dress and I knew my underwear was showing—and then I would cry, and my mother would come to my rescue, calling for him to stop. "Al, you're hurting her. You're playing too rough!" His face would look shocked and innocent. "I am not!" he'd protest. But if I kept wailing, he'd pull himself off the floor and with a long, sad face trudge out of the room and up the stairs, like an old bull or that dragon by the sea who knew Jack would come no more.

Up the stairs he went, one sad shoe at a time. And then even his shoes disappeared from view. No more play—would we ever play again?

When he returned, the fun would begin anew, though it would be muted at first, for he was like a chastised boy. But soon he would be sitting with us at the piano (though he didn't know how to play), banging out notes, saying this was a composition he had written specially for us, entitled "Reflections on a Garbage Dump in May." If we started giggling, he'd look astonished and cry, "This is a very serious composition!"

The playing father, the one who would wrestle with us, or make up songs at the piano, or suddenly start singing instead of speaking, so our dinner table sounded like an amateur opera with each of us joining in the fun and trilling, "Please pass the peas," that father was a continual delight to all his children—he was wilder than we were! But for me, that father wasn't as potent, as desirable, as the father in the suit. Almost every night at dinner, that man held court. Amid the clatter of silverware, my father would launch into a story about his day at Yale. (What stories did my mother have to tell? We knew her day. She'd spent it with us.) My father was like one of the four winds returning to the firelit cave in Hans Christian Andersen's fairy tale—the South Wind, perhaps, who had chased ostriches in Africa all day—reporting to his mother and brothers what he'd seen on his travels.

*   *   *

In the spring of my eleventh year, the Black Panthers came to New Haven. My older relatives sounded scared, and I'd never heard them sound scared about anything before. So at first I thought they were talking about an invasion of animals. I imagined scores of them, sleek and shadowy, as they leaped over the hills and trotted across the New Haven Green. Looking for shoppers.

It was my father who set me straight—men not beasts, he explained. Bobby Seale was being tried in the New Haven courthouse for the murder of Alex Rackley, another Black Panther. Seventy-five thousand people were expected to arrive for a weekend of protests. Yale had decided to feed and house as many of them as they could; my father was on the planning committee.

As we dug into our meat loaf and mashed potatoes, he told us that Nixon had sent paratroopers to Rhode Island, a seventeen-minute helicopter ride away from New Haven, and that the National Guard had troops stationed a few miles from the New Haven Green, "in full riot gear with bayonets fixed to their rifles"—a firsthand description he was able to offer us because he had driven out to the armory to see them.

Yale students and faculty left town in droves as the weekend approached. Downtown stores and restaurants closed. Signs in their windows read, "Our insurance company has canceled our coverage for the weekend—please don't break our windows."

"All of the administrators went out and bought dungarees and flannel shirts and loafers," he told us, laughing. "So there they are, and they've got the spanking-new blue jeans, the pressed flannel shirt, the polished loafers, trying to blend in with the crowd." But not my father. "There's no way I'm gonna hide," he said. "I'm an administrator. I've got a job to do. I'm gonna wear my suit."

He had a job to do, but he also had a whole newsworthy world unfolding in front of him. He went everywhere, checked out everything, and brought the stories back to us.

That Friday night, to kick off the weekend of protests, a big rally was held at Ingalls Rink. Huey Newton and William Kunstler would speak. When my father got there, the auditorium was packed. Speaker after speaker took to the microphone on a stage ringed by armed Black Panthers, Huey Newton's bodyguards.

With each speaker the crowd grew louder and angrier. "They were trying to inflame people, to get them into a riot mode," my father said. "Of course, all cops were pigs, anybody who wore a uniform was a pig, and any white male was a motherfucker."

"Al!" my mother warned, but he overrode her with a flashing glance, impatient, almost scornful; he was in full storytelling swing. When a student tried to walk onstage, Huey Newton's bodyguards grabbed him, threw him to the ground, and started kicking him. The other students yelled, "Stop it! Let him talk! Let him talk!" The guards stepped back. The student went up to the podium.

"And then he just stood there. He didn't say a word," my father told us. "The crowd went absolutely dead silent. One minute they were roaring, the next you could've heard a pin drop."

At the dinner table, we too were struck into silence. The student wavered at the microphone. Our forks were suspended midair. Six Dobie children watched and waited, just as hundreds of Yale students had done.

My father's stories mesmerized me; they were as colorful as any fiction I was reading in books. But I always dreaded the moment when the storytelling ended, because that was when the discussion of current events began.

My father would bring up a topic—the death penalty, women's lib, "youth-in-Asia," something the President had done that day—and then we each had to take a turn at giving our "opinion." I didn't have any. I scoured my brain but I could never find even one small opinion lying around in there. I didn't even like the word, it was colorless and it cramped itself up at the end: *oh-pinyon*.

Topic and *current events* were also dull and frightening words; they reminded me of scissors slicing into construction paper. I preferred *moonlight* and *sonata, swan lake, snow queen*. But they weren't opinions—they weren't even thoughts! I didn't "think things out." I daydreamed, I drifted out to sea in a beautiful pea-green boat with the owl, the pussycat, and a five-pound note. . . .

Although I would do my best to make up an opinion, if my father didn't agree, he'd pounce, arguing with us as if we were twenty, not nine or ten or eleven. Sometimes I'd break down and cry. Once or twice, even my mother ran weeping from the room. Each time he would look astonished, and then both angry and ashamed. He'd forgotten we were children; forgotten how sensitive my mother was. He was just looking for a good sparring partner, but suddenly he'd become a bully.

"I bet you don't even know who the President of the United States is," he said to me at the table one night, fixing me with his hot blue eyes. "Do you even know what *year* it is?"

My father could be hard on me, it's true. I believe that there was something about my nature, my dreaminess and forgetfulness, that alarmed him. Perhaps it was his Germanic background, a trained distaste for both disorder and vulnerability. When I forgot to turn off lights or the bathwater, broke and spilled things, left my clothes lying around, he would leap on my mistake—"*Where* is your brain?"—and then, to make matters worse, I would only stare at him, dumbstruck. I was defenseless at those moments; a sleeper shaken awake. That vulnerability set off something inside of him, and I feared his temper then. And yet he greatly inspired me. He wanted us to read the newspapers, be informed, have opinions, *live in the world* and not inside our heads.

Well, I wanted to live there, too, even more than he wanted it for me. That was where all the action was taking place, not here inside our house; strikes, rebellions, noble battles. The world according to my father was a very democratic place. His stories were peopled with dishwashers and chefs, plumbers, professors, college deans, the police chief and the mayor, every class and color of people.

Listening, I felt that life itself was democratic. Everyone had a part to play, the lowly cop in trouble, the princelike president of Yale. Life liked life, plain and simple, and as long as you were willing to live it fully, it wouldn't abandon you. It would pick you up, throw you into the fray, again and again, give you trouble and joy; ravish you. The entire world outside our family seemed to be in agitation. Everyone else was blossoming and becoming themselves. I wanted to join them, to enter that world. But how to get there?

On that question, I was completely in the dark.

When I think about those final years of my childhood, I remember a story my father once told me, one that now appears to me to be about an inheritance, a gift passed from my grandfather to my father and then to me. In the story, my father was a young boy, stranded in bed with a broken ankle, restless and bored. Every afternoon, Grandpa would come home from the Winchester gun factory on his lunch hour to take his meal by his son's bed. One day, he rigged up a mirror by the window, slanting it so Albert could see the world outside.

I like to imagine that boy propped on his pillows, watching that flickering mirror hour upon hour . . . sky and sky, an occasional cloud plowing the blue sea, a gusty branch, wind-riding birds. The boy growing impatient, seeing in that framed rectangle, that living picture, how gorgeous the world was, how tempting, how perfect.

What my grandfather gave to my father, my father gave to me—a vision of the world's richness. He was my mirror in the window. I watched him as he left us every morning to go to work, to more adventures, as fully charged as a racehorse, and I was filled with wonder. What if I could live like my father lived, like I thought all men lived, a large life filled with drama?

"Someday . . ." I began to tell myself, my eyes following the flag of car exhaust sailing by the kitchen window as he backed quickly out of the driveway, going as fast backward as he did forward. But *someday* must be a long way off, I thought. It was hard to imagine that I could ever leave us that easily.

As it turned out, it wasn't me after all but Bill who broke away first. That it was bloody and hard is only a testament to the power and glory of The Family.

8

An A for Creativity

THE FIRST TIME THAT BILL RAN AWAY FROM HOME, WE WERE ON A family picnic at the lake at Chatfield Hollow. There were only six of us that spring Saturday, my mother and father, Cindy, Beth, little Stephen, and me. I was thirteen and about to graduate from St. Rita's, which only went to eighth grade. Bill was a freshman at Notre Dame High School; he'd just turned fifteen.

My parents had driven our new sky-blue Pinto, the one Grandma Callahan and Great-aunt Bert had helped them buy, and they'd left the big station wagon at home that day for Michael to use. As the oldest, with places to go and important, college-bound things to do, Michael was sometimes allowed to skip out on family outings. Bill didn't have any plans we knew of. He just didn't want to come with us, and my parents, surprising me, had let him have his way. He was supposed to stay at home.

When we pulled into the driveway after our day at the lake, Michael appeared at the front door, looking flushed and even a little wild-eyed. In his hand, he had one of the pieces of scrap paper my mother cut up and made her grocery lists on. Such a small scrap of paper and on it nothing but *I'm leaving. I'm sorry. Don't worry about me. Bill.*

For a second, everything took on the bright, flat colors and simple lines of a children's drawing—Michael's orange hair and white face, the rectangular doorway behind him, the green grass where we stood, the blue sky and round yellow sun high over the pointed roof of the house.

Michael had found the note on the kitchen table when he got home that afternoon, he told us. Immediately he'd jumped into the car and gone to look for Bill until he spotted him walking down a nearby street. "When he saw me, he waved me away and then he started running. I tried to catch him but he cut through the woods."

Later, Bill would give his own version—Michael was chasing him with the *car* and so intent on bringing him home that he almost ran him over. "I was running for my life," Bill said. It was the usual Bill version, funnier, darker, the complaint hidden in humor—Michael's blind ambition, his big-brother panic, the station wagon bearing down; Michael, the good son, almost killing him.

My sisters' faces were blank, astonished mirrors of my own. He ran away? Wrote a good-bye note and . . . went? Where'd he ever think of that? There was only The Family in our family. There was the big blue station wagon and the big blue tent, the dinners every night at six, chores on Saturdays and Mass on Sundays, spring picnics, summer campfires, sing-alongs in the car, Aunt Barbara, the great-aunts and uncles and grandparents, the lavish, sparkling Christmases. Bill's picking up and leaving all of that behind was a daringly original act, the most creative act performed by any of us, in fact, since my father-less mother, that only child, dreamed up a big, happy family back when she was nineteen.

After my parents raced out the door to go look for him, Cindy and I put one of our forty-fives on the record player in the living room. We sat in the two armchairs, rocking and listening to "Which Way You Goin', Billy?" sometimes looking down into our laps and sometimes staring at each other as solemnly as owls. Every time the record ended, one of us would get up and put it on again.

Where did the trouble begin? I thought we all knew that it was there, but then why were my parents so bewildered? Cindy and I knew, knew in the same deep, wordless way that we knew each other's skin and scars and faces when asleep. It was just there, the trouble; we could smell it.

Bill had always been hungry, hungrier than the rest of us. He had my father's romantic nature, and a reckless heart that was ever ready to fling itself open. Even his temper tantrums as a two-year-old were extravagant: Bill would hold his breath until he turned red, then blue, and then finally, horribly, mercifully pass out, crumpling to the carpet and lying there in a heap.

But he was as tenderhearted as he was reckless—a combination that could only lead to trouble, far more trouble for him than for anybody else. When Bill did something wrong, even the most minor of infractions, he was tormented with guilt and would obsess over his disobedience until he was driven to confess. His sneaky siblings couldn't understand him—tell on yourself? No way, José!

When he was sad or hurt, Bill looked sadder and more hurt than anyone I knew. When my parents yelled at him, his mouth would drop open like a trapdoor and then hang there, the hurt and humiliation naked on his face. As he got older, he began to work on his defenses. A big shrug of his shoulders, a quick retort. But he wasn't fooling anyone—or at least not Cindy and me.

When we were little, my mother was always having to tell Bill to leave the two of us alone. He teased us with knuckle punches to our shoulders, elastics sent zinging toward our heads, wet dish towels twisted into ropes and snapped at our bare legs. Cindy and I ran like hell. We hated him and adored him without end. He was quick and sarcastic, handsome and cool. And even then, running from flying elastic bands, we knew.

He had dirty-blond hair, floppy bangs, a closemouthed smile that tilted to the left, dark blue eyes, and my mother's coloring—cream with a bit of coffee—so he tanned easily. All of my girlfriends, and Cindy's, too, fell in love with him.

Once, when he was eight or nine, he stood at the top of the attic stairs wearing only a bath towel, performing for Cindy and me. We watched from below as Bill sang to us, using his fist as a microphone.

"Come on, baby, light my fire . . ." He slid the towel open quarter inch by quarter inch. Cindy and I were wide-eyed, giggling, beside ourselves with terror and glee, ready to run at any moment. He sang the words as suggestively as he could. "Fire" became "fie-ahhh." His bangs were still wet; his chest, smooth and shiny as a seal. The towel crept open, like a stage curtain . . . his hipbone, his thigh . . .

Cindy and I shrieked! We turned to run. We didn't go anywhere. The towel hung between his legs; he stopped there. He was a great big tease. He entertained *and* tortured us at the same time; he combined the two beautifully.

Another day, he shut me in the kitchen broom closet. Pushed me in there with the mops and brooms and rags and slammed the door. I tried to shove my way back out, pushing as hard as I could on the door; it didn't give an inch.

"Billy, let me out!" I yelled, this time throwing my whole body against the door. I got a shuddering inch of kitchen light and air before the door banged shut again, closing me inside. I had to get out! I threw myself into the door again and again. I knew if I started screaming, I would never stop. I covered my mouth with my hand.

Then, as if someone had waved a wand over me, I melted into the floor, down amid the mop heads and rags, and went quiet. It smelled of Endust and lemon furniture polish.

A minute went by, and the door cracked open. A sliver, then a wedge, of kitchen table and cool linoleum, the dining room doorway beyond. . . . I made a dive, but it closed too fast. I could hear him whistling.

I'd been on the other side of this door when he threw Cindy inside the week before, so I knew he was examining his fingernails while he whistled, then polishing them on his shirt. He might even bend over and retie his sneakers, holding the door closed with his buttocks. We knew one another's little tricks and gestures better than we knew our own.

It wasn't until my mother came into the kitchen and Cindy told her that he'd trapped me in the closet that I was released.

* * *

What Bill remembers is my coming out of that closet like a beaten dog, shoulders slumped, face paper white, and going straight to my chair at the kitchen table without making a sound.

What I remember is the look of dumb surprise on his face when he saw me, followed by pain, and then by guilt. As my mother scolded him, he looked so hurt that I was instantly set against my own best interests— *Poor Billy*, I thought, and I even felt bad for being so terrified in the closet.

But as the scolding continued, he stuck out his chin, held up his empty hands, and shot back, "I didn't even touch her." And then I didn't feel sorry for him anymore.

He was the second-oldest brother, and he walked in Michael's footsteps every day of his childhood. Michael went first, Bill one year later—to Cub Scouts, Boy Scouts, piano lessons with Mrs. L. down the block, St. Rita's basketball team, Little League, first, second, third, fourth, fifth, sixth grades . . .

In a family, everyone has a role to play: If Michael was the brainy son, the successful son, what was Bill to be? Second best at everything that Michael did? He was the second-oldest son with nothing to call his own. And so he carved out another role for himself—the rebel. He had the courage for it, the buried anger, the creativity, but he didn't really have the heart. He disguised that fact with bravado whenever he could.

From first through sixth grades, he and Michael fought in the school yard at recess at least once a week, fistfights in front of an audience of cheering boys that always ended with a nun sailing into their midst to grab one of them by the ear. One good yank and both of them howled and went soft, like puppies.

In seventh grade, my parents let Bill leave St. Rita's and attend Blessed Sacrament Junior High. Now he had a school of his own. He joined their basketball team, got straight A's. My sisters and I weren't surprised—we always knew he was smart. Basketball trophies began to fill the shelves over his desk. He joined the school band. When Bill and my girlfriend Terry Wright played their trumpets to each other out their attic windows, they sounded like they were announcing themselves to the world in triumphant blasts: *Here I am!* I think of that moment, that happy, brassy blowing, as the end of an era.

The following year, the battle of the blue jeans began. Bill wanted them; you'd almost have to say he *needed* them. He might have been the only boy his age in Hamden who didn't have a pair. My grandmother offered to buy them for him but my mother refused. She feared losing us to the world. If we went skipping into it in our bell-bottoms and blue jeans, not only would we disappear, but she wouldn't be able to follow. I believe she must have sensed that the very world that would welcome us with open arms would hold her in contempt.

A few years earlier, posters showing a gray fist had begun to appear on telephone poles all around New Haven, advertising a nationwide women's strike—a strike for day care and equal wages in the workplace. Now militant-sounding women were everywhere on the news. At the dinner table, my Catholic father asked us what was the difference between euthanasia and abortion, and under his hot bright gaze we could find none. Another night at the dinner table when my father was working late, my mother turned to the six of us and insisted that she was *not* a housewife.

"I'm not married to this house!" she proclaimed, at once bold and beseeching. "I'm married to your father," she added. "I'm a wife and a mother of six and I think what I do is important!" I'm sure it was Beth who spoke then, who said something encouraging. Stephen wouldn't have understood her agitation, and the rest of us had begun to harden our hearts against her. We had to, for she had set all her hopes and dreams, her sense of worth, on the idea of a big happy loving family. And we were going to crush her dream. It was unbearable to think about, so we did our best not to.

Our parents never considered anything but a Catholic education for their children. Bill's school, Blessed Sacrament, went from seventh to ninth grades, after which all of his friends were going to Hamden High, the big public high school. Whenever we drove past Hamden High, which stood right on Dixwell Avenue next to the mall, we'd see the lawn filled with students, some lounging on the grass and smoking cigarettes, others making out against the brick wall, hundreds of kids, each dressed differently, in halter tops and hip-hugger jeans, Farrah Fawcett hair, khakis, tennis shirts, funkadelic afros that shimmered like halos, painter's overalls, huge bell-bottoms rippling like flags in a breeze—a chaos of color and expression. To parents like ours it must've looked like a mutinous place. Your child might end up being a stranger, speaking a different language altogether. He might end up feeling scorn for you—a businessman in a suit, a housewife in an apron. So Bill was forced to leave Blessed Sacrament after eighth grade, a year before his classmates, and go to Notre Dame, once again following in Michael's footsteps, even though he begged to stay.

My mother and grandmother fought about it. Their fight was short and swift—and fierce. It left them cagey around each other for years. Grandma took Bill's side, telling my mother that he needed something of his own. The rest of us kept our mouths shut. Standing up to our parents just wasn't possible.

The year Bill started at Notre Dame was the year he began to rebel. He played the coarse, stupid boy. Played it angrily. He'd drink straight from the milk carton, burp loudly, mumble all his words, say "ain't" and "duh" and "it don't matter to me," making my mother flinch.

Then he ran.

Cindy and I wondered if he was camped out in the woods across the street. What would he do without a sleeping bag?

Beth Ann kept her worries to herself, asking only if we knew how much money Bill might have with him, revealing, at nine years old, a deeply practical side. How far could Bill stretch twenty dollars? Her blue eyes were blank and as round as nickels, but I could almost hear her brain clicking as she added up the price of bologna and cheese and milk. In the last few years she and the dog, Sebastian, had become exceedingly close. "Hey, little buddy," she said to him that afternoon, and together they went upstairs to her room, closing the door behind them and staying there until dinner.

Our parents came home empty-handed that night.

The next thing we knew there was a police officer in our living room. He stood there taking notes, judging us, it seemed, and I knew my mother wanted to tell him about the picnics, the camping trips, the six of us wrestling with Dad on the living room floor when he came home from work, the dinners she made for us every night that always included two vegetables, one yellow, one green.

My father and mother began to put together a list of Bill's friends, none of them from Notre Dame. They called and spoke to the boys, to their mothers. Bill was nowhere to be found.

That night it rained. A cold spring rain.

"Dear God, please keep Billy warm and dry and make him want to come back home," I prayed. In my mind, God was the perfect Dobie cop; God would fetch him and bring him back, not by his collar but his heart.

Bill passed the night on a wet park bench at the same ball field where we had taken Danny Moore to meet Julie. The next day he came back. And that, we thought, was that.

When Bill left the second time, a few weeks later, summer had begun. As a week passed without a word, my parents' shock gave way to shame. They had failed, their beautiful family wasn't perfect after all. So my sisters and I began to tiptoe around the subject, tiptoeing even in our thoughts, as all good Catholic children learn to do.

Then suddenly one night he was back. Home again! But not to stay, only to get his clothes.

A dark-windowed van idled out front.

Bill had slipped upstairs without anyone noticing and thrown some clothes into a grocery bag. He was heading out the front door when my father spotted him from the kitchen. He ran into the living room, hard on Bill's heels.

"Where do you think you're going?" he yelled. Bill quickened his step, shoved open the front screen door.

"You're not leaving here again!" my father shouted, following him outside. "Get back in the house!"

Bill wouldn't stop. My father shoved his shoulder and Bill whirled around. My father's large freckled fists were clenched. His face was so close, Bill must've felt his heated breath. When my father was angry, the trees bent down.

The passenger door of the van swung open and I saw Bill's friend Joey at the wheel with his veil of black hair, taking it all in. There was an audience now; a silent, judging witness. Bill had an ally, someone besides us.

He looked straight at my father and put his arms up, still holding the grocery bag in one hand.

"I won't hit my own father," he said. Who was this brother? He'd become someone outside of us, our care, our games, our knowledge of each other. He sounded completely sure of himself, of what was right and what was wrong. He'd obviously kept his own counsel, come to his own conclusions. He had a moral code, spoken aloud now, same as my father.

With his hands still raised, Bill took a step backward toward the van. Then the most shocking thing happened in a night of shocking things—my father-in-the-suit fell to his knees on the lawn.

"Just tell me what's wrong!" my father howled. Bill looked like he'd been hit. He covered his eyes for a second, then turned and went stumbling toward the van.

When he leapt inside, I saw a third boy in back, another slice of deadpan cheekbone and lank hair. The door slammed and they took off, wheels screeching. I could imagine the three of them in that van, quickly lighting a joint, cranking the music up, listening to something raw and angry enough to beat grief down.

Five times Bill ran. Five times came back. Here again, gone again, all through that spring and summer and into the fall.

I was enthralled by the drama but found it overwhelming, the weeping and breast-beating, the shouts and teary professions of love and bewilderment. It provoked my own emotions, heartbreak and confusion and awe, but left no room for them.

My mother seemed to have become someone else, some wan and pining lover out of a book. Late one night, I saw her flitting noiselessly into the bathroom. Or, to be more precise, I caught a glimpse of the corner of her pink nightgown before the door closed, and then I heard her crying. She had been so determined to be a better mother than hers was—had she failed?

"If Bill doesn't quit this business, she's going to have a nervous breakdown!" I overheard Grandma whispering fiercely to Bert not long afterward, and I wondered what that was and if my mother had already had one. I kept picturing her pink nightgown slipping through the doorway; it was so ghostlike. And in a way she had become a ghost—vanishing behind closed doors so she could cry where no one would see or hear her. My father fought on, redoubling his efforts— he wanted his son back, he wanted his wife back. Though my mother was afraid his temper might drive Bill away even further, I preferred it to her sorrow.

I remember another day, when Bill and my father were upstairs in Bill's room fighting while my sisters and I sat huddled together on the living room floor.

"You're destroying this family!" my father yelled. Cindy, Beth, and I stared at one another's faces, as raptly as if we were watching the scene unfold there.

"You're killing your mother! Do you ever think of anyone but yourself?" And then the clatter of footsteps, the sound of a body falling into the accordion fold of the closet door. Cindy dug her chin into her chest, squeezing her eyes shut.

It was easy for us to imagine Bill caught in the door, hands at his side, saying nothing, accusing Dad with his innocence, and to imagine our father looming over him, white-faced with shame. They were like two giants roaring and stumbling about, breaking their own hearts.

With her chin still buried in her chest, Cindy opened her eyes and looked at me, her face long and strained. The three of us moved closer and then reached for one another with our feet, pressing them together in the center of the circle.

One night that fall, when Bill had gone missing again, my father jumped up from his chair in the living room, returned the papers he'd been reading to his black attaché case, and snapped the lid shut.

"I'm going to go find him and bring him home," he announced to my mother with sudden decisiveness. All in a moment, he'd thrown off melodrama, befuddlement, impotence. Years later, when I heard the phrase "the nervous system is meant to act," I would remember my father's face that night. He was thirty-nine.

Within hours he was back. He had one arm hooked under Bill's shoulder and with the other he was trying to open the door.

"Watch the step here," my father said gently, and Bill's feet slid up and over the doorstep like snakes.

As they came into the living room, Bill grinned straight at me, and I started to smile back. But then I realized he was grinning at everything. When my father maneuvered him to the foot of the living room stairs, he called out to my mother and she appeared wearing her nightgown.

Bill smiled up at her, an astonishing smile, then stumbled and grabbed the rail. He made it up one stair, two, slipped, straightened, held on tighter, never taking his eyes from my mother's face, never dimming his blazing smile. Another stair, and another; gamely he held on. Nothing would stop him from reaching her. When he finally made it to the top, she folded him in her arms.

They put him in a shower to "straighten him out" and asked me to make a pot of coffee.

I was in a dark mood in the kitchen. My parents thought he was drunk; I knew he was as high as a kite. I felt bad for them and bad for him, and it was as if the two feelings, warring inside of me for so long, canceled each other out. A bewildering coldness filled me. It was clear that my days as a witness, as "handmaiden with the coffeepot," as I called myself that night, were coming to an end.

9

Scorpios and the Sacred Heart

AS I TRUDGED UP THE HILL ON MY FIRST DAY AT MY NEW SCHOOL, THE white blouse I'd put on that morning for the first time was so stiff I could hear it crinkle when I moved my arms. The blouse was tucked into a regulation brown-and-white checked skirt, the brown knee-socks I wore were pulled up tight, and the laces on my soft-soled shoes were tied into a bow and then a double knot. I felt plain and serviceable, and not much else. It was as if my insides had been washed clean, and now on this bright September day I was ready to be filled, transformed, made into something better than this plain, pale self.

At the tree-covered top of the hill, Jesus stood on a pedestal and opened his chest, displaying his thorn-pierced heart next to a small sign reading, "Sacred Heart Academy"; the school itself was invisible from the road.

The long driveway in was a perfectly smooth, velvety black—did good Catholic men repave it for the nuns every night? On either side was a cropped green lawn, thicker and plusher than any front yard I'd ever seen, its manicured expanse shaded by big oak trees with rustling leaves and tall pines pointing their spindly fingers toward heaven. Walking up the drive in my dull uniform, I felt as if I were approaching a rich man's house—not as a guest, but as someone newly hired for some menial position. The religious statues that lined the road, chalky-white faces staring blankly over my head, were like doormen who had to keep their opinions to themselves.

At the end of the driveway, the paved surface opened into a big circle, the trees dropped away, and the school came into view, white-bricked, two-storied, shaped like an L. The parking lot was filled with girls, scrubbed and shiny, God's girls, all dressed alike because that's the way He loved us, evenly. Books were clutched against breasts, hair tucked behind ears, socks pulled high, only the knees showing and a few inches of thigh, and God notwithstanding, there were pretty knees, ugly knees, knobby ones like skulls, fat and freckled ones, and some so beautifully shaped they could take your breath away.

On my way in, I saw two of my St. Rita's friends, Marisa and a black-eyed girl named Lisa Guardino, but I knew I wouldn't be seeing any of the boys from St. Rita's. Sacred Heart was an all-girls school, no boys to distract us, to make us silly and stupid, vain or jealous—that was the theory, anyway, though we were perfectly capable of being all these things without boys around. Still, the hope was that without boys or pretty clothes, makeup or jewelry, we could pay attention to what mattered: our souls, college. It made me feel important and serious, like I was off to my first day of work.

In homeroom that morning, there was nobody I knew. At the desk in front of me, however, was someone who immediately caught my interest. She sat straight in her chair and her raven-black hair, which fell to her shoulders, was brushed to such a high sheen it was almost blue. Her hands, which she kept flat on the desk, were small, olive-skinned, the nails filed into perfect moons; she wore one gold ring. She was paying strict attention to our homeroom nun. She didn't fidget once. In fact, she hardly seemed to be breathing.

The nun was welcoming us to Sacred Heart. "Young Christian women" she called us, and it was the first time I'd ever heard myself described as a woman, not a girl. I was thirteen.

When the bell rang and we packed up our books to leave for our first class, the girl in front of me turned around. She had sable-colored eyes, black eyebrows, and thin, curved lips. She was small-boned, so the uniform was almost cute on her. "Like lemmings," she said, as we began filing out. Her eyes were worried, but there was a snicker in her voice. We exchanged names.

"Sylvia," she said, sounding out each syllable, so the S was a whisper and the *a* tilted up, and I knew that was how her mother said her name, and that her mother loved her.

She repeated my name in the same precise, silky way—"Kathee"— and we became friends.

I only have three photographs of Sylvia DeAngelis now. It's hard to believe that I don't have more. She was my closest friend through all four years of high school, and for a while it seemed we shared everything, even birthdays (almost). We were excited when we found out our birthdays were just one day apart, and both of us were Scorpios. It was Sylvia who told me what that meant—we were powerful, we were difficult. She never mentioned that we were supposed to be intensely sexual, too. That didn't interest her as much as our hot temper and talent for revenge. Sylvia had only two books in her house when I first knew her: the Bible and *Linda Goodman's Sun Signs*.

"Don't cross a Scorpio," she said, cocking one inky eyebrow so she looked knowing and dangerous—like someone in one of those old movies she liked to watch. She had a wiseass attitude but a wide-open heart. Sometimes when she looked at me, her eyes would literally shine with love.

In two of the photos I have, she sits at the piano that was tucked in a corner of her family's living room. In the first, she's curled on the bench, elbow on one knee, face resting on her hand. Her bangs swoop over one half of a neatly plucked eyebrow as she stares moodily off into space. In the second, she's banging away on the piano, an unlit cigarette hanging from one corner of her mouth. Her lips are slightly parted as if she's about to say something to me—the photographer. I can almost hear her: "Of all the gin joints . . ." She just couldn't hold the deep angst pose for long.

In the third photograph, taken in the fall of our fifteenth year, she and I are standing in front of a brick wall in winter jackets, unsmiling, our fists raised in the Black Power salute. Both of us wear our hair parted in the middle, and it hangs flat on our heads. We look as limp, as slatternly, as laundry in the rain.

But I'm getting ahead of myself here. At thirteen, Sylvia and I weren't posing for the world. She wasn't trying to subvert her impishness and become someone *serious*. I hadn't yet brought Ayn Rand and *The Virtue of Selfishness* into our lives. I had no need for Rand's elitism or Black Power salutes or any fuck-you gesture to the world. Not yet. Not then.

The first time Sylvia came over to my house for dinner, shortly after we met that fall, she was shocked to see us all sit down at the kitchen table together and wait for my father to lead us in prayer.

"In the name of the Father, the Son, and the Holy Ghost . . ." Sylvia made the sign of the cross and bowed her head with the rest of us, but she made bug eyes at me from across the table, nervous and admiring. I was delighted. In fact, I was bursting with pride—in her, in my family. I couldn't wait to discuss them with her later.

After everyone had been served, we began to make up limericks, with each person at the table contributing a line. Sylvia couldn't believe that she was expected to join in, but of course she was; even little Stephen played.

"There once was a man named Jack."

"He liked to eat on his back."

"He put soup up his nose."

"It smelled like a rose."

"Stephen! Your turn!" we called out in unison, every voice artificially sweetened for our little boy child.

"And it smelled good," he said triumphantly, brandishing his spoon. Sylvia laughed aloud, her laugh ending in a purr.

"He's so cute!" she kept exclaiming. She was the youngest in her family, so Stephen and Beth Ann were amazingly adorable to her.

Sylvia thought my family was perfect. Somehow she seemed to have missed all of the storms raging around Bill. She noted the prayers and games at dinner, the way everyone, even the boys, helped clean up afterward, and then how we each set about our chores—one of us making our sandwiches for school the next day, one mixing the pitchers of powdered milk, another mixing the frozen orange juice in the blender for breakfast. Sometimes Sylvia said we were like the Brady Bunch, sometimes like a well-run army.

"Your parents are so young!" she used to exclaim. "Everyone's so smart!" She was amazed at the bookshelves that were everywhere—in the living room, the dining room, and each of our bedrooms. She saw our dinner table games as deeply competitive and highly educational. She had a working-class view of us—she thought we were always sharpening our wits on one another, always having to perform. She figured we'd each go far.

If Sylvia saw my family as a shining army, I saw hers as a renegade division hiding out in the woods, quarreling, snickering, deeply loyal to one another, suspicious of outsiders, and weary, weary to the bone. They ran a little grocery store in New Haven and worked six and a half days a week; later Sylvia would call herself "the original latchkey kid."

Night came early at Sylvia's house—there was no effort to hold it off as the daylight hours grew shorter with the advance of fall. After dinner, Mr. DeAngelis went through all the rooms of the house, checking the lights and doors and windows like a sentry on patrol. He was a short man with wide, plaintive eyes and furry eyebrows. Before he closed the curtains, he peered out each window. He opened and closed the front door, relocking it. He bent over each lamp and clicked it on, then off.

Behind his back, Sylvia saluted him. "Reporting for duty, *sir!*" she said, but Mr. DeAngelis was almost deaf so he didn't hear her. She marched stiffly behind him, hands clasped at her back, bowing from the waist into the lamps and then cocking her head as though to listen as she switched them on and off, on and off. Mr. DeAngelis noticed nothing. He was lifting the phone from its cradle, checking for a dial tone. Sylvia saluted a standing lamp. "All quiet on the Western Front," she announced.

Our families seemed like perfect opposites, so we were deeply drawn to each other's. In my house, night and day were cleanly divided. At bedtime, doors were shut and lights went out; quiet reigned in every room, on every floor, the house a no-man's-land until dawn. Morning was sunlight and raucous cheer, little Stephen throwing himself on top of me in my bed, crowing like a rooster to wake me, and then all of us racing about to open the venetian blinds and curtains and chase away the gloom.

In Sylvia's house, drapes kept the living room shrouded from every sunny day. At night, the room was locked in permanent twilight. The watery gaze of the TV flickered over the walls, the chairs, the flowered couch, the figures of her parents and of Albie, the older of her two brothers. Albie couldn't have been more than twenty-five then, but his receding hairline and heavy jowls gave him the bare, humble look of a much older man. Stretched out in the gray flickering light, mouth wide open, he seemed like a figure in someone's dream, or in a painting. *Drowning Man* you might have called it, or simply, *The Grocer's Oldest Son*.

Mr. DeAngelis would sit tilted sideways against the arm of the couch, his hands folded meekly between his legs, while Mrs. D. nodded off at the other end. Notch by notch, her head would fall toward her chest until suddenly with a snort, she'd crank it back up again.

"It looks like a mortuary in here," Sylvia would say in her Boris Karloff voice.

Then she'd shake her father's shoulder. "Dad! Dad! Go to bed! Go up to bed now!" I could imagine many a strange thing, but a girl ordering her father to bed was not one of them.

Albie lived at home and helped out at the grocery store whenever he didn't have an outside job. I liked him a lot. He was very sweet and very paranoid. He thought someone was snooping in their mail and bugging their phone.

"The FBI?" Norman, the younger brother, often teased him. "Think the FBI wants you? Or maybe the CIA? I think it's the nut farm that wants you."

Both of Sylvia's brothers had gone to boot camp at Parris Island, but Albie had had to be shipped home.

"They broke him," Sylvia told me, initiating me into some of the DeAngelis family mythology, for that was the explanation they used to account for Albie's paranoia.

Norman survived training and became a marine. The first time I saw him, one afternoon that fall when Sylvia and I had just started to become friends, he was bent over a bowl of pasta, hair in his eyes, as he sucked strands of spaghetti into his mouth. I'd come in the front door, looking for Sylvia, and there he was in a white tank top, sitting at the kitchen table, facing me but looking into his pasta bowl. Only the living room was between us. His lips were shiny with oil. His cheekbones looked like Indian arrowheads. I was glued to the carpet. Sylvia hadn't told me she had this kind of a brother. He had muddy eyes and a marine's blue tattoo on his arm. He rode a Harley. Even his name seemed significant to me—Nor*man*. He was my first, astonishing experience of love at first sight. The feeling was like a black-and-white film suddenly going full color. Or the other way around.

When he finally looked up and noticed me standing there, he said nothing, just stared at me in silence for a long moment, then went back to his pasta. He was hungry, I could tell. Very hungry.

A strand of leather was tied around his left wrist. He had long fingers, a man's large knuckles, the skin darker there—oh, I noted it all.

Norman could tame a wasp with those fingers. I saw him do it on a warm autumn day a few weeks later. He was working on his bike in their driveway. The wasp had flown into a narrow piece of pipe where it was turning itself in circles, lifting its long legs and making a furious buzzing sound. Norman slipped his finger inside slowly, slowly, and then he was petting the wasp, its soft back end, and when he withdrew his finger, the wasp followed, hanging on almost wistfully.

"See?" he said. "He likes it."

I felt sure I would kiss him someday—it came to me in a flash.

Then I put the idea away. Impossible. I was just his little sister's girlfriend. He hardly noticed me.

"So the CIA's after you?" Norman asked. It was early October, a
Sunday, the only day the store was closed, and we were eating in the
dining room at the big table where an oilcloth had been set over the
white lace tablecloth to keep it looking nice. We helped ourselves to
the bowl of ziti and sauce, the plate of fried eggplant, the tomato and
bread salad soaked in olive oil and salt. There was a bottle of soda on
the table, forbidden in my house because the sugar would ruin your
teeth.

Albie giggled, and then went owly serious. "They might be."
Norman looked at him hard. "You know what? You're screwy. You're
messed up in the head."

Albie laughed. "I got a screw loose," he said. He looked appealingly
at me, then at Norman. "Right? A screw loose in my head."

Norman relaxed. "One screw? You got a whole toolbox rattling
around in there." Even Mrs. D. laughed.

"A whole toolbox in here," Albie said happily, childishly, pointing
to his head.

"What do you think, Kathy?" Norman asked, jerking his chin at
me, his eyes clear as rain. "Time to commit?"

They were constantly asking my opinion, as if glad to finally
have a witness to all their crazy goings-on. I loved it. I felt like they
needed me.

"Pa!" Norman shouted. "Pa! They're coming to take Albie away!
They're taking your son to the funny farm, Pa!"

Mr. D. looked at me, raised his eyebrows, and tapped the side of
his head.

"You don't care, Pa? I'm talking about your son. You know what
they say—the fruit don't fall far from the tree." Suddenly, Norman
smiled. The smile lengthened and narrowed his jaw. White teeth
flashed; a lickable wolf.

"Don't you talk to your father that way!" Mrs. D. said, and then, just like that, she was mad. She went lipless, hawklike, black eyebrows arching up into a furious V.

"He works fourteen hours a day, a slave to that store, all he does is work and sleep so you can sit there with your smart mouth and—"

"Who asked him to?" Norman said, shoving his plate away, then his chair. "I'm leavin'."

Outside in the driveway, the Harley exploded into life. Then came the earsplitting chocka-chocka-chocka as he rolled past the dining room windows where we sat. He hit the shady street, ploughing it with noise. The roar faded, but so slowly that after a while I wasn't sure if I was hearing the last sounds of the bike crossing the New Haven line or just a stunned echo in my ears.

For a few minutes I couldn't see anything clearly. There was the sound of silverware on plates, of Albie saying . . . what? What did he just say?

The late-afternoon sunlight lay weakly on the table, across half-empty plates, oil smears, a wadded-up napkin. How dull it all was.

The only signs that Norman had been there among us were a crumpled Marlboro pack and the scent of Aramis on the phone receiver, which I noticed when I called home later that evening to ask my mother's permission to stay over. I closed my eyes and held the receiver against my lips. My breath slowed, and there was a sensation of warm water running down the nape of my neck and my spine. I had no idea when I'd see Norman again. Sylvia had already told me about a time he'd gotten so mad that he took off and drove his Harley straight across the country to California.

But there were wonderful nights when Norman made it through a whole dinner, lazily snapping at Albie, Albie happily egging him on, Mrs. D. laughing and Mr. D. asking what I thought of it all. Then Sylvia and I would clear the dishes and Norman would light a cigarette, and I'd pray he would stay around.

One night when he did, I watched him as he sat there in his white tank top, his jeans and motorcycle boots, playing with their dog. She was an Alaskan malamute, a silvery, blue-eyed creature he'd named Queenie. Norman buried his face in her fur, roughing it up with his hands.

"Who's my girl, huh? Who's my girl?" he said, his voice suddenly high and sweet. Queenie barked, jumped up on him, ran her wet snout through his long hair.

"She likes to smoke," Norman told me, lighting a Marlboro. "Watch this, Kathy." (My name in his mouth!)

"Sit, Queenie, sit!" he said, and she immediately went down on her haunches, watching his face for her signal.

As soon as he took a long drag off the Marlboro, her tail started sweeping the floor. He held the smoke in, looked hard at her, and then jerked his chin up. Queenie jumped on him again, her mouth open, and he blew the smoke in. She slurped and bit the air. And then she licked his lips with her long red tongue. Barked for more.

10

Little Woman

MY BROTHER BILL'S FIRST GIRLFRIEND REMINDED ME OF A CUPCAKE.
Becky was dark-haired, dark-eyed, round-breasted, and so sweet and
softly feminine at thirteen that I could see why Bill was always pulling
her onto his lap. Whenever my parents went out, Becky baked cakes
in our kitchen, chocolate with pink icing, letting the rest of us lick the
batter off the spoon. Every cake she baked was in the shape of a heart.
The day I'm remembering she and Bill were wound tightly around
each other on the living room couch, snuggled in the corner, kissing.
She was wearing a white blouse with little ruffles along the neckline,
and she seemed to fit perfectly into Bill's arms. While Cindy and I
watched unnoticed from the stairway, enchanted and jealous—but of
which one?—Bill worked his hand into her blouse, then her white
bra, rubbing her breast while she made mewing sounds like a kitten.
The nipple was tawny-colored, like a doe's eye. I didn't have any
breasts to speak of yet. Once again Bill was our scout, leading the way
into strange new lands.

I was on my own scouting expedition one day not long after that,
snooping around my parents' bedroom, when I made a strange dis-
covery. It was late afternoon, the light liquid in the big mirror over
their dresser, no one in the house but me. On the dresser top was a
mirrored, gold-framed tray and on it, my mother's lipsticks, all deep

shades of red. Except for the occasional dab of powder on her nose, that was the only makeup she wore.

One by one, I opened the lipsticks, sniffing them, examining the subtle differences between Rose Red and Geranium. I rummaged through her jewelry box, picked out a pair of jet-black earrings and held them up to my ears, checking myself out in the mirror—pretty. In one of her dresser drawers, I found her pastel-colored nightgowns and her panty hose. Thick white cotton socks were piled next to lacy bikini underwear, and on some of those the elastic bands were frayed. Since I preferred a completely romantic vision of my mother's femininity, I closed the drawer and moved on to her closet. Her dresses hung neatly there and I ran one hand over them, like I was stroking a harp, and they released her scent. They smelled of Dove and Secret and Alberto VO5 and, underneath, some essence that brought me back to childhood when my mother seemed like some large, warm animal with tiger-colored eyes and miles of downy skin.

Then I noticed two books on the overhead shelf, peeking out from behind some shoe boxes. We never hid books in our house, so of course I had to look. *The Godfather* and *Valley of the Dolls*. I glanced through them quickly—I didn't know when my mother might come home—and put them back.

Over the next few weeks, I returned to her closet again and again until I'd read both books from beginning to end, and then one more time to reread page ninety-seven of *The Godfather.* Sonny and the bridesmaid. He lifts her up onto the sink. A hard thrusting, and all the while the bride and groom smile and dance for the guests downstairs. "Insides like pasta," the wives cackle. I stumbled around the house in a daze.

My parents said I lived too much in my imagination. My head was in the clouds. Or in a book. To them, it must've seemed as if I'd tucked myself into a dream, far, far from reality. But books weren't a hideaway, they were an invitation. Even their titles seemed to me like inscriptions on stone archways, doorways to . . . well, something more real than the world around me. *The Power and the Glory, Long Day's Journey into Night, The Heart of the Matter.* Those were my mother's books, the ones she left lying out on the coffee table or arranged neatly on shelves, co-conspirators in plain sight.

On the bathroom radiator was my father's copy of *Pale Fire*. It sat there for a year, picking up the smells of Fantastik and Ajax. I thought it was a key to my father's mind, and when I couldn't make heads or tails of it, I was deeply impressed.

I read erratically, racing through some books cover to cover, abandoning others after a paragraph or two. When I cracked open *The Heart of the Matter*, I was intrigued by its first lines: "The police van took its place in the long line of army lorries waiting for the ferry. Their headlamps were like a little village in the night. . . ." But then I came to the phrase "red laterite slope," which I didn't understand and didn't like the sound of anyway, and I closed the book, put Graham Greene aside.

Reading this way was like seeing the countryside through the windows of a fast-moving train. Drunken priests, knife fights, donkeys on a trail, a thief in the house—the variety, the possibilities out there were staggering. I found *The Outsiders* on my own, and soon I was filled with visions of boys in gangs, boys living dangerously, romantically, on the streets.

That spring, I began to notice the shaggy-haired boys in their Army coats and dungaree jackets hanging outside the old firehouse on Putnam Avenue, only three and a half blocks from our house. I'd heard the adults debate whether they were juvenile delinquents or just bored kids. I hoped they were delinquents. The town of Hamden had refurbished the firehouse, put in pool tables, a soda machine, and a youth counselor, and officially named it the Teen Center. Every time we drove by in the station wagon, I'd sneak a look at them, those wild, beautiful boys, and I began to wonder what it would feel like if they were trying as hard to sneak a look at me.

Almost every book I read, except for *The Outsiders* (and *Little Women* and *Christy*, of course), was written by a man. I assumed the role of the protagonist in each, and if most of them were men, so what? It made no difference to me. I, too, would swoon at the sight of a beautiful woman, bare-shouldered, in a silver dress. Who wouldn't?

The women in the stories I read incited lust, memory, hope, despair. That was fine, but it wasn't a life. Being the one who *felt* those feelings, that's what mattered.

Secretly, I had begun to think that my father and I were alike, if for no other reason than the fact that I didn't want to be stuck in the house like my mother. My father wouldn't have thought that he and I were alike; he couldn't think that way, couldn't because he was a man and I was a girl. But I could slip my skin at will.

I was fourteen and the world was whispering, whispering. I thought it was talking to me in particular.

One day when my father was driving us home from church, all of us in our Sunday clothes in the blue station wagon, we passed a girl wearing dungaree cutoffs walking up Clifford Street. She had long, tanned legs and long blond hair that brushed her hips as she walked. From the backseat I saw my father's head swivel, my mother's shoulders tighten. My father didn't even notice that he had turned to look. He went on talking like nothing had happened.

She was a part of spring's beauty, that girl, same as the forsythia blooming. I, too, wanted to drink her in with my eyes. Study her until I'd had enough. And I wanted to be her, too, collecting stares as I walked down the street, pulling fathers from their suitlike selves. I was confused, but in a completely interesting way.

There was a sort of destiny in this moment. Watching that girl through my father's eyes, I sensed the future, the day when I, too, would saunter down the street in cutoffs. But unlike that girl, when my time came, I would be conscious of my effect. Fourteen, and it was getting harder and harder to wait.

11

Jailbait

"I WANT TO EAT YOUR PUSSY." AS HE DROVE THE TRUCKER HELD THE SIGN up to his window for me to see. He'd printed it out in large capital letters, and must have carried it with him to relieve the loneliness and boredom of the road. To me, it read like an SOS in a world of strangers.

There we were, rolling across the country that summer of my fourteenth year on a six-week vacation in a motor home, my father at the wheel of the lumbering beast, sitting up high over the road, my mother and Michael his copilots, Henry Mancini thundering from the stereo speakers. My father liked his music loud.

We still had a long road ahead of us. First we'd gone north to Niagara Falls, now we were heading west across Canada, all the way to Vancouver, where my father wanted to tour the university. After that, our destination was the university at Long Beach, California, where my father would be attending the National Association of College and University Food Service conference.

There was a kitchen table in the middle of the motor home, which folded into a bed for Cindy and me. During the day, Cindy and Beth spent a lot of time at that table, working on their vacation scrapbooks or playing Mad Libs, while Stephen sat next to them coloring. Above the driver's seat was a big, glossy-looking cabinet that opened into a bunk bed for my parents. At night, we could hear my father snoring.

\ skinny corridor led to the back of the motor home, where overhead cabinets opened into beds for Bill and Michael. Beth Ann and Stephen slept on the couches underneath. "Six weeks in a tin can with all you boneheads" was how Bill described our trip.

When Henry Mancini filled the motor home, Bill directed the orchestra mockingly—if he was in a good mood. But mainly he wasn't. He didn't want to be with us. He spent most of his time stretched full-length on one of the foldout couches in the back, his eyes closed, perhaps asleep, perhaps just wishing he could be asleep, asleep like Rip Van Winkle, waking in six weeks when our vacation was over.

I spent a lot of time in the back, too. Sitting there at the wide window, I could make contact with the men driving behind us, and my parents couldn't see what was going on. Truckers saluted me with their horns. Men followed in their cars. I carried on conversations with them, first mouthing the words, then writing them notes. They rode our bumper so they could read what I'd written.

When the trucker showed me his "I Want to Eat Your Pussy" sign, I thought quickly, and wrote out a reply: "Meow." His eyes went wide and then he blasted his airhorn.

In the middle of one of these conversations, two dark-haired men in a red car held up a piece of paper reading, "Jailbait." I bent over my pad of construction paper, and carefully printed my response: "Want to Go Fishing?"

For a couple of seconds their faces went blank; then they laughed in astonishment. I could see them talking animatedly to each other. The driver had a mustache and a wide white smile, the passenger's hair was tied back into a ponytail. They followed us for miles down that sunlit highway, through the late afternoon. Henry Mancini gave way to Billie Holiday, Billie to Neil Young, he and the Beatles my parents' only concession to us kids, and still they were there. So there I was, stuck in the back window like a mannequin.

I was stunned by my effect—grown men, good-looking men!—deeply flattered, but no longer happy. Didn't they have somewhere else to go? We had just met and suddenly we were going steady, me and these two men in their red car. As the sun lowered, I squirmed in my skin, more worm than hook now. There at the back window, I'd run out of postures, run clean out of things to say to them. As Jailbait, my conversational topics were limited.

When we exited the highway, they did, too. When we turned in at the KOA campground, they were right behind us. By the time they'd paid the campground fee, I was beside myself with agitation. They were too close, too close . . . right there with me and my family. Cinderella and Lolita were not compatible roles.

They parked in the campsite next to us, and when my father went out to hook up the electricity and water, they started chatting with him. "How many miles per gallon do you get in this thing?" My father noticed nothing, not even the fact that these men were tentless, trailerless, extraordinarily idle.

For a long time, I was too nervous to leave the motor home, and when I did, I grabbed my baby brother's hand and dragged him with me like a prop. As soon as we came to the door, the men's faces flared up, but I bent down to Stephen and whispered in his ear. I took him and his trucks to the picnic table set up at the edge of the parking lot. While he played, I caressed his hair.

When I felt their impatience growing, I put my feet up on the bench and rebuckled my sandals, brushing invisible dirt from my leg. Once or twice I dared a glance, a look that I hoped was like a rope, saying, "Hold on." I hoped some form of action would occur to me. Perhaps, by nighttime, when my family had fallen asleep

They left the campground in an angry scud of pebbles and exhaust. In one hour's time, I'd gone from being the most desirable bit of jailbait in the world to a stupid cocktease.

For most of our trip that summer I wore hip-hugger jeans, halter tops, big hoop earrings, and an Army cap Sylvia had given me as a going-away present. I had two halter tops, one candy-striped, the other a yellow mesh that clung softly to my breasts and allowed glimpses of skin to show through the little holes, quick peeks of snow white and shell pink. I didn't wear a bra; my mother said there wasn't ything there to support yet, and, technically speaking, she was quite right.

As soon as we'd left Connecticut, she and I had started arguing about the halter tops. She forbade me to wear them in Vancouver or at my father's conference in California.

"I'm ashamed to be seen with you," she said. "Do you have any idea what you look like in those?" Before I could think of a reply, she went on. "You look awful. You look like—"

"To *you* I do," I broke in quickly. "I don't care what you think. I'm not dressing this way for you."

"Who *are* you dressing that way for, then?"

"Myself," I said haughtily. "You dress the way you want to dress, I dress the way I want to dress. I don't make fun of your clothes."

"Kathy, I'm not making fun of your clothes, and besides, I'm a grown woman and you're—"

"And so? I'm a woman, too."

"Kathy, you are not! You're a fourteen-year-old girl."

Almost a decade after the fact, my mother had suddenly begun to regret allowing me to skip kindergarten. "That's where the trouble began," she explained to me. She shouldn't have listened to the nursery-school teacher who had told her I was ready for real schoolwork, she said, because "emotionally, you were too immature."

Never mind, I told myself, tying my halter top at my back; even if what she said was true, and part of me thought it was, I was not going to live in her vision of me. That summer I'd discovered another gaze, the gaze of boys and men, and in that shining light I felt myself blooming. No longer Kathy, oldest daughter, big sister, mother's helper, I was feeling the first whiff of real freedom in my life: Who might I become?

"Beaver." The day after I'd disappointed the men in the campground, two men at a truck stop spoke the word when I walked by on my way to the ladies' room. Their faces were brown and red from the sun. They were smiling at me but talking to each other. Beaver? To be honest, I didn't know what these men were saying half the time. When I took a stab at the meaning of "cleaver beaver," I pulled back almost immediately. *No, can't be*, I thought. But maybe it was. There seemed to be a continent of men out there who had made up a language that was as dirty, as strange, as the thing itself. Makin' bacon. Jelly roll. Busting cherry. They said it aloud. They said it to me. They figured I knew.

And I could fake it pretty easily. I just stuck with the metaphor of the moment and riffed.

I know we stopped at all kinds of state parks with mountains and glaciers as we headed west, but I don't remember any of them. Canada was nothing but truck drivers to me; harbingers of the world to come. Prosaic by day—red duckbill caps, *Playboy* Bunny stickers, sweat stains, sunburn—they changed into pure spirits at night as I lay awake in the motor home, listening as they rolled down the highway, riding high, headlights bent into the dark country ahead. When the sun rose, they would take on human shape again, call the waitress "doll," ask for a cup of "diesel fuel."

My mother argued with me over my halter tops, with Bill over his grammar. "It don't make no difference to me," Bill would say and burp loudly.

"It *doesn't* make *any* difference," she'd correct him, looking pained.

"That's what I said. It don't matter neither way."

My mother knew her English, knew what a dangling participle was, a split infinitive, how to diagram a sentence and write a term paper. For a long time, we had been in awe of that and her piano-playing and her ability to pronounce the French words on a menu, but in the last year, her older children had begun to tease and harass her. The harder she tried to maintain her dignity, the more we went after her. She must have felt like she was trying to run from wasps.

One night when we were all camping out in the big blue tent, my mother spoke in her sleep, clear as a bell. "Bah bah, black sheep." We stifled our giggles, called out, "What's that, Mom?" We wanted to lead her deeper into it, but she got cagey, even in her sleep, and said stiffly, "Never mind. You wouldn't understand."

That had us rolling inside our sleeping bags. We couldn't wait until the morning to give her a hard time.

She was my mother, but that year, after an entire childhood of being close to obsessed with her, trying to read her every thought and feeling, admiring her to the point of adoration, she ceased to be anything more for me: not the Catholic schoolgirl feverishly writing her high school essay on blacklisted Graham Greene, not the eighteen-year-old my father met who, on their first date, rolled the car window all the way down and let the wind play havoc with her hair. Or for that matter, the nineteen-year-old who dropped out of college and married my father against her mother's wishes, then had six kids, one after the other, while Grandma Callahan cried, "It's just too many!"

Her act of rebellion had spawned us, a big happy family, and now the rebellious girl was a mother, shepherding, correcting, corralling her teenage children. Even now I sometimes wonder why my parents were so surprised by the mass mutiny of our adolescent years—an act of rebellion was our very genesis.

In San Francisco, we escaped the motor home for a couple of days and checked into an old hotel. Bill and I found ourselves alone in a room on the third floor one afternoon. All across Canada, Bill's restlessness had plagued me. I had tried to be interesting to him, to fill in for his long-haired friends with their hash oil and their windowless vans. When he talked about running away back to Hamden, I volunteered to go with him. He wanted to be with his friends, and I wanted to be with him.

I sat on the windowsill that day, watching him as he pulled out a cigarette. A dirty neon sign blinked and buzzed outside. A breeze stirred the velvet curtains, moth-bitten and maroon. The sill was covered in soot. I straddled it, one leg suspended above the jangling street below, one in the dimly lit room.

"I smoke, too," I told him.

"You do not," he said absently. He paced the floor, frowning.

"I do, too! How would you know?"

"Okay," he said, coming over to me and holding out the cigaret
"Go ahead, take a drag."

"Drag" was a clue, but I couldn't read it. At the first puff, th
smoke leaked out of my mouth. He laughed. "You smoke like a girl,
he said, "and you walk like a boy." I decided I would learn to smoke
like a boy and walk like a girl.

It was tricky figuring out the best way to be a girl. Love and
loathing were aimed at her in equal strengths. Wearing a halter top
was teaching me that. But at fourteen, I thought I could reap the desire and dodge the loathing.

The morning we arrived at Long Beach for my father's conference, there were several other families pulling into the parking lot at
the same time. The fathers were shaking hands, the mothers standing
by with their smiles, and then I saw him—a teenage son, long and lean
with big, lazy eyes. He looked as silky and clean as a cat. He stood behind his mother and father, taller than either of them, his face blank,
like he was taking a break behind it. But then those big, lazy eyes
landed on me. He blinked.

When I went into the dormitory where we'd all be sleeping, the
boy followed me.

"My name is Greg," he whispered, lips close to my ear. "What's
yours?" All over my body, little hairs stood at attention. Our families
were coming down the corridor, carrying suitcases and piles of
clothes.

"We'll be together for three days now," he said, like we'd met long
ago and had been waiting for just this chance. As soon as I slipped inside one of the rooms assigned to my family, I fell down on the bed. I
lay very still; my body chattered excitedly.

Of all the feminine role models I had in my head, the woman in the
whipped cream dress on the cover of my father's Tijuana Brass album
was my favorite. Dark-haired and large-breasted; long-lashed and coy.

was a bit of cream in her hair, and more she was licking from her
. She was like a window into men's brains. When we were seven
ight, Cindy and I used to put on our white go-go boots (a present
Grandma and Great-aunt Bert) and dance in the living room,
ng over the shag carpet and twisting our hips to the *sexeeee!* lady
ne whipped-cream dress, to nakedness and dessert.
In the dorm room shower that night, I arranged the shampoo
her over my breasts and posed in front of the mirror. My breasts
emed bigger, one pink nipple peeked out of the cream. Something
beautiful and it would never be seen. Something so powerful and it
ould always be hidden. Why? It seemed almost sad to me that I had
ecome this creature—beautiful, sexy—and no one would see me as I
was in this bathroom, naked and covered with cream.

I had always looked at girls with a boy's admiration, a very young,
very inspired boy. I admired girls' angora sweaters, their painted nails
and puzzle rings, the patchouli oil and silver bangles, their sharp little
bones and hilly breasts. I looked at my girlfriends' teddy bears with
their button eyes and stitched-on smiles, fuzzy bedtime companions
waiting to be tucked in, and thought them the very picture of dumb
luck. I watched a silver crucifix slipping into shadow and felt I'd never
seen anything more beautiful. *Boys must go crazy for this girl*, I'd think.

I could put on hoop earrings and a flowery blouse, but being
female still felt like a bit of an act to me, an act my mother discour-
aged and my grandmother encouraged. My mother didn't want me to
care what I looked like, didn't want her fourteen-year-old to look sexy
or even know that she could. My grandmother simply wanted me
dressed in the latest styles. She liked accessories—bone bracelets,
wooden beads, smart-looking belts, clever little pocketbooks. I didn't
want my clothes to be that thoughtful. A halter top went straight to
the point; it started its own conversations. Wearing one was as good as
having a personality.

I don't know where the haunted house was, but we were all in it
the next day, all the mothers and kids on a day trip, following a tour

guide down a hallway, when Greg's hand folded itself around mine. How long his fingers were! No one looked down; nobody saw.

Then we were in a high-ceilinged room and they shut off the lights—everyone gasped—and he bent down and kissed me on the lips. Petal soft, his lips; petal soft, his hair swinging against my face.

When the lights came back on, we looked straight ahead, unseeing. Greg was still holding my hand.

Back at the dorm, Greg asked me if I wanted to meet him that night. I nodded yes. I felt as cool and shivery as a bowl of jello.

"You know the field past the parking lot?"

I nodded again.

"Meet me there at ten o'clock."

I was absolutely certain I was going to meet him and then, when the time drew near, absolutely certain I wasn't. I was terrified. I didn't know how I was supposed to act, how to tongue kiss, where my hands were supposed to go, which clothes would come off and when. I didn't even wear a bra! I was an impostor, not a girl at all, and Greg would know.

From inside the motor home, behind the big window, I could leer and beckon, but out on that field, there would be nothing between him and me. This boy was sweet and normal-acting—he would expect me to do or say *something*. But if the lady in the whipped cream dress opened her mouth, what would she say? "Meow"? My imagination stopped there.

It didn't matter, though. I *couldn't* go to him, no matter how much I wanted to, because . . . why? Because my mother and father had locked me in the room. Then I locked the door myself so my lie would become the truth. And then I paced, door to window, window to door, cursing my parents for locking me in. Nine-forty-five, nine-fifty . . .

By ten, my body was electric. I pictured Greg arriving and standing alone in the field, looking for me. I sat down on the bed. By tenfifteen, I was wishing for a cigarette. By ten-thirty, I wished I were another girl altogether. I wished Greg would burst in through the window, and that he had never existed at all. When the clock struck eleven, I jimmied the window screen open and slipped outside.

I crouched low until I'd passed the lighted windows, then I ran. The field was empty. I sat in the grass for a while, torturing myself with his absence. But the grief I felt disappeared every time I heard a twig snap—oh no, he's coming back! As soon as the silence returned, I let myself feel lonely again.

Finally I left the field, slid back in through the window, and went to bed. As I lay there thinking about the evening, I was relieved to be done with it. And frustrated, disgusted. To rob from yourself! Is there anything more bitter than that?

The next morning, we dragged our suitcases out to the parking lot. The conference had ended. Greg and his family were packing up their car. Every time he bent to pick up a suitcase, his hair fell across his eyes. He wouldn't look at me. Finally, I found a moment to approach him.

"What happened to you last night?" he said accusingly.

"My parents locked me in the room," I whispered. "I couldn't get out! When they fell asleep, I snuck out the window but you were already gone."

"I waited for you for an hour," he said sorrowfully, as though he hadn't even heard me. He was looking off into the distance, at the image of himself perhaps, shining and then hangdog in the grass. Just then his mother called him and he walked toward their car.

"Okay, guys, time to saddle up!" my father announced. Our families pulled out on the road at the same time, with everyone hanging out the windows, waving and yelling good-bye—everyone except for Greg. He had settled himself in the backseat and was busy looking in the other direction. As we headed down the highway that day, the tires flapped on the pavement: *last chance, last chance,* they said, *blew it, blew it, blew it.*

There was a phrase the adults sometimes used if you missed a game or a day of fun, reading perhaps, or hiding under the dining room table listening to the little people you were sure lived inside the wood. "The parade's passing you by!" they would call out cheerily, cheerily, in singsong voices, a darker note underneath—warning? disapproval? It always broke my heart.

* * *

One evening after we returned to Hamden at the end of August, my father showed our vacation photos to a man he worked with at Yale. They were sitting on the living room couch while I watched from the piano bench across the room. My father came to a photo of me, posed on a rock in a black bathing suit, my hair long, almost gold after a summer of sun, my skin still shockingly white. "Chickenskin" was the Dobie word for a pale complexion.

"Cheesecake," the man said. And the word hung there, absurd and tantalizing, over the coffee table, the blue-green shag carpet, the upright piano. My father cleared his throat, avoiding my eyes. He looked startled, embarrassed. Quickly he went on to the next photo.

Cheesecake was a door opening, but I had to walk through it alone.

12

Initiation

THERE WAS A MOMENT OF ABSOLUTE CLARITY BEFORE THE STORM OF boys, fingers, tongues, dirty words whispered hotly in my ear, then shouted at my face—the day I decided to lose my virginity.

A warm September day, a summer day almost, the green grass sharp and sticky against my fingers. Sebastian was at my side, an alert little presence, his sturdy white chest and thumping tail; the sheer friendliness of him! And in front of me, as far as the eye could see, rolled the black rivers of Treadwell and Clifford. The traffic, the boys, the men! If my mother was watching from the window, I was finally (triumphantly) indifferent to her gaze, free of worrying about what she thought of me. Sitting there on the lawn that day in my candy-striped halter top and hip-hugger jeans, I was the picture of optimism, the very definition of goodwill toward men.

That evening, when the sly, long-haired stranger I had fished from the street came to pick me up, my parents were waiting in the living room. I'd told them I was going to go to the movies with someone I'd met while running an errand at the grocery store. As soon as Brian walked in the front door, he seemed to speed into fast motion, jerking forward, thrusting out his hand to my father, "Hi-uh-how-you-doing. Glad-to-uh-nice-house." He acted overjoyed to meet them, and kept tucking his long hair behind his ears.

He mentioned his mother, telling them she lived nearby, that we'd be home as soon as the movie was over. My parents' faces were bright with discomfort or confusion, it was hard to tell which. I'd caught them unprepared. Cleverly I'd never used the word *date*; it was just me and a neighborhood guy catching a movie. Brian had almost ruined it with his nervousness and his formality, but he hadn't the time. We were there in the living room for less than three minutes, and then we were gone.

I don't remember how I dressed for the occasion. I know that I had no idea what sex might be like, though I had some of the vocabulary down. The books talked of sucking, biting, plunging, riding, thrashing, so I figured we'd both be pretty active. But it happened much faster than I expected.

We went to the drive-in where *The Godfather* was playing. Another sign! The wedding had just begun when Brian leaned over to kiss me. I was surprised by how slippery it was. He didn't so much kiss as lick me and roll his wet lips over the lower half of my face. I didn't know what to do in return except let him. I couldn't believe I'd been so in the dark—I thought tongues went *inside* mouths!

Before the wedding scene was even over, we left the movie and drove to a small parking lot behind a brick building. When Brian discovered I was having my period, he said, "Wait here," and left the car.

I'd never seen this parking lot, though it was only blocks from my house. A locked metal doorway was labeled "Deliveries" and next to it on the reddish brick, a black scrawl read, "Suck This." Somewhere in the tall wild grass behind the car, a cat cried. I felt like I'd been transported to a different town, a town of back alleys and stray cats and stranded cars. A new map of Hamden was drawing itself in my head—sketched in black and silvery gray.

I couldn't imagine where Brian had gone, but when he came back, he had a towel in his hand.

"Where'd you go?" I asked.

"My mother's house, over there," he said, pointing absently across the parking lot and the street to nothing I could see.

The mother and the towel made things fussier than I thought they'd be. I had to tuck it under me like a coaster. He had trouble getting himself inside and asked, "Are you a virgin?"

"No, of course not."

And then, "Are you *sure* you aren't a virgin?"

"I've had lots of boys," I told him. I wasn't just lying, I was bragging. He told me to stay still.

When I got home, I took a bath because it seemed more reflective than a shower. So I lay there in the bubbles and reflected. I didn't feel any different. I'd thought that sex was something you'd like no matter what. Still, I wasn't disappointed. I had posed and passed my own initiation rite into the world—losing my virginity. I figured now I was ready for my life, the real one, to begin.

The next afternoon, I walked down Treadwell Street swinging my hips and licking my lips. I wanted the boys to know I'd had sex. I was experienced. They didn't have to be careful with me anymore. I'd picked the most surprising sensation from the night before—Brian's mouth gliding wetly over my lips, cheeks, chin—and decided to wear it. I thought wet lips were a universally understood signal, which I alone had failed to recognize. If I could have worn a sign that said, "We're Open. Come On In," I would have. I licked my lips; I swung my hips from side to side.

"The way you used to walk!" my mother told me years later. "I wondered what message you thought you were trying to send." My mother saw me as a bumbler, a girl so solitary and odd that she only *thought* she was trying to send a message. But men heard my message loud and clear; they understood it perfectly.

One day that week, I missed the school bus and walked to Sacred Heart, late for classes and happy about it. I sauntered up Treadwell feeling like a hole had been cut into the day and I'd wriggled through it. My checked school skirt was rolled up high above my knees and my knee socks pushed down at my ankles. I used the heavy school pin to pull my blouse open, though I still wore an undershirt.

After three blocks, the houses and their yards and flowering bushes disappeared and Treadwell began to curve and climb, thick woods on the left, an abandoned factory on the right set below the road. The parking lot was empty; the black tar was cracked and buckled and shimmering with broken glass.

A car stopped and a man leaned over the passenger seat to say hi out the window and ask if I needed a ride. He was in his forties and dressed for golf. Checked pants, an alligator on his white shirt. His clothes were corny to me, even creepy, but his confidence was laid on thick. His eyes were bold and amused. I became aware of my undershirt, a placard on my chest that said, LITTLE GIRL. I hated it.

I leaned into the car and ran my eyes over the upholstery because I couldn't think of anything else to do at the moment. He talked; I gave him a glittering smile. Whatever Brian was, skittish, long-haired, thirty-three-year-old Brian who still lived with his mom, he wasn't a grown-up the way this man was, and losing my virginity to him gave me no clue as to how to behave now. I was a novice all over again.

The day was hot; the light strong and bland. From the trees, birds squeaked monotonously. Occasionally, a car drove by, a woman at the wheel, a child strapped in next to her. A perfectly pleasant and boring sort of day until this man slipped into it.

He was explaining how much sense it made for him to drive me to Sacred Heart—he had time on his hands, I needed to get there—but his eyes, blue as cornflowers, were saying something else. He acted like he knew me, like we were playing a game by rules we both understood. I didn't, but I was mesmerized. I'd never been at the other end of a man's cynicism. It transformed me; suddenly I was worldly-wise. Knobby knees, tiny breasts? Homework? Tricks I pulled to fool stupid little boys. He drove me to school and came back that afternoon to pick me up, suggesting we go to Knudsen's Dairy for ice cream cones.

His name was Victor. He wore a belt, drove a car, had a thick wallet—how can I capture what a grown man feels like to a girl? His flesh is pale and heavy, disgusting and exciting.

He ordered our cones, paid for them; his wrist was tanned and strapped with a heavy gold watch. He was incredibly casual about his maleness. Even when he wasn't looking at me, even when he was busy ordering and paying, I felt his awareness of me, his plans for me on my skin. It was more thrilling than being touched.

We ate our cones sitting at one of the picnic benches outside so we wouldn't mess up his new car. That's what I think we talked about that day, his car and my preference for chocolate ice cream. When we had finished our cones, he said he'd come pick me up at Sacred Heart again tomorrow.

That day I brought a dress to school and changed into it before meeting Victor in the parking lot. It was a backless black wraparound sundress my grandmother had bought for me, a dress for double takes and wolf whistles, and I was sure Victor would be bowled over. I laced my wedged-heel shoes up my ankles. My hair hung loose, covering half of my bare back. I wanted to appear grown-up to Victor. In that dress, I imagined myself as a beautiful, sexually confident woman, the perfect match for a forty-two-year-old man, never realizing, of course, that my schoolgirl uniform was exactly what a man like Victor would prefer.

That afternoon he took me straight to his condo. Victor didn't work. He lived on a trust fund, he said—not that I knew what that meant. He played golf. The rooms of his apartment were pin neat; no dust, no music, not one window cracked open to the outside. The things he talked about left me tongue-tied—golfing tournaments, tennis, money. Except for the huge mystery of what would happen next, an event completely in his hands, I would have been bored, bored in the excruciating way only children can be. But I was too nervous to be bored; my whole body was humming. What did he want from me? When would I know?

Finally, he suggested a massage and told me to take my shoes off and lie facedown on the couch. It was as if he were mocking me. Up until that moment, I hardly recognized myself. I was performing without a script and doing a pretty good job of it, I thought. But once I unlaced my shoes and lay down, I felt drab and ordinary, nothing more than a slow-witted child. "Aren't you going to take your panty hose off?" he asked sarcastically.

He said it like I was being a prude, like "Come on, girl, you know the game," said it and my panty hose became Great-aunt Emma's girdle, and I had to take them off. Then he helped me unwrap my dress and that seemed to be enough for him, to massage me as I lay there in my girl's white underwear. If he had wanted more, I would've gone along, his attention and his scorn my guides.

When I got home late that afternoon, I hardly knew what to feel about Victor. *Thinking* about him was out of the question; there was no analyzing and coming to conclusions, as an adult might do. Every time he appeared in my head—blond, large-thighed, with thick, manicured hands—a dark wave rolled down my body, but I couldn't tell if I felt excited or repelled. If he asked, I knew I'd have to see him again, but I hoped he wouldn't.

Brian didn't have Victor's terrible weight and so when he called and asked me to meet him, I said I couldn't. I didn't understand why *he* wanted to. He'd made sex seem difficult, irksome, like he was trying to do a job with the wrong tools. When he came, he gave one short grunt and right away warned me to stay on the towel until I'd wiped myself off.

On the phone, he sounded surprised that I wouldn't see him, and a little peeved. "Why not?" he asked. I answered truthfully for a change: "I don't know. I just can't."

13

A Democracy of Boys

MEN USHERED ME INTO MY SEXUALITY, BUT I WANTED BOYS, BOYS with light in their eyes, hoarse voices, hard arms, silky chests, bodies that were my size. And the boys I wanted were the bad ones—the confident, aggressive, dirty-minded ones. They put me at ease, the willfulness of their desire excited me. Timidity, awkwardness, efforts to converse, the nicely dressed boy at the door made me feel clumsy, like I was an unwieldy package they would have to get their arms around.

The bad boy was sneaky, clever, always thinking one step ahead. He was kissing me, whispering, "Baby, baby," while he raised his hips to unzip his pants and then fiddled with the snap on my jeans, all the time acting as if I might be so preoccupied with his tongue and his voice that I wouldn't notice what was going on below. I didn't even mind that they assumed they were tricking and pushing me into sex. I was dangerously careless of their opinion of me.

In my impatience for boys, I decided to run away from home. I wrote my good-bye letter, but unlike Bill's terse, heartbreaking notes, mine was an epistle. It went on for pages, though I have no idea what I wrote there. Complaint? Manifesto? A five-year plan? I only remember going into Bill's bedroom, waking him up, and handing him a sheaf of papers to give to our parents in the morning.

He told me he didn't think Mom could handle it.

"Are you sure you have to go?" he asked, clearing his throat and pushing himself up against the pillows. His hair was smashed against his head, his eyes, clearly visible in the streetlight shining through the window, were cloudy vials of blue. He looked unhappy to be the message bearer, but who else could I ask? I thought he would understand.

"It's gonna kill Mom," he said. "I don't think she can take any more."

I thought it was unfair that he had used up all of her resources and now I wasn't supposed to get my chance. Couldn't he have run away four times instead of five? He didn't ask where I was going or how I was going to survive. He was so guilt-stricken all he could think about was how Mom and Dad would handle this—a second Dobie child running away!

"I've got to get out of here," I told him roughly, for this wasn't what I'd expected at all. He was supposed to see me as his ally, and then ask if I was wearing warm enough clothes, give me money, tell me to meet him later in the week on some street corner.

He took the letter with a sigh, slid it under his pillow, and lay back down.

"Okay, good luck," he said, a little rip cord of pain strung between his eyebrows. I went downstairs, sliding through the silent house, lonelier than I'd expected to be. But as soon as I stepped out the back door, any doubt or guilt I'd felt vanished in the cold night air, the rush to get out of sight. Halfway down Clifford, my heart unknotted and let loose all ties to the sleeping house behind me. I made straight for the Hamden Teen Center, straight and unthinking, as if it had been written down in a book beforehand.

I passed Tom's Market, which stood across from the one-room town library, and then Putnam Avenue Grammar School, hurrying every step of the way until I crossed the street to the empty parking lot that stood directly opposite the center. I sat down on the curb, crouched there, my eyes glued to the door. I had complete faith . . . but in what? I suppose only in that something would happen to me.

While I waited on the curb, one block away Grandpa, Grandma, and Great-aunt Emma would've been tuning in to the evening news while Emma sat in the stiffest chair in the living room, sitting up so straight you thought one day she'd break her own back, sitting as she had sat for forty-five years, smack in the middle of Grandpa and Grandma's marriage.

Two blocks to my left, Great-aunt Bert and Great-uncle Jim would also be watching the news, silently and in their robes. Upstairs, Grandma Callahan would be playing solitaire in front of her TV, an icy glass of Coke on the table next to her, the percolator in the kitchen filled and ready for the following morning when she would rise at dawn to drink her coffee and read the *New Haven Register*, happy to be alone.

But did I think about any of them as I sat on the curb, waiting? Not for a minute. My whole being was craned toward the Teen Center door.

I hadn't taken anything with me that night, no money, no food, no extra clothes. I wore no makeup, nothing sexy—just a T-shirt, jeans, and my fake leather jacket with its fake fur collar, for the September nights had gone cold. I'd thrown off every inessential thing. I walked like a girl but I was running away like a boy. I sat there thinking (without thinking): *Here is where it all begins.*

The Teen Center door opened. Four or five boys and girls came out, then a larger crowd behind. Right away, they caught sight of me. Of course, I was hard to miss. The whole street was empty, no cars, no one walking, just one girl, crouched on the curb across from them, watching.

They turned away and started talking to one another. In the clear autumn night, their voices had a harsh edge. Some of the girls sat on the low cement divider that ran between the firehouse driveway and the little sidewalk leading to the door. The boys stood there talking to them, but they were casting sideways looks at me, sly and curious.

The girls huddled close together, sometimes hugging each other and shivering violently. They couldn't have forgotten I was there, but they acted like they had. Then three boys broke off from the rest, lit cigarettes, and, glancing over at me, drew into a huddle. One of the boys had a baby face and white-blond hair, short and straight and fine and almost colorless in the streetlight. He was wearing a dungaree jacket; the other two had on Army coats. They laughed and smacked their arms against the cold. They acted like all boys seemed to act, as if no one ever watched them. *They* were the watchers, all unaware. They threw down their cigarettes and without any further consultation, crossed over to me.

"Want one?" The blond boy was smiling and holding out his pack of Marlboros. He said his name was Timmy. He kept pushing the bangs off his face only to have them fall back down again. "A sheepdog," my grandfather would've called him.

When they asked if I was from around here, I told them I was running away. Offered it up as tribute and membership dues.

"Where you going?"

"California or New Jersey."

They took that in silently. Smoked. The boy Timmy lifted his chin and blew a perfect smoke ring into the sky.

A man came out of the center, locked the door, and walked away. The others were beginning to drift off, but the boys didn't seem in any hurry to go and I was glad.

"When are you leaving?" Timmy asked.

"Sometime tonight," I told him, wanting to keep things open.

"How you gonna get there?"

"Hitching." I shrugged.

He squatted down next to me. "You can come over there with us if you want," he said, tilting his head toward the group across the street. The other two boys stood there, suddenly looking uncomfortable, like his crouching down next to me had left them unsure of the act of standing. When I stood up to join them, they seemed relieved.

But almost as soon as we walked up to the small group left in front of the firehouse, a girl said, "Timmy, we got to go home now." She was as white blond as he, with the same sunless skin, like they'd been raised under the earth, picnicked in the moonlight on milk and mushrooms.

"My sister," Timmy said gruffly. He had to go.

The other boys said they had to shove off, too. It hadn't occurred to me that my outlaws would have curfews. They told me that if I ever came back, I could find them at the center.

"You want some butts for the road?" Timmy asked. And then I was alone.

What now?

Every lie I told I had to live out. It was a kind of Catholic curse. I hadn't really planned to run away to California or New Jersey, but now I would have to. *I'll go and come right back*, I thought, and then I could hang out with them at the Teen Center.

But I had no idea which highways went to California or New Jersey. I didn't even know how to get to the highway. I thought, *I'll stay at Sylvia's tonight, sleep in her garage or something, and hitch a ride away in the morning.* Maybe she would know where the highway was.

The route to Sylvia's house cut through the reservoir on a small cement bridge that shone white in the streetlight. Then the sidewalk disappeared and the road swooped up, went by shady streets where rich people lived and wrapped itself around one corner of East Rock Park. I was climbing that hill, the park rustling darkly on my right, when a police car pulled in front of me. An arm beckoned from the driver's window. The man inside was middle-aged with gray hair and a wide, worn face, freshly shaved. He was the enemy; anyone really cool would've called him a "pig." But I was happy to see him. It was lonelier out there than I'd thought it would be. When he asked what I was doing, I told him I was going home.

"Do your parents know you're out this late?"

"Oh, yeah. But they're expecting me home now. I think I might be late."

"Well, get going, then. You shouldn't be out here by yourself at night." I waved good-bye and kept walking. Though I told myself I was only going to Sylvia's to sleep in her garage, I had a vague picture in my head of kitchen light, food and talk, macaroni salad, a comradein-arms. But when I got to Sylvia's, the house was dark. I threw some stones at her bedroom window but they landed, clattering, on the side of the house instead—her mother!—so I fled.

I headed back toward the Teen Center. I didn't know where else to go. I'd had visions of camping out in the woods with a tribe of kids. Moss bed, breakfast of berries. Caves. I realized I hadn't thought it out too well. How did Bill do it? Obviously, I had the wrong friends—no long-haired, reckless boys with couches in the back of their vans. No boys at all. No one with even a driver's permit, never mind a car. All Sacred Heart girls had long ago done their homework and were now tucked safely away in bed.

When I got back to East Rock Road, I spotted the figure of a man up ahead, climbing the hill. He was tall and slim-hipped; yellow-blond hair hung to his waist. I recognized him as someone I'd seen at the Teen Center earlier. It was the same brown leather jacket, the same astonishing mane of hair. He'd been looking for someone who owed him money. He hadn't seemed too happy about it, either. He was older than the others, lean and unsmiling, cool as a movie cowboy.

"Hey!" I yelled, and went running after him. But it was as if one of us was a ghost, because he kept walking swiftly up the hill. His long yellow hair shone in the streetlight, swinging from side to side like a woman's dress. I ran faster, my feet slapping the pavement, setting off echoes, hollow and sharp, like pistol shots. My breath scraped the air. In a few easy strides, he reached the top of the hill where the drive entered the park and then, with a last shimmer of yellow, dropped out of sight.

"Hey, wait!"

I was chasing him as fast as I could when the police car appeared again, its red light flashing over me. That's all he did, no siren, just a flash, then a U-turn to my side of the road. It was as if the cop and I had found some secret code to communicate with each other.

"I thought I sent you home," he said.

"Oh, I'm going now," I told him. "I wasn't really before. I was going to my girlfriend's house. Sorry, I lied. But now I'm really going home."

"Okay, I've had enough. Get in. I can't spend the night chasing you all over Hamden, listening to your stories." He didn't sound angry and I was grateful for the way he put it—chasing me *all over* Hamden when really it was just up and down the same hill. Somebody had to put a stop to it, but I couldn't.

He told me I had a choice. Either I would tell him where I lived and he would watch me walk in the front door and see that door shut behind me, or he'd bring me to the station house, find out who my parents were, and call them down. I gave him my real address and when we got there, he waited until I'd gone inside and locked the door behind me. I slipped up the stairs as quietly as I could, woke Bill, and asked him for my letter back. My bed felt like heaven that night; everything had turned out perfectly.

I'd run away from home and returned before anyone knew I was gone. It was almost as good as being invisible. I was living in a dream. I acted without consequence, walked without a sound, left no finger-prints. But my imagination was cooking up real boys, real cops, grown men ready to take me away in fast cars. My parents couldn't pull me away from this new mystery; I wouldn't let them.

The next day when I got out of school, I slipped out of my uni-form into my jeans and returned to the Teen Center. As soon as I reached Tom's Market, I could see a big group of kids gathered out-side. As I got closer, I heard laughter, boots scraping the pavement. This time, I walked right up to them.

"Hey!" The boy named Timmy smiled. "I thought you were going to California."

"This cop picked me up," I told him, and every face turned in my direction. "He picked me up twice! The first time, I told him some story and he let me go, but the second time he was pissed. He said he was gonna give me a choice." I paused, having learned a few things about storytelling from my father.

"He said I could either tell him where I lived and he'd bring me home, or I could have sex with him and he'd let me go. Yeah, he did.

He said if I had sex with him right then, he'd open up the car door and let me go. So I said forget it, take me home."

The boys were astonished. They made me tell the story again and again. They asked me what the cop looked like, and I said he was a young, fat cop with a red face, keeping the real man, who had actually been nice to me, out of it. The boys began to tell stories about cops who had hassled them, while I sat there smoking one of Timmy's cigarettes. Their laughter and talk closed around me. Just like that, I was taken in.

Then we were all walking into the firehouse together. After the light outside, it was as dim as a cave. A stony coolness came off the concrete floors. Under the high ceiling, boys in jeans and boots studied the two pool tables; the balls spun and clacked.

"Fuckin' A," a voice said.

At the back wall, a doorway was filled with fluorescent light. I caught a glimpse of more pool tables, many more slouching, studious boys. No cathedral could have filled a true believer with as much awe.

To my right, I heard chirping, then laughter, from a couch that had been pushed up against the wall and was overflowing with girls. At first glance, they all seemed to have long, dark hair, sharp nails, and full, womanly breasts. I was impressed. They invited me to hang out with them, but it wasn't much of an invitation, since there was no more room on the couch. I had to sit on the floor at their feet.

They must've known one another forever—they kept talking about girls I'd never heard of. "That fat whore," one of them said, and the two girls named Chrissy grabbed each other's breasts, squeezed, and shrieked. That took me aback. They held the laughter for a long time until they distracted all of the boys from their pool games. I sat there awkwardly, not even able to smile. I didn't understand what was so funny.

The two Chrissys were the dark, pretty ones, commanders of the couch. Timmy's sister Lucy was more of a tomboy, stripped down and toughened up in a family of ten. She and Timmy had eight younger brothers and sisters, each one paler than the one before, so that the very youngest seemed to glow like a firefly.

All of the girls went to Hamden High, except for Joan Connolly, who was at Sacred Heart with me.

Joan was big and raw-looking, with ash-blond hair. Her eyes were a light, sharp blue, her fists as large as a man's and bright red. When certain names were mentioned, Joan would growl, "I'll kick her snotty ass," and then, clenching one fist inside the other, crack her knuckles. The girls told me that Joan had broken one girl's nose and another's ribs.

Joan had a real taste, a talent, you might say, for violence. I couldn't help but think of the girl named Georgie as her sidekick; they seemed like bodyguards for the pretty girls. Georgie was short and pigeon-toed, so when she walked, her ass waddled after her. She had a small round head, buck teeth, white skin, and black freckles, like a baseball someone had drawn a face on. Every time the Chrissys brushed their hair or snapped each other's bras or blew each other big, mocking kisses, Georgie's face turned wistful and hurt for a moment, and then she'd come up with a story about what some stupid bitch had worn to school that week, or how some other girl never shaved her armpits and how bad she smelled.

But when push came to shove, they were all good friends. That was something I'd have to come to terms with later, that the people who hate you are always friends to somebody else; their fathers love them, their sisters depend on them, they cry when their grandmothers die.

That first day the girls tried to teach me how to behave. "You smoke like a gangster, Kathy!" they said. The beautiful Chrissys showed me how I was supposed to smoke—two fingers making a V, the cigarette held between. They puckered their lips like they were going to kiss it, and smoked from the dead center of their mouths. They liked Virginia Slims and Mores. I liked Marlboros and smoked them out of the side of my mouth, sometimes letting them dangle there while I zipped up my jacket. I held the cigarette backward, the lit end cupped in my palm. I tapped the ashes onto my jeans and rubbed them in. And when I'd smoked a cigarette down to its filter, I flicked it away in a reverse snap.

The girls didn't like the way I dressed either. "Don't you ever wear a bra, Kathy?"

I didn't think they would ever just let me be. But I hadn't come to the Teen Center to find new girlfriends. I had no desire to nest with a bunch of girls on a big couch.

There were so many boys at the center—playing pool, spitting, cursing, coughing, shoving—that I felt happy as soon as I walked in the door. When I strolled to the soda machine, the air seemed to vibrate. The boys talked louder, stood taller, shoved one another harder. When I played with the zipper on my jacket, boys watched keenly. I laughed aloud and plucked grins from their faces. It was fall but I was still wearing my halter tops. I was ripe for the picking and it showed.

One boy in that lively group was a beat behind the others. He didn't know what was going on, or he didn't want to know. It seems there is always one boy like that. He turned to the others, all watching me, and asked petulantly, "Give me a smoke, man." He had to ask twice. And then, for no reason at all, it seemed, he muttered, "Motherfuckers." One day, I would know that boy—Ben—all too well, but at that electric moment, his surliness didn't even register.

"Kath! Tell him what that cop did," Timmy said, and as I was telling it yet again, other boys gathered around.

"Where did he want you to do it with him?" Timmy's friend asked when I had finished.

"Right there. In the backseat of the car," I told them, shrugging it off.

"Damn," someone said with feeling. "Fucking cop. He had balls!"

"So he just let you go?"

"Yeah, he wasn't mean or anything. He thought he'd just take a chance—see if he got lucky."

"Lucky!" the boys laughed.

They told me they were going for a beer run. They were waiting for some guy who had a car and was old enough to buy the beer.

When the older boy arrived, we piled into the backseat of his car.

This was the beginning, the first of many rides I'd take in the next six months—the only girl in a car full of boys.

There were too many of us to fit in the back, but the driver, whose name was Nicky, didn't look like he wanted anyone crowded up in front with him.

"Here, sit on my lap," one boy said, hitting his leg.

"No, she can sit on mine," another boy cried.

I sat carefully on the first boy's lap, feeling his two legs like a wobbly dock underneath me.

"Am I too heavy?" I asked him.

"Hell, no, you're light as air," he said. "I could hold ten of you." And taking a big breath, he pulled me farther back on his lap.

And then we were off! Flying down Putnam Avenue, windows cracked, cigarettes sparking and sparks sailing. We swung wildly to the right, then to the left, but I was held secure in my bundle of boys.

In the rearview mirror, I could see that Nicky's eyes were on me. Coal black and unsmiling. He was giving off a man scent just sitting there, steering.

I heard Nicky ask one of the boys in front who I was.

"What's your name again?" the boy asked, turning around in the seat. "What's her name, Timmy?"

"It's Kathy, you brain-dead moron. What's your name?"

"Fuck you," the boy said to him, and to me, "I'll remember it now."

From the start, the boys made me feel at home, with their jokes and their boasting, their tall tales of fights and cops and car crashes and someone's father chasing them around with a baseball bat. Their scattered, coarse energy warmed me, entertained me, let me in but asked no questions, made no judgment. There was something democratic about the boys, something I'd been looking for my whole life, it suddenly seemed.

It was just a matter of time, two or three days later, until Eddie Flynn walked me home one night and lingered by the front door. He backed me up against the wall next to the door and began to kiss me,

bending his knees and pushing his body against mine. He was as sup-
ple as a snake. He slithered and pressed, herding me into place, and
then he held me there. I'd never been kissed like that before. The way
he used his body, it was like someone had tied his hands.

Eddie had a longish face, a thatch of black hair, a peppery sprin-
kling of freckles along his nose and cheekbones, the soft beginning of
a mustache on his upper lip and that half-sweet, half-nasty manner of
some mother's boy bulling his way into manhood. He was completely
appealing to me. Not that it really mattered. Any bold, half-handsome
boy could've done what Eddie did next.

"Come down here," he said, and jumped off the stoop. Then he
pulled me behind the bushes. Here where my brothers and sisters and
I had hidden from one another as children, here where Cindy and
Beth and I had made little houses, knocking on the tree trunks to be
let in, Eddie unsnapped my jeans and put his hand inside, his finger
up in me. His hand scraped back and forth along the zipper.

He called it "finger fucking," and so that's what it was then. It was
all brand new to me, anyway; speeding car, open country, crash
course. "Baby, touch him, he likes you." Penis as puppy dog. "Baby, you
got to let me do it. I can't stop now." Desire as runaway train.

14

Party Time

THE HOUSE FILLED UP QUICKLY WITH LONG-HAIRED, SHARP-FACED boys, and girls wearing thick black mascara and turquoise eye shadow. Like partying nomads, they arrived carrying cases of beer and bottles of scotch, vodka, and gin. Some of the girls had thought to bring plastic cups. The music blasting from the living room stereo could be heard from the lawns across the street—the J. Geils Band singing, "Take out your false teeth, mama, I wanna suck on your gums." Sebastian looked like an especially eager host, trotting from room to room on stubby legs and swinging his feathery tail so hard his rump wagged.

It was still September, but already the night had sharp, cold edges where it touched my skin. My parents had gone away for the weekend with Cindy, Beth Ann, and Stephen, and Michael was off somewhere with a friend. So Bill had decided to throw a party.

When he'd told me about it that morning, he said it as a warning, not an invitation. He was hoping I'd clear out—sleep over at Sylvia's perhaps. But instead I went straight to the firehouse and invited everyone there to the party. I hardly knew them yet, but I was going to show them that I was as cool as they were. I was excited to have something to give them.

What I didn't know was that Bill's friends and the firehouse crowd were rivals, for no other reason than the fact that they lived in different parts of Hamden—Bill's friends in Spring Glen, the firehouse kids in Whitneyville. In every other way, Spring Glen and Whitneyville boys were exactly the same: working-class kids who all went to Hamden High (except for Bill, of course, since my parents had forced him to go to Notre Dame); who all wore the same Levi's, boots, and leather jackets; who all drank the same booze (Johnnie Walker, Schlitz, Budweiser, and anything else they found in their parents' liquor cabinets), smoked pot, and occasionally took speed but preferred 'ludes. The only discernible difference in their taste was that Spring Glen boys seemed to have a preference for vans; Whitneyville boys liked their muscle cars.

In the kitchen that night, the girls were making screwdrivers while the boys were doing shots with their beer. Smoke hung from the ceiling and someone must've spilled a drink, for my shoes stuck to the floor when I walked, sucking and popping at each step. I'd never drunk alcohol before, so it didn't occur to me to start then. Instead, I planted myself on the couch in the living room to wait for *my* friends to arrive. There bottles were being passed, bongs were burbling, and J. Geils gave way to Jethro Tull. On the coffee table in front of me someone had placed a paper plate piled high with brownies. It seemed funny to me that at a party where no one had brought even a bag of chips, never mind some onion dip, someone had thought to make dessert. "Eat me," the brownies seemed to say, and I did.

When I glanced up, Michael and his friend were standing there in shorts, holding tennis rackets. They looked flushed, naked, and appalled.

"Tallyho!" a voice called out from across the living room; the crowd parted to reveal the speaker, a long-haired boy-man sprawled in my father's rocking chair, a girl with black hair on his lap.

"Where's Bill?" Michael asked stiffly. Bill's friends drew around him. "Nice socks, Mikey." Putting on British accents, they asked about his backhand.

"Where's Bill?" Michael asked again.

"Billy can't see you now."

"He's otherwise occupied."

"I think he's rolling a joint."

"Tapping a keg."

They looked up at him innocently, shrugged.

"Hey, Mikey, where can I get one of those shirts with the little alligators on them? They're keen."

"Neat-o."

"Jim Dandy." Just like that—the captain could be made a clown. It was terrible. But I felt there was a kind of justice in this. Michael couldn't be king everywhere. He was on Bill's turf now, a place where straight A's and good behavior didn't matter. In fact, they were a black mark against you.

Just then Bill walked in, surprise written all over his face. "Oh, Mike, hey, I forgot—"

"You're responsible for anything that happens here. I'm leaving," Michael said.

"Whhhoa! Can you handle it, Billy?"

"You better have it all cleaned up before Mom and Dad get home tomorrow," Michael said. "I'm not covering for you this time." And then he turned away. Bill looked like he'd been slapped. Had he expected Michael to join in? Or give him a brotherly pat on the shoulder and ask to be introduced to his friends? Bill let out a loud belch, but Michael was out the door, gone.

"Fuckin' . . ." Bill muttered, swallowing the next word in his beer.

I was reaching for another brownie when a flush-faced boy sat down heavily next to me. "You'll be flying tonight," he mumbled, and when he saw the quizzical look on my face, he let out a laugh. "Oh, shit," he said. "You didn't know? They're hash brownies." Who would've thought? His laughter made me laugh and so we sat there, the two of us, looking at each other and laughing, though I'd already forgotten what had started us off.

Then I was in the upstairs hallway with its towering doors, all closed, and some other boy was holding me against the wall, thigh to thigh, pressing, digging, teasing, torturing his own hard-on. His tongue slithered into my mouth. I took it like a climber takes a rope;

it focused me. He yanked open the nearest door and pulled me into my parents' bedroom.

In there, the air was hushed, the bed barely visible in the dark. When we had stripped off our clothes, the boy pulled me onto the bed and lay on top of me. I felt the whole weight of his boy body on mine, felt his struggle, then the thrust in. Once inside, a holy pause, before the action began anew.

It was so secretive, so intimate; he seemed to be whispering in my ear, but all he was saying was, "Uh-uh-uh-uh-uh . . ." Then the door cracked open, and ghoulish faces stared at us from the light—"He's fuckin' doin' her!" Laughter followed. The door closed, and we lay in darkness again. "Fuck them," he said, pulling me close as I tried to break away, but I could hear the despair in his voice. The moment was over, and he knew it.

I dressed and slipped down to the kitchen, where Sebastian had licked the floor as clean as he could and was now walking sideways, bumping into cabinets, feebly waving his tail. He seemed to be trying his best to tidy up after us, keep us out of trouble. Bump, wave, bump, wave; he finally made it over to me.

I emptied the beer someone had poured into his dish and refilled it with water. "Better stick near me," I told him, cupping his narrow head, but he lay down sideways on the floor in front of the cookie cabinet, one apologetic eye watching me. His tail tapped the floor, *sorry, can't do, sorry, sorry.*

The front and back doors to the house were open. There was no center to the party anymore, people were everywhere, on all the floors of the house, on the back porch, on both lawns, out in the driveway, down the basement—inside the closets, for all I knew.

Suddenly, there was trouble out front. Word passed like electricity from room to room, and everyone rushed to the door.

Battles were erupting on several parts of the lawn, curses and grunts filled the air. I saw two figures tumbling across the grass and onto the sidewalk. The firehouse boys had arrived.

Up and down the street, lights came on. Doors opened. Men stood on their front steps, looking our way, their fists clenched, as if they'd like to toss off their responsible adult selves—just one more taste of youth!—and join in the brawl, show these punks a thing or two. Across the street, old women in nightgowns and robes watched from the other side of their screen doors.

Then, out of nowhere, a boy came charging across the lawn, roaring and swinging a log. Everyone jumped back.

I knew that log! It was the driftwood my parents had brought home from Cape Cod and put in our garden. Now this maniac was using it as a weapon, whirling around the lawn, scattering the fighters. Grinning from ear to ear.

"What the fuck?" I heard Bill mutter. "We got fuckin' Paul Bunyan here." His voice was rough and careless-sounding, but I could see the panic in his eyes.

Sides were forgotten. Every guy on the lawn crouched around the log swinger and took turns dashing toward him, but no one could get close. He had dark shadows on his jaw and his green eyes were lit. His brown leather jacket flapped open every time he swung. I recognized him from the firehouse. He laughed and, grabbing the log with one hand, sliced hard at the air, practically knocking himself over. No one was having as much fun as he was. I watched in wonder.

"Jimmy, you fucker!" Now I knew his name.

Then we heard the sirens, and dozens of kids went running . . . across lawns, into cars, over fences, through the hedges. I ran along with the rest of them; but unlike the others, I couldn't run home.

It had been my first big party, and as I headed into the woods across the street, I knew it would be my last. I didn't like the crowds or the aggressive ugliness of the music, the way the boys drove Michael from the house and got Sebastian drunk, the whole great sea of carelessness. I kept picturing Beth, not my parents, walking into that party, and I could see her face, astonished, then grave, as she bent over Sebastian and spoke tenderly just to him: "Okay, little buddy, I'm here now."

No, I hadn't liked the party. But the boy upstairs, his tongue in my mouth, his skin hot and bare, yes, I liked that. The wild, handsome man on the lawn, his reckless energy, yes, yes. No one could touch him, not just because of the log but because he had no restraint, no fear, no guilt. He wasn't even fighting because he was angry. He was having fun. I wanted to see him again.

From my hiding place in the woods, I looked out at our house, all lit up and deserted, the front door ajar. The log of driftwood lay in the middle of the lawn like a giant, half-eaten bone, and two police cars were parked at the curb. When the cops pulled away, I crossed the street and went home.

Late that night, Bill and I wobbled over brooms and mops. I was happy to be cleaning up with him, thinking we were partners at last. But he, big brother, black sheep, wasn't happy at all. He cleaned with a grim determination. As he swept broken glass from the kitchen floor, he was silent. I mopped and watched his face. My brother looked the complete opposite of Jimmy on the lawn; he was all grown-up at sixteen, already paying for his freedom and his pleasures.

"You shouldn't have been here," he finally growled. But I knew better. I had my own life now. He didn't know about the boy upstairs, didn't know that it was I who had invited the Teen Center over.

That night I was given two glimpses of my future: Jimmy, charismatic, careless Jimmy, jumping straight into the chaos on the lawn; and the ghoulish faces peering in at me through the bedroom door, laughing. But I had no hint of what the future held for me, and though I was given these two signs, I couldn't read either one of them.

No, instead I lay on my bed and composed a poem to the outlaw on the lawn with the streetlight in his eyes. By the fourth verse, my outlaw was surrounded by police, washed in a red, swooping light. They were blind to his wild, free spirit; they were going to put him in a cage. In my poem, I imagined Jimmy as someone bighearted and hungry, blissfully unaware that he was heading for trouble.

15

The Real Girlfriend

I WAS WATCHING A POOL GAME IN THE BIG FRONT ROOM OF THE firehouse, wearing my yellow halter top, when Nicky Pineda asked me if I wanted to go for a ride. One minute he was standing with a group of the older guys by the front door, the next he was coming across the room to me, saying my name. I was pleased he remembered it, and I agreed immediately. He had been our driver on the beer run and was one of the man-boys at the firehouse. Nicky, Jimmy, and Patrick Cahoon: These three made a nation.

The man-boys always arrived at the firehouse at dusk. You heard the roar of their cars outside. The firehouse doorway shrunk; they loomed, all leather and stubble.

The man-boys ruled the Center. It was as inevitable as anything else in nature. They had dropped out of school and had jobs that callused their hands, money in their pockets, tanned, muscular arms, confidence, cars, a case of beer in the trunk, a bottle of Johnnie Walker pushed under the front seat, and a divided Hamden in their heads—Whitneyville versus Spring Glen.

I didn't know if I liked Nicky Pineda or not. I liked what I knew about him so far—his full lips, olive skin, coarse hair. Sometimes the other boys called him "Nick the Spic" to annoy him. I liked the nickname, too. Everything about him seemed thick and bullish. There was nothing flirtatious about his lust; it was simply rude and strong. His T-shirt looked pressed. I was excited.

When I got in the car, Nicky drove straight to West Rock Park in West Haven. He was that sure. I watched him with pleasure—a silent boy! Driving! Smoking!

We seemed to drive up many hills, aimed each time for the slice of dark sky at the top, until finally we reached the peak of West Rock and parked at a low stone wall, a flutter of tiny lights far below us. He kept the motor running but shut the lights, turned his full, unsmiling lips toward me. "Come on over here."

When we kissed, his hand got up between us and held my breast. Then he was breathing hard and pulling my T-shirt out of my pants.

His other hand was getting busy with himself, with *it*, our reason for being here.

He unbuttoned his jeans to let it breathe and it poked straight up in his underwear, trying to get out. It was suffocating in there. He yanked his underwear down to his hips. "I've got a real boner," he said, and the word fit perfectly. I thought I'd never seen anything so ridiculous and so admirable in my life. "Let's get in the back," Nicky said urgently. It wanted what it wanted. He had trouble tucking it back in.

As soon as we were in the backseat, he unsnapped and unzipped my jeans. "Take them off," he said. Everything was happening too fast, like someone had just set out dinner and then, just as suddenly, cleared the plates and threw down dessert.

"Uh, could I have a cigarette?"

I wanted to give Nicky whatever he wanted, but taking off my pants just now? And only my pants? It didn't seem very sexy.

My capacity for desire was in its baby stages, just beginning to un-furl; instead of coaxing it, teasing it out of its nesting place and then stirring it up, Nicky was bulldozing over it, flattening my desire with his. But he had no use for my desire, and his disregard matched my own, for I had no idea what I was missing.

"A cigarette?" he said. His laugh was a snort. "You're gonna start playing shy *now*? After letting me go this far?"

With every breath, his chest rose to meet mine; heat came off his body in waves. His black eyes had turned deadly serious.

He softened enough to say my name. "Kathy," he said. "Come on, Kathy . . ." I was deeply flattered by the heat and heaviness of his wanting. He told me we couldn't stop now and then he told me why. . . . At fourteen I found it easy to believe in blue balls, in wanting something so badly that if you didn't get it, you'd be poisoned by frustration. Yes, I could believe in that.

Nicky and I had sex every night for a week, and each time he seemed unfriendlier. I couldn't get the desire and the unfriendliness to mesh in my head. It seemed a mistake had been made, and soon things would be set right.

One of those nights, he muttered the word *chinga* in my ear and my skin prickled. I didn't know what the word meant but it opened like a door anyway—and through that door I could see Nicky's mother and his sisters in a kitchen wearing aprons. The women sang to each other in Spanish, a nest of sparrows. The flowered curtains, the laundry basket, the patter of pretty feet blackened his lust. "Chinga," he said, and I felt his anger and excitement as if they were my own—the flowered curtains trembled, the mother's hands flew up, his body jerked, a shot and a soiling. Ah ha! So that's how it was.

On the seventh night, Nicky asked me to skip school in the morning. He said to take the bus as usual and he'd pick me up in the school parking lot.

That morning, I tumbled down the steps of the bus with the rest of the girls, all of us in our brown-and-white-checked skirts and knee socks, our stiff white blouses and soft, brown shoes, God's girls, dressed like Toll House cookies. Marisa and the two Lisas, Guardino and DiRosa, walked by me in the parking lot—"Hi, Kath!"—their voices friendly but embarrassed. They hesitated a second. What to say? Should they wait and walk in with me? Walk away?

Marisa and Lisa Guardino and I had been good friends since first grade at St. Rita's. As soon as we got to Sacred Heart, we gathered a group of like-minded girls, including Lisa DiRosa and Sylvia, until there were about nine of us at our cafeteria table. We ate lunch together, had sleep-overs, bicycled, played volleyball, fell in love with one another's older brothers but in a public, jokey way. We didn't seem to have any secrets except the kind we quickly shared. Everything about us was as plain as paint.

It went on that way until the end of our freshman year. Then school let out, and I started wearing halter tops and short shorts; I'd become "boy crazy," as they would've said. Since I spent much of the rest of that summer on the cross-country trip I took with my family, I didn't see any of my girlfriends until the fall.

In September, when we returned to Sacred Heart, they immediately sensed that I had changed. Marisa, a redhead with sugar-and-cinnamon skin, started blushing whenever she looked at me. Slowly, she and Lisa and the other girls gave me up that year. There was no meanness to what they did, but no choice, either. I embarrassed them, I know, confused, maybe even saddened them. I never stayed after school anymore, not for drama tryouts or the Latin Club. I swore aloud. I walked with a sexual swagger.

But they were a kind group of friends. They said nothing, let me sit with them at lunch and drift away little by little. Only Sylvia and I remained close, but she knew nothing of my nightlife, didn't even sense it, unlike the rest of them. And if she had? It wouldn't have mattered. The tie between us was stronger than that.

Meanwhile, two of the black girls in our class had begun to court me, and I them. Leslie and Linda were in my homeroom that year—Sylvia had been switched to another—so the three of us were in all the same classes. We often found ourselves sitting together in the back of the classroom. They were always joking and playing with each other, and after a while they began to include me, first by playing *to* me, a most appreciative audience. Leslie was tiny but her afro was huge, seventies-style, with copper-colored highlights. She kept her pick inside it. "That's so . . . country, Leslie," Linda would say, cooing it so you didn't know if that was a good or bad thing.

One day in Christian Womanhood class, Linda raised her hand, fluttering her fingers in the air, trying to get the nun's attention. When she was finally called on, Linda said, "I'm sorry, Sister, but as a nun how can you teach us about being women?" Shock rippled through the classroom, and several girls turned around to shoot her angry, appalled looks. But I was impressed. Within a week the three of us were playing Mod Squad in the hallway between classes. Shortly after that, Sylvia and I moved over to their cafeteria table. But meanwhile, the old gang and I couldn't just pretend our friendship hadn't existed.

So there was Lisa DiRosa waiting for me as I stood in the parking lot that morning. "Hey, Kath, aren't you going in?" It took a tomboy to cut to the chase. Marisa was blushing wildly and Lisa Guardino seemed to be watching my shoes, but DiRosa was looking me straight in the eye. A tiger in the field and on the court, a great stealer of bases and rebounds, she had short black hair and an athlete's slouch to her shoulders.

"I'm waiting for someone," I told her. "A guy I know. I'm skipping today."

"Okay, uh, well, good luck . . . I guess," she said, patting me on the back clumsily, her hand cupped like it had been molded permanently by her catcher's mitt.

Just then, Nicky's car slid into the parking lot, dented, dark, engine growling low. The door swung open. I slipped inside. Girls stared, astonished, then quickly looked away, ashamed of their naïveté. No one would tell.

We went into the woods that bordered Treadwell Street. There, in a patch of needles and sun, Nicky spread out a blanket and we got completely undressed. I liked that he had thought of the forest and the blanket. His forethought became our foreplay. There wasn't any other kind—just a kiss to get it out of the way. He pushed himself right in without any notice of our nakedness. We were completely bare in front of each other for the first time. And it was daylight. I wondered if I should be wriggling or something. The pine trees telescoped into a perfect circle of blue, Easter egg blue, and from somewhere behind us came the sound of a work crew clearing a patch of forest. I couldn't help thinking that I should have been happier than I was right then. *You are naked in the woods, making love on a school day,* I said to myself, and though that sounded like a fine adventure, it didn't feel like one.

Overhead, a bird screamed. Nicky was putting on his pants. For a moment things went very flat, and I got scared. I had staked all my bets on this new world of mine, thinking that there I would come into my own. What if I was wrong?

Nicky wanted to leave right away. "I have to get to work," he said. He was already late. But I had nowhere to go. Home was out of the question, and I couldn't just walk into school in the middle of the morning.

"The nuns aren't even gonna notice you were gone," he told me impatiently. But of course they would. Unlike Nicky, the nuns noticed everything.

I said he could take me back to school. It was a silent ride. I spent it staring out the window, making plans.

When we got to the long drive that led through the grounds, I told Nicky to drop me off. He never asked what I was going to do, and there was obviously no point in asking his advice.

I settled in behind the statue of Jesus where the bushes hid me from the road. I'd wait here for the bus that took us home, I decided, and just try to blend in with the crowd of girls when they started to board.

Now that Nicky was gone, I began to feel a lot happier about him and me. It was amazing how quickly my natural optimism could reassert itself. Nestled in the soft grass, I suddenly realized that Nicky and I had been going together for eight days now! By tomorrow it would be nine. Making love in the daytime suddenly felt like an anniversary celebration. I would have to call his attention to that tonight.

When I thought about what we had just done in the woods, I became intensely aware of my skirt and my bare legs. A dark delicious humming started up along my skin. I thought of all the girls in school, rolling up their sweater sleeves and writing their equations down. I thought of Nicky lying on top of me, his thick thighs and bulletlike head, his pushing in and out while in the distance, other men hacked away at the edge of the woods. I remembered hearing the shriek of their saws, then the sharp cry of a blue jay high up. Blue on blue, I thought. I took out my notebook to write it all down.

There was the tiniest bit of unease in my mind about my ability to enjoy my "adventure" now when it was over and not at all when it was happening. It seemed a little tricky, this, a little dubious. But the vivid aftertaste was real, this pleasure, this savoring as my pen set out across the page.

The despair I'd felt in the woods was vanquished. I was writing my way out of it, without knowing that that was what I was doing. I wondered how you spelled *chinga.*

That night I said something to Nicky about being his girlfriend for more than a week now, and he looked at me with contempt.

"You're not my girlfriend," he sneered. "I've got a real girlfriend. She won't even let me kiss her."

He was driving me home from West Rock Park, and I turned and stared out the window (I couldn't bear to look at his face) but saw nothing. The fences and houses and trees had been swallowed up by a dense fog. The only image to appear out of that mist was *the real girlfriend*—lips first. They were painted bright red, set firmly together. Immediately, I assigned her all the other attributes of femininity I found most beautiful—long dark hair, high cheekbones, womanly breasts.

She was a prize, I was absolutely sure of that, but an alien creature. I couldn't imagine telling a boy *not* to kiss me, *not* to lay a hand on me. Why would I? I must have heard girls talk about not having sex so boys would respect them, but that notion held no attraction for me. All in all, it had a hollow, dusty feel to it, like a glass jar on a shelf—DO NOT TOUCH. No, not for me. The respect of a sixteen-year-old boy couldn't hold a candle to his desire.

That was the last night I spent with Nicky. I moved on.

16

The Most Beautiful Boy in the World

DOWN IN THE BASEMENT, THE STROBE LIGHT PULSED ALONG THE cement walls and floors, Led Zeppelin played on the stereo, and pool balls spun straight across the green. "Gonna make you sweat, gonna make you groove!" Timmy sang, as I took aim for the corner pocket. When a skinny boy named Pete tried to block the shot with his hand, Timmy wrestled him from the table. The old pinball machine my father had gotten from a colleague at Yale clicked and flashed and rang until Ben shoved it with his hip, sending it into Tilt mode, all of its lights shutting off. Six of the boys from the Teen Center had come home with me that day.

The basement was our turf, a Dobie Teen Center all its own. My parents had given it over to my brothers and sisters and me that year, making a strong bid for our presence on the home front.

The pool table, with a big red bow around it, had appeared as the surprise gift at the end of a long treasure hunt on Christmas morning. Together we'd gone in search of it, following the clues my father had written in rhyme and hidden all over the house late the night before. During winter break, Cindy had painted wavy Day-Glo stripes down the walls and across the cement floor. With the black light on, you moved across the room as a set of glowing clothes. If you weren't careful, you'd trip over one of the beanbag chairs slumped on the floor. When our relatives first saw the room, Great-aunt Bert pronounced it "groovy," savoring the ridiculous word, and Great-aunt Emma gamely tried out the pinball machine, amusing us to no end.

I'd brought the boys in through the side door, the one that opened from the backyard directly onto the basement stairs, so that we could avoid the kitchen—and my mother. But suddenly she appeared at the top of the stairs in her flower-covered apron and her high heels. Her face was pink, her hazel eyes blazing. I turned the music down, but not off. I felt cocooned by my crowd of boys and their instantly sullen faces.

"Aren't you going to introduce me to your friends?" she asked, her voice stiff with false brightness. A hundred sullen boys couldn't protect me from that. I gave their names, the ones I knew, with a great show of nonchalance. The boys barely bothered to nod.

It was the seventies, the seventies in a small town, which meant that the sixties had just begun to influence us, and so we had more drugs to mix with our alcohol, a free-floating anger at authority, contempt for conformity, and no real tolerance for anything. God help the housewife in her apron and high heels, trying so hard.

I no longer saw my mother as young or beautiful. I saw only the old-fashioned apron, the dark support hose, the beauty parlor hair, dyed blond now; my critic, my uncomprehending mother. It must have been terrible for her, all our loving gazes receding from her that year. But I didn't want to know what she was feeling anymore.

After she went back upstairs, slamming the door behind her, the boys decided to take off. This was no Playland; this was a house with parents.

"Let's go," blond Timmy said, and when I told them I couldn't come with them, they bounded up the stairs and out the side door as eagerly as if I were the mother and they were fleeing me.

When I walked into the house a few minutes later, I found my mother cooking dinner. Her eyes were wet.

"Why didn't you bring them in the front door and introduce them to me?" she demanded. "Why do you feel you have to sneak around all the time?"

"I didn't think about it." I shrugged. "They're just some boys I know."

I couldn't explain that mothers and boys just didn't go together in my mind, family and sex, kitchens and backseats. I thought everyone knew that was so but pretended it wasn't, said "Nice-to-meet-you, nice-house-you-have-here," and "Why-thank-you-very-much" while one person was thinking, *How do I get out of here so I can fuck your daughter?* and the other was trying not to think about it too much.

"Are you ashamed of me? Do you think I'm too square?" Her voice was pitched high, imploring and protesting all at once. Behind her, the kitchen walls were plastered with inspirational posters she'd bought in the New Haven mall, quotes from Kahlil Gibran and Martin Buber printed on fields of wildflowers, on sunrises and ocean waves. Every few months, she bought a new one, as if she were trying to cheer herself up, so that over the last couple of years the kitchen had become more and more like a teenage girl's bedroom. Less a setting for the Dobie family dinner than the place where my mother strove to project her personality against motherhood, wifedom—that promised land that had become a black hole.

"No, I'm not ashamed of you," I said angrily, fighting back an enormous wave of pity. I wasn't going to feel that for her. Rage was better. Drop-dead coldness. Not pity. Not for your own mother. "It doesn't have anything to do with that."

And it didn't. There was no sense in bringing them together. I didn't want to see the boys go sullen and stupid under her gaze, didn't want her to shrivel and protest under theirs.

"They're your friends. They're in my house," she was saying.

"They're not my *friends*," I replied, dripping scorn.

"Well, then what are they?"

"Just some guys I know."

"You were the only girl!"

"So what?"

"Why weren't there any other girls with you? Why were you the only one?"

Then I thought she was insulting me, thought it was a clever way of asking why I didn't have any *girl*friends, and an even more clever way of doubting the boys' interest in me.

"The girls at the firehouse don't like to play pool," I said as airily as I could. "So they wouldn't come over."

I was feeling very sticky and strange by then. This is what could happen to the beautiful adventure if you brought it home—it could suddenly look tawdry and shameful. I had to get out of that kitchen before my dream crumbled to dirt.

I told my mother I was going to Sylvia's, though I didn't think I was. I headed swiftly up Clifford, crossed Putnam, not slowing down until I was well away from the house. As I wandered up and down the small streets that crisscrossed a hill back behind the avenue, I began to feel calmer. Men were raking leaves, kids leaping into the yellow-and-orange piles, dogs barking as I passed.

When dusk fell, and all the leaping children were called home, I headed toward the firehouse. The boys weren't there, so I went to see if they'd gone over to Pete's house, a favorite gathering place because his parents were never home. Pete's older brother answered the door. His hair was still wet; he'd just stepped out of the shower.

He went to the refrigerator for a couple of sodas and I took off my jacket and sat down on the couch to drink mine. He just stood in front of me, rolling his unopened can back and forth across his stomach thoughtfully. Because of his wet hair and the smell of soap coming off his skin and the silence that he held and held, the air was heating up, a thousand agitating molecules.

When he finally sat down, he leaned back against the arm of the couch, legs sprawled wide. He lit a joint. Squinted at me.

"Where are your boys tonight?"

"Oh, they're around."

"Aren't you cold wearing just that?" he asked, holding the smoke in and talking over it, his voice strained. He jerked his chin at my shirt, a polyester blouse that tied at my waist, leaving my belly bare. It was silvery, shimmery, printed with blue flowerpots and pink flowers; a disco blouse that never went dancing.

"No, I'm never cold," I told him. "Usually, I'm too warm. That's why I like the winter and the fall." He exhaled the smoke with a big sighing sound, then carefully pushed the glowing end into the ashtray and pinched whatever fire was left between his fingers.

"You *look* cold," he said quietly.

"What do you mean?"

Then he leaned over and with his fingers barely touching the side of my breast, brushed his thumb lightly over my nipple, the same thumb that had just put out the joint. It left a faint smudgy track on my shirt.

"Goose bumps," he said.

"Maybe that's not because I'm cold," I said, trumping his boldness with my own. If he was going to be outrageous, I'd be right there with him. It was almost a point of pride with me.

He looked shaken awake. "How old are you, Kath?"

"Fifteen," I lied, but I would have my birthday soon.

He went over to the front porch windows. I heard him murmur to himself, "Down, boy." Maybe he didn't think I was listening, maybe he didn't care whether I heard him or not.

When he came back, he stood over me, rubbing his stomach with his hand now. He let out a whistling sigh.

"I see what they're talking about." He smiled at me then and shook his head. "Trouble."

I was happy I'd made him sweat, happy to see him smile, but he told me I'd better leave, and I wasn't so happy about that.

Maybe it was a test, but if it was, I'd passed *and* failed, for the next thing I knew I was out on the street, wandering around by myself, nowhere to go but home. When I got to the house, I found I wasn't ready to go inside yet. Instead I went around to the backyard and sat on one of the swings, gently rocking myself back and forth with one leg. As I took a cigarette out of my pocket, I saw a light go on in the house. A figure appeared in the window of the living room, then disappeared on the way up the stairs. Then someone else ran by the same window, the smaller faster shape of Cindy or Beth. Now the sunporch, windowed on all three sides, was filled with light. Who was in there? Suddenly I imagined little Stephen bent over his trucks all alone, clearing his throat to make engine sounds. Grief pierced me, and I wanted to cry. I felt as if each person inside that house was secretly, terribly lonely.

What I needed right then was for some kind, sensible friend to give me a good shake and say, "Don't be silly, they're inside that house all together—you're the one out here alone. Your little brother is playing with his trucks, having fun. The loneliness you feel now is your own."

Maybe the talk started right away, started with Eddie Flynn when he emerged from the bushes that September night: *"She let me finger-fuck her!"* Maybe the boy in my parents' bedroom was a firehouse boy. All I know for sure is that Nicky talked, couldn't stop talking, in fact, and Nicky hated me. The girls did, too. I must have been driving them mad, for they heard what the boys said about me, the contempt in their voices, and then they'd see one of those boys come into the Teen Center to get me, and off I'd go with a grin and a wave—the chosen one.

They hated me for getting away with it, even though I was only "getting away with it" in my own head. But that's what must have been so infuriating. To them I was trash—it was obvious. Everyone knew it but me. As far as I was concerned, I was doing exactly what the boys were doing, which meant I was as alive, as bold, as free, as they were. What the girls would have to do, and they probably sensed this already, was pull me out of my head and into the light of day, make me see things *their* way.

"He ate her out!" I was waiting for my turn at the pool table when I heard them behind me. The boys stopped their game and looked at me to see how I would react.

"Ecchhhh . . . gross!" the girls screamed, and when I turned around, the couch was writhing—girls grabbing themselves and falling into one another's laps, laughing. "That's so disgusting!"

I was taken aback. I didn't think anyone shriveled around sex but spinster aunts and little kids, certainly not beautiful girls like the two Chrissys. I thought that even if you felt that way, you tried to hide it because it was so uncool. You weren't going to see *me* talking about sex like a little girl with a frog waved in her face.

The girls succeeded only in making me feel worldly-wise, which was, of course, exactly what I wanted to be. In fact, the only time I ever felt ashamed was when I wasn't "in the know," a peculiar kind of shame that went straight back to my dream-clouded childhood. So when Patrick Cahoon had asked me to do "sixty-nine" the night before, I was mostly concerned with not knowing what that was.

Patrick was a big blond boy, built like a football player. One of the man-boys. He had a military haircut and thick lips that gleamed every time he passed his tongue over them. We were lying half naked in the backseat of his car.

"How about we do sixty-nine?" he asked.

"Okay, sure," I whispered, and then wondered why he was turning himself around and heading down there. . . . I actually started to follow him.

The day after the girls had made their scene on the couch, I got to the Teen Center early. It was right after school, the quiet part of the afternoon. None of the girls had arrived yet, and none of the man-boys, either.

The only people there were a few of the quiet, anonymous boys who hung around the fringes of the action, studying the pool tables like they were doing their homework, and the four black boys who sometimes came around, four dark faces in a sea of white.

They always appeared at the firehouse together and went straight to their table, which was the one just inside the entrance. If they weren't playing pool, they stood with their backs against the big firehouse doors watching—and more than the pool game, as I found out that day.

When I walked in, Fat Roscoe was taking a shot while Craig and the two younger black boys leaned on their sticks and waited.

"Hey, Kath," they called out, and then Craig handed one of the younger boys his pool stick and came over to me.

"Kath, we need to talk to you," he said. "It's important."

Craig was tall, whiplike, soft-spoken. He was handsome, but his handsomeness had no currency here. Fat Roscoe was fat; he was wrinkled with it, like a bulldog. He had gold teeth and a big walking stick. Roscoe made ugly cool, cooler than any white-boy prettiness. Behind his back, some of the white boys referred to him as "the coon." They were afraid of him and they adored him. He was like some kind of mascot, he so perfectly fulfilled their idea of a nigger.

"Come take a ride with us," Craig said. "So we can talk with you alone." This must have been in late November, right before I began seeing Jimmy.

Their car was parked out front. It was an old car, low-flying and high-finned, wide as a bed. Craig got behind the wheel. Roscoe opened the door for me. "Slip in the back, angel," he said, and motioned the other two boys to get in there with me. Then he sat in the front, the car bowing down like he was royalty.

As soon as we hit Hamden's main drag, Craig began.

"Kath, everybody's talking about you. You got to start being careful."

"You're getting a rep," Roscoe said in his gravelly voice.

They talked to me over their shoulders, keeping their eyes on the road. The two young boys next to me were quiet. They were about my age, maybe a year or two older, and they were listening closely, their faces deadly serious, like they were in training to be men, and I suppose they were—black men in Hamden.

"You can't trust any of them," Craig said. I turned my head toward the window, trying to hide the pleasure I felt—not only at his and Roscoe's concern, but at the very idea of being well-known. A rep. A shadow, a ripple. Something's there in a room before you enter, and still there after you're gone. I couldn't have been happier. My name would have the force, the thunder, of Roscoe's walking stick, set down with a thump every time he took a step.

He and Craig advised me to slow down and to watch out. There was nothing judgmental in their words, nothing that said I was wrong or dirty, or that having sex was. It was all about the treacherous company I was keeping. To this day, I marvel at it. Four boys in a car with me? They could've imagined a very different scenario—but all they tried to do was protect me.

Until that ride, I'd assumed that they wanted to be friends with the white boys. I thought Roscoe didn't know what they said about him. I even felt sorry for them and pictured myself as their ally. It was laughable. What did I have to offer them? A girl so foolish she didn't even know she was alone. No, it was they who allied themselves with me. They saw the danger approaching and took sides—not with the crowd, with the pretty girls or the rowdy boys, but with the weakest link in the chain. A bravery wasted on me.

I had no caution in me then, just as I had no sexual shame. And so late that afternoon, unwilling to heed their advice, I walked straight into New Haven in search of a new adventure, and soon enough I found one.

It was about four miles from my house to the New Haven Green. When I got there, I sat down on the grass and smoked a cigarette. Dusk was falling, and the old-fashioned lamps that lined the green lit up as I sat there, and under them crowds of people rushed home, dark-suited men swinging their attaché cases like boys with schoolbags, women clustered in groups, holding their coats closed at the collar and laughing with each other for no other reason, it seemed, than that it was five o'clock and they were free! Their eyes sparkled in the cold of a November evening; leaves crunched under their heels. And then a boy came across the grass toward me, the most beautiful boy in the world. He had green eyes and a fistful of blond curls on his head. His cheekbones were high; his full lips had perfect Cupid peaks. He looked like an angel, but dusty.

I had the distinct impression then of his being a wanderer. There was something worldly and carefree about him, something not Hamden. To me he seemed like a boy who rode the rails or stowed away on ships; he'd watched the prairies roll by, seen the northern lights from the deck of a fishing trawler. But perhaps he was just from New

Haven; a city boy. I don't remember what we talked about, but I know I invited him to come to my house later that night. I told him to knock quietly on the basement door and I would let him in.

It was late when he arrived, lights out and everybody in bed for the night. On the eight-track tape player, Steppenwolf sang softly about his snow-blind friend, and the most beautiful boy in the world was climbing up the beanbag chair from the floor, climbing up my legs, my belly, my breasts, his hands sliding up inside my shirt as he rose, climbing through the black light and the strobe light, looking like a water creature making his way onto land.

When he had finally worked himself up every inch of my body and lay full-length on me, he whispered, "Hey, girl," like we had just finally now and truly met, and then his mouth was on mine.

How sweet he was, how slow, how sensuous, how totally unlike Brian or Victor, Nicky or Patrick. Who had raised him that he didn't think sex was his to experience alone? That he thought there were two of us there? I had a sudden image of a spangled fat lady from the circus, holding him on her pillowy breasts.

When he left that night, he disappeared altogether, on to another town perhaps, but he would stamp himself on my brain, and so he would resurface again and again through the years, in other boys and men. Once the mind knows something exists, there's no stopping it from finding that thing again, especially when that thing is a slow, practiced, shamelessly hot and tender boy. Occasionally he appears in my dreams—he's always on a high wire, performing for a crowd. He wears a dusty bowler and will take no money for his show. He does it for the love of it; he's as light as air.

17

A Distant Coyote

THE SACRED HEART CAFETERIA HAD A FLOOR OF MARBLED GREEN linoleum—sea green with clouds of white moving across it. Dozens of windows lined the two long sides of the cafeteria, with one wall of windows looking directly into the seniors' parking lot. The room was full of light in January, and cold.

Linda, Leslie, Sylvia, and I sat together; Leslie and Sylvia across from me, Linda at my side. I was taking Spanish that year and I knew Linda's name meant *pretty*, but I thought it hardly captured her. I searched hard for the right word to describe her looks. Elegant? She wore her hair natural and cropped close to her head. She had smooth rich skin, a face that was almost flat in profile and so serene you could print it on a coin, long arms, strong legs. Finally the word *lovely* came to mind—lovely Linda—but that hardly seemed to capture her.

She was tall and sinewy, haughty as hell when she wanted to be. If she saw some of the snobbish girls from our class in the hallway, she'd crank her chin up so high you could see the outline of her windpipe and swish right by them, not even granting them a glance.

"Come on, girls," she'd call out airily to us. "We'll be late for our manicures!" Or our tennis lessons. Or the opera. Swish, swish, swish, nose in the air. But she could never keep up the act for long. Soon enough her whole body would double over and shake with laughter until tears flowed down her face. Linda could make you laugh until you cried or until *she* cried, but if the wrong people were laughing or laughing for the wrong reason, she would shut down fast. She had only to make her face go expressionless—a still black face—and the laughter would freeze midair.

There was only a handful of black girls at Sacred Heart, four or five out of five hundred, including, in our class, Linda, Leslie, and a worried-looking girl named Rita, who served on the student council. In our senior year, Rita would become class president.

At the table diagonally across from us in the cafeteria, Joan Connolly sat with a group of loud, gossipy, good-looking girls, once again playing bodyguard. It was as if she was working a double shift. Her large red hands twitched on her lap. Cuffed in the stiff white blouse, they looked as incongruous as lobsters on a leash.

From freshman year, this group of girls had elected themselves class royalty. They thought the choice was obvious, that the peasants knew they were peasants. There was Louisa with her long brown Barbie doll tresses, little Stacie, very pretty and brimming with aggression, mascaraed Rose, her dark eyes bulging slightly out of a face that was greasy with makeup, and four or five others. Like frat boys, they were always in a pack, so their presence was felt en masse, a dense and glittering force of female confidence.

They went to Florida at winter break and came back and compared their tans. They wore Notre Dame class rings on chains around their necks. They went steady. With seniors. Any fat girl, any plain or pimpled one, immediately felt their contempt.

The fact that they didn't like me was no surprise. The previous year I'd been so far beneath their radar, I might as well not have existed: I never wore makeup, it was obvious I read books, I studied Latin, didn't have a boyfriend, and I cared about doing well in school. Sophomore year I changed, and they noticed me, but they didn't much like what they saw. Recently Rose had cornered Sylvia in the bathroom and told her, "If you were smart, you'd stay away from Kathy. You're too nice to be hanging out with a girl like her."

That afternoon, as I was eating my usual lunch—Hostess cupcakes and chocolate milk—I heard little Stacie let out a yelp at something Joan had said: "You're kidding! Really? That's disgusting." And they all looked over at me. I was sure Joan was telling them about me and the boys at the Teen Center. But I didn't care. The very fact that they were gossiping canceled out anything they had to say. My mother's lessons about never saying anything bad about anyone had gone very deep.

While I'd decided to ignore the girls, I could see they'd gotten Linda's attention. Without having any idea why they were snickering—not that that mattered to her—she began to plan a response. Linda liked to play with the class queens, like a cat plays with a mouse. At first, all she did was drum her long, ringed fingers on the tabletop. Her fingers made a spiderlike sprawl—she had strong fingers, many silver rings, even on her index fingers—and they struck the table harder and harder, beating out a drumroll to . . . what?

She lowered her head to ogle the girls, and when she did, her glasses slid down to the tip of her tiny, flared nose. Improbably, they hung there. Sylvia, Leslie, and I turned to follow her gaze.

The class queens had finished discussing me and were now oiling their arms and legs. Protecting their winter vacation tans. If enough sealant was applied, perhaps they would make it until early spring, when they could hit the backyards with their aluminum reflectors.

"Ugh! I'm peeling!" one girl cried.

"Hmmmmm . . ." Linda murmured, pressing her lips together like she was seriously pondering something.

"Uh-oh," Leslie said.

"Excuse me, girls. Be back in a jiffy," Linda said in one of her peppy white-girl voices.

"Linda, don't . . ." Leslie warned, sounding alarmed but looking interested.

Linda was already sliding away in her chair. She didn't get out of the seat, just pedaled the linoleum with her large handsome feet until she had pulled up to their table.

She put her arm next to Louisa's and said, "Why, you're blacker than I am!"

"I am . . . *not*!" Louisa replied, jerking her arm away as though Linda's touch had soiled her. She had a look of revulsion on her face she didn't even try to hide. "This isn't . . . *that*! It's a tan!"

"You forgot a spot. Better rub some cream on," Linda continued helpfully while the girls buzzed. "You're getting a little ashy there."

Then she came pedaling back, waving to us as she came.

"Just having a little chat with the girls," she explained, docking at the table with a thud and reaching for her Coke at the same time. "Trading beauty tips." She smiled her close-lipped doll's smile and wagged her head back and forth, like one of those electric doggies you used to see in the back windows of people's cars.

Leslie was giggling into her little cupped hands.

"Linda, you're so droll," she said. It was a compliment they handed back and forth to each other frequently.

Then Leslie took her pick out and began to fuss with her hair. When she was done, she patted the back of her head coquettishly and announced, "I'm a lover, not a fighter."

When we left the cafeteria that afternoon, Leslie hooked an arm over my shoulder, pulling me into her.

"Hey, chum," she said and then, nestling her lips in my ear, she began to sing, "Jimmy Mac, when are you coming back . . ."

"How is that bad boy?" she asked affectionately, though she had never met Jimmy, and never would.

Later I would say that I went out with Jimmy for three months, so maybe I started seeing him in early December. But I probably cheated on the time. It might have been the end of December or early January, two and a half months that we went out or even less and I rounded it off. Three just sounded better because almost from the start I was trying to imagine telling someone the story of what happened that night in the car with Jimmy and the boys, and I didn't want the listener to take Jimmy's and my relationship lightly. So two and a half months became three. And even though I'd turned fifteen that November, in my story I was still fourteen. That's the way I would tell it, I decided, if I ever did. Because if I said I was fifteen, the listener might say what happened wasn't so bad or that I should have known better.

Whenever it was that Jimmy and I started seeing each other, I remember our first night very well. We'd had sex in his car, and as we drove out of East Rock Park I was sitting over by the door, ready for a drop in the temperature. Wasn't that how it had gone with Nicky, hot, hot, hot, then cold?

"What are you doing way over there?" Jimmy had asked, tilting his head sideways at me. "Don't you like me anymore?" *The boy asked me.* I slid across the seat and under his arm. He pulled me closer, his leather jacket crumpling softly against my back.

"Do you want to steer?" he asked.

The next day he called and we went out that night, and the night after, and the next one. . . . By mid-January, Jimmy and I were as thick as thieves.

I'd given up rubbing my legs, chattering my teeth, and stamping my feet, and now I was huddled into a tight ball on the cement steps in front of my house. But as cold as it was that winter, and it could get very cold waiting there for Jimmy, sometimes for ten or fifteen minutes at a stretch, I still wouldn't be caught dead wearing gloves or mittens, a hat or a scarf. I didn't even wear a coat, just my leather jacket, which was so short it didn't cover my hips. Socks, I had decided, were uncool, so I always wore panty hose under my jeans.

Winter break had ended and I was back in school, but the rhythm of my evenings remained the same: dinner, dishes, then out the door or back upstairs to my bedroom. I spent three or four nights a week with Jimmy, the others doing homework, chatting with Linda or Leslie or Sylvia on the phone, reading, dreaming—and thinking of Jimmy.

As I sat there shivering on the front stoop, I craned my neck toward Clifford Street. I knew that was the route Jimmy would take, because he always stopped at the Teen Center before coming to me. I could hear his engine the minute he made the turn from Putnam Avenue—a throaty, grinding noise, like the car was chewing up the street.

As soon as Jimmy pulled up, I saw that the car was full. Most of our evenings began this way, Jimmy coming for me with a carload of boys, usually the younger ones, the little brothers moving up, flunkies or friends, but none of them with cars of their own or money in their pockets or a man's need to shave—or a girl like me at their disposal.

Timmy stepped out of the front seat. "Howdy, ma'am," he said, tipping his bangs like a hat. I slid in next to Jimmy; Timmy followed.

"Hey, babe," Jimmy greeted me, kissing me on the mouth. Ben and Stevie and Neal were crowded together in the back. Hey, hey, hey all around.

"Kath, you want a beer? We got a case back here if this motherfucker gets his big feet off it."

"My feet ain't big!"

"Where we going?"

"Fuck, anywhere! Let's go!"

When they got Ben's feet off the beer, they handed me one. A can of Schlitz, wet to the touch. I popped the tab and put it on my index finger, wiggled it, watched it wink in the streetlight. Jimmy took my hand and moved the tab from my index finger to my ring finger. It was like a chorus of birds opened up in my chest, Jimmy, my love, my heart, *my man.*

"With this beer, I thee wed," Timmy said, smiling crookedly and pushing the bangs from his face. I knew Timmy had a crush on me, but he seemed to have resigned himself to the role of witness to Jimmy's and my romance. To me, Timmy was like a twin brother; he was my age, my height, school-bound, curfew-bound, always underdressed and so always cold, such a familiar combination of enthusiasm and awkwardness that I found it impossible even to imagine him pursuing a girl, or making that first move.

When I bent my head and took that first sip of Schlitz, my mind played a magician's trick, and it was Jimmy's breath I was tasting, his cold lips, and I drank it slowly in a smoky kind of swoon.

Jimmy turned the music loud, draped his arm around me, and we took off with a sense of expectation so strong you might have thought we were actually going somewhere.

The heat was blasting from the floorboards. The little pine tree hanging from the rearview mirror whirled round and round. Jimmy turned to smile at me, so close I could smell the beer and Marlboros on his breath. He hadn't shaved. His jaw was furred. From the back, a voice as deep as a drum said, "No shit." Oh, I was happy then. I'd been with all three of the man-boys who ruled the Teen Center. That didn't spell trouble to me.

Jimmy liked to drive slow. It drove the boys crazy sometimes, but it made me feel like we were king and queen of the streets, out surveying our kingdom. When he took the corner at Dixwell Avenue, he turned the wheel using only the palm of his left hand—the master of one-handed driving because he liked to keep his other arm around me. He had green eyes, charcoal lashes, and close-cropped reddish-brown hair. When I brushed my hand up the back of his neck and head, I could feel each bristle. His jaw was square—a man's jaw in profile, which was how I saw him most often, there at the steering wheel—and he had hard, thin lips, a tight James Cagney grin. His hands were rough, the fingers callused. He'd dropped out of school before I met him and worked as a car mechanic at a gas station close to the New Haven borderline.

If I were making up the story, I would have chosen sullen Nicky or rude-boy Patrick to play the part that Jimmy eventually played in my life. Call it a failure of the imagination. But Jimmy was so playful, so lighthearted, and always, until the end, affectionate toward me. I can't remember a single sharp word from him, any hint of coldness or contempt. I knew he was a troublemaker, of course, but saw no anger or despair in him, no twisted psychology. Trouble just seemed to find him, and when it did, most likely he'd be grinning at it, as if trouble

was just one more guest at his party. It was his loose and easy gen-
erosity—everybody along for the ride!—that drew people to him. It
made you think he was never really doing anything bad, just up to
some boy's mischief.

From the backseat, Ben was yelling, "Close the fucking windows!"

"Auntie Ben!" the boys shouted back.

Ben was called Big Ben and sometimes Ben Gay. Bulky, dark-
haired, and still carrying his baby fat, Ben always had something to
complain about. When the window was open, he wanted it closed.
When it was closed, he was suffocating.

Sixteen, but with his heels dug in hard. He was determined to be
cranky.

I didn't know enough yet to realize that he was what my mother
would have called a late bloomer. He didn't yet feel what the other
boys were feeling about girls. That confused and angered him. I knew
he didn't much like girls but I thought if I was nice to him, he would
treat me the same. I know I treated him better than the boys did.

"Jimmy, it's like fucking Alaska back here!"

"You pussy," Stevie said.

"Kathy?" Ben asked.

"Kath, don't close it!" the boys yelled, but I reached over Jimmy
and cranked the window up.

"Thanks, Kath," Ben grumbled. "Fuckin' assholes."

Jimmy gave me a sly smile. "The boys are acting up," he said.

"Yeah," I said happily, and we listened, proud as parents, prouder
even, while they argued in the back.

Jimmy wasn't the quickest one in the car, but he was always the
one having the most fun. He slid a Gladys Knight tape into the deck
and started singing along. "She's leaving on a midnight train to
Georgia . . ." he sang to me, changing her words so they would come
out right, "I'd rather live in her world than live without her in
mine . . ." until the boys began yelling for some Zeppelin. He gave
them the Allman Brothers instead, and the car fell into a stillness so
that there was only the music, the bass throbbing, the heat coming up

at us in waves. My hand began sneaking up Jimmy's thigh and the boys exploded into another argument. "Get off my fuckin' foot!"

I ain't on your foot.

Yeah, you fuckin' are. What's this? It's my foot.

That's a fucking snow shovel. No wonder I'm steppin' on them—look at 'em! You could plow roads and shit.

Fuck you. My feet ain't big.

Kathy! Kath, look over here—are these big feet or what?

Jimmy was laughing the way a man laughs when something funny's going on, but he also has a hard-on and a hand secretly stroking it; that is, with about as happy a laugh as I'd ever heard.

"Big feet, big dick," Ben shouted in self-defense.

That's when Jimmy decided to drop them off at the Teen Center. When we pulled up to the curb, they didn't want to get out of the car.

"Ah, come on, Jimmy!"

"Why the fuck we gotta get out?"

They knew why and they weren't happy. Jimmy paid them no mind. He gave them a big cartoon grin—*what can I do, boys?*

"Party's over," he laughed. "It's past my bedtime!"

"Where you two going?"

Stevie gave Ben a shove toward the door. "You know where they're going."

And then Jimmy and I took off for East Rock Park.

Once inside the park, we left the road. The trees took us in and then stood guard over our car. They were heavy with snow and hung with so much dazzling ice that on a sunny day, it would have hurt your eyes to look at them. A deep hush came out of the woods, deeper and denser the longer you listened, and then you could hear tiny pops and cracks, ice shifting, a squirrel hunting, one bough letting go of snow deep inside the forest.

"Look, he's sitting up, he's begging," Jimmy said after he unzipped his pants. The flat belly, the stiff hairs on his thighs, the hard dick with its snake head; a triangle of warm, white flesh, almost glowing in that dark car.

He was begging to be petted, so I did. Jimmy put his head back and yowled softly, like a distant coyote.

Jimmy explained all kinds of things to me. No one else had bothered. They all thought I knew. Or didn't care whether I did or not.

He told me a man's semen built up in him so that if he went a long time without fucking, he would have so much to shoot, he would fill you up. Legs up made it easier for him to get in. Legs down, tighter and nicer. I wouldn't get pregnant if I took a hot bath when I got home.

Whenever I slipped my hand under his balls, Jimmy would say, "Aren't they heavy?" He was joking but he wasn't. He liked to think that his five o'clock shadow hurt me. "It's sharp, isn't it?" he'd ask, rubbing his jaw. "Did I scratch you all up?"

The windows steamed over and then the steam froze in a child's drawing of snowflakes. Outside this crystal curtain, there were owls in the trees, wolves in the snow, moonlight like ice, shadows like ink. Inside, we were bare-skinned, warm to the touch.

One night, he wove his fingers through my hair and gently pushed my head down, whispering fervently, "Suck it, baby, please." When I took it in my mouth, he leaned back and petted my hair, saying dreamily, "Like your Popsicle."

After he came, we always laughed, as if each time it was a complete surprise. Then we lay holding each other in the backseat. Sometimes he fell asleep gripping my hand so tightly that I was sure he needed me to save him from something, and I knew that I would.

Back then I didn't know girls could come, too; I thought what I felt was the apex of sexual sensation, the warm and shivery tingling when he touched me, the profound jolt when he pushed himself inside; shock and sense, revelation and rightness hitting all at once.

On the ride home, I sat under the curve of his arm, the fingers of his right hand falling over my right breast, all very casual, but we were slinky with pride. He steered with his left hand, a Marlboro hanging from his lips. When he glanced sideways at me and grinned, the cigarette pointed up.

"Am I your man?" Jimmy asked me, as if he had to. But that was the thing about Jimmy—he asked anyway.

He dropped me at the front door and was there again the next night. We could hardly bear to be apart. If he ran into my parents, he was as charming and clumsy as some shaggy dog, but to me he was the epitome of masculinity, and in retrospect the first wholly successful challenge to my father's dark suit and tie.

On Sundays, Jimmy and the boys and I would visit the Teen Center director, a big, fleshy woman named Donna with brown hair down to her hips. Donna was half hippie, half shit-kicker, and she lived in the only apartment complex in Hamden. It was practically across the street from the firehouse, looming seven stories above Whitney Avenue. She had a black boyfriend and they were always in bed when we arrived. They lay there naked under the sheets and we raided their refrigerator and then, Cokes in hand, pulled chairs up around their bed.

When Donna and her lover spoke to each other, their voices hummed with self-satisfaction, and I could feel their pleasure, naked under the white sheets and our gaze. She'd lean back against him and he'd reach over her to grab the menthols or lighter from her night table, pausing, it seemed, to let us see his black arm against her marshmallow skin. He was all ripples, lean and long, and she was a mountain of whipped cream.

"So what are you boys and girls up to today?"

"Boys and *girl*," Timmy said.

"Kathy and her merry men," the boyfriend said.

"Hairy men," one of the boys cracked.

"So you two are together now?" Donna asked Jimmy and me.

"Every night," Jimmy said to laughter, pulling me close.

"Better watch out for that one," the boyfriend said to me.

"Kathy's the one you got to watch out for," Donna told him. "She's a free spirit, right, Kathy? Like me."

"Better not be too free, baby," her boyfriend reminded her.

Back home, I sailed around the house singing "Midnight Train to Georgia." I told my sisters that it was Jimmy's and my song. I was madly in love. It was Jimmy, of course, but it was also the gang of boys who came with him. My tribe in the woods, the one I'd been looking for the night I ran away. My brotherhood.

Sometimes I worked on the poem I'd begun the first night I saw Jimmy, swinging a log on our front lawn. In the latest version, he was standing on a windswept cliff at midnight, still surrounded by police. *They didn't care that he loved me—and I him—or that his whole wild life was mine,* I wrote, and then those very unimaginative cops put *my man's proud body* in handcuffs and led him away.

We didn't seem to *do* much, Jimmy and I, but we did it almost every night. Once in a while Jimmy got to my house late or had to leave early. "I gotta go see my old lady," he'd say, and always with such regret, I thought he meant his mother.

I don't know how long it took me to realize that he was talking about a girl, but when I did, I wouldn't let myself feel anything about it. Then I heard the name Chrissy and knew she was one of the two Chrissys at the firehouse. I'd never seen Chrissy by herself and it was strange to think of Jimmy approaching her through a forest of shining hair, long clicking fingernails, smoke, bubble gum, and whispers. He would be an intruder there. He would have to beg. I was sure Jimmy was grateful to have found me, his true love, and equally sure he would soon break up with Chrissy. That he didn't do it right away made sense to me. At fifteen it was easier just to slide from one moment, one adventure, to the next, carried quickly, almost violently, by your deepest feelings. It would all get sorted out eventually, I thought, and the unwanted girlfriend would just disappear, along with any other inconvenient bits of reality.

On Valentine's Day, Jimmy presented me with a little white teddy bear wearing a T-shirt that said, "I Wuv You." Wasn't that the truth of the matter? His heart revealed?

By the end of February, the snow was piled high in the yards. Donna had been fired by the town of Hamden right after some of the boys at the center torched the girls' couch and pushed it down the stairs. She was replaced with a nervous-looking man named Alan.

The hostility of the firehouse girls had grown thick as brambles. When I walked in, it was so intense that if none of the guys I knew were there, I'd turn and walk out. I'd never been hated by girls before, and the ugly look on their pretty faces came as a shock. I wasn't happy about the situation, but I wasn't as worried about it as I should have been. I just stopped going to the firehouse and started spending all my time with "my boys," as I'd come to think of them—Jimmy and the shifting cast of characters that came with him.

Some nights they picked me up at home. Sometimes, in my impatience, I met them halfway to the Teen Center. I waited on the corner of Putnam and Clifford, stamping my feet against the cold. Under my boots, the lawns were crunchy with frost; my breath was a warm, moist cloud. If I was early or they were late, I'd sometimes wonder what it would be like to be stranded out here, connected to no one, belonging nowhere. But as soon as I climbed into Jimmy's car, I left the loneliness and cold behind. We made a warm, jostling world of our own, one completely cut off from the day-lit world, the world of parents and other teenagers where your behavior was closely watched and carefully controlled. Outlaws and rebels, we had each other, and nobody outside of that car mattered.

That's the way I felt then, though now I can see how it really was. The boys were still hanging out at the Teen Center, even though I wasn't. Jimmy was still best friends with Nicky and Patrick. Chrissy was Jimmy's official girlfriend. The boys who went out with us at night, and the girls who hated me, were all full-fledged members of the Teen Center gang; I was the only outsider.

The ground was eroding under my feet, but I never noticed. In fact, as my world became smaller, each aspect of it became more precious, every moment alone with Jimmy, every festival shout from the boys, every time they said "Kath" with affectionate familiarity and Jimmy held me close and whispered, "Babe."

18

Bad Cop, Bad Cop

IN MARCH, I WAS STILL BABY-SITTING FOR FAMILIES IN MY NEIGHBOR-hood—a good little girl when they all started hiring me the previous spring, who would've thought I wasn't by wintertime?

I was an excellent baby-sitter, of course, a popular one. I worked for five families and had a waiting list. It was a job I was well suited for. I knew how to change diapers, give baths, bandage cuts, I enjoyed playing with invisible friends, talking to shoes, singing lullabies. If the children wanted to stir a pot of blocks and feed me out of it and do it again and again and again—and each time I was supposed to exclaim "Yum! Yum! Pudding!"—I would.

This particular night, I was working for the Luganos, my favorite family. One boy and a baby girl. Nina was rosy-cheeked and sturdy; the boy, Johnny, was pale-faced and fragile, enchantingly serious. He found a ready nest in my heart, the place Stephen had carved out six years earlier, which has been open ever since, a place for small, unearthly boys who seem, even at five years old, to keep their own counsel. There were never any scenes when the Luganos left the house. In fact, that night Johnny waved them out the door so he and I could get back to flying planes off the living room furniture.

When someone started knocking at the Luganos' front door, I'd already tucked Johnny and Nina into their beds and I was wandering through their living room, shoeless, sliding my feet across the sage-green carpet and drinking chocolate milk. Even though I liked being in other people's houses when they weren't there, after an hour of exploring the Luganos' refrigerator and kitchen cabinets, reading their grocery list and their wall calendar, and trying out each chair in the living room, an itchy kind of restlessness had come over me. There were no books in this house! I was ready to go home, but it was only nine o'clock. Two more hours to go.

The knocking started softly, with a stuttering rhythm, tap, tap-tap-tap, tap-tap, like the person at the door was signaling in a secret code.

When I'd told Jimmy earlier in the day that I couldn't see him that night, he was unhappy. "What do you have to baby-sit for?" he'd asked in a plaintive voice. "I need you to take care of *me*." I didn't think he was upset because he was desperate to see me—he just didn't like being told that he couldn't. So when he asked me where I'd be, I gave him the address, assuming that if he did stop by, we'd have a quick, quiet visit, two young lovers stealing some time. Maybe we'd huddle outside on the steps, share a cigarette, kiss.

Before I could even get to the door, the tapping changed into a harsh knocking and I flew—he'd wake the children! There was a window set high in the door and when I stood on my toes and looked out, I saw Jimmy and the boys huddled in their coats, faces pinched with cold and lifted toward the window.

"You can't come in," I mouthed through the glass. Could they even see my mouth? I shook my head but my heart was already stricken. I had never refused Jimmy anything.

But why, why did he bring all of them?

"Kathy, it's coooold!" they cried, their voices getting louder and louder. "Come on, open up!"

I unlocked and cracked the door.

"You have to go—" I started, but they pushed the door wide and piled in, Jimmy, Timmy, Ben, and Stevie, beer cans in their coat pockets but already rolling drunk. They went straight for the kitchen. Opened the refrigerator, the cabinets.

"Where do they keep the booze?" someone asked, while Jimmy snaked an arm around me and planted a cold, beery kiss.

There was nothing good to drink and nothing handy like brownies to eat, so Timmy picked up an egg, yelled, "Hey, Jimmy, catch this!" and threw it across the kitchen.

The egg splattered against the wall and dripped down.

"The kids are sleeping!" I hissed frantically, but it was as if a gong had sounded; mayhem.

"Batter up!" Stevie cried, gripping a spatula. Another egg went flying. "Strike!"

Jimmy grabbed a plate from the counter.

"Frisbee?" he asked Stevie. I tried to grab his arm.

"Fucking flying saucers!"

Timmy went reeling out of the kitchen, bounced off the hallway wall, and disappeared into the living room. I got there in time to see him lurch sideways as if the floor had tilted underneath him; a table tipped, a vase exploded.

"What the fuck?" Timmy said, looking puzzled.

He dropped to his knees and wavered over the broken glass.

"I'll clean it up, Kath, don't worry, make it nice and clean and nice," he mumbled. He dove for a piece, missed, dropped his cigarette on the carpet.

"Timmy, it's okay, I'll do it. Come on, Timmy, you gotta go now," I told him, trying to pull him to his feet.

From the kitchen, the smell of beer and burning. When I went back in there, Ben and Stevie were sliding around on the eggs like figure skaters. Then Ben's legs flew out from under him, and he landed like a rock.

A beer can lay leaking on the floor. A cigarette had been ground out on the linoleum.

"Jimmy, you gotta get out of here! Please! Please, you have to go! The parents are gonna be here any minute!" And with *parents*, not *children*, I herded them through the hallway and out the door, shutting it behind them.

I was turning back to the kitchen to clean, heart tripping with panic, when Jimmy started hammering on the door.

"Kathy!" he yelled. I froze.

"Kathy?" In the silence that followed, I could hear him listening to me listening to him.

"Kathy, let me in! Kathy, please!" Boom, boom, boom, his fist beating out a protest. Then he howled: "Katheeee!"

He'd forgotten he had a car to go to, a home, friends, days and years ahead, another night to see me. "Kathy!" he called out again. My feet were nailed to the carpet. I wanted to cry.

Then his fist plunged through the window on the door . . . glass, blood, winter wind.

"Wh-who is that?" And behind me at the top of the stairs, Johnny stood owl-eyed and shivering in his baseball pajamas.

When I jerked open the door, the boys were falling into the car, yelling, "Jimmy, let's get the hell out of here!"

Jimmy just stood there, swaying slightly and looking down at his bloody hand, his face soft with wonder.

When he looked up at me, his eyes were filled with gratitude. In his play-around, fuck-around boy's life, he'd stumbled upon something real in himself, something running deep. It was there, but by tomorrow he'd forget.

"Sorry, babe," he whispered, then turned and stumbled toward the car.

I closed the door and locked it, but an icy wind tunneled through the broken window and into the rooms of the house. It was as if the outside had come inside: Furry black tree branches looked close enough to touch with my hand, snowflakes gusted through the hallway, and the streetlight spilled onto the carpeted floor. In the window frame, jagged claws of glass were splashed with blood. Suddenly it seemed that I had always known this would happen someday, that I would bring chaos into a home, set fire to the curtains, flood the family room, hurt a child. Known it from the day Frank Lee leaned over Henry's seat with a look of great anticipation on his face and a pencil in his hand.

Upstairs, Johnny was huddled in bed. His fist clutched his pajama top like a fretful old man.

"What do they want?" he asked, his scared eyes glued to my face, still depending on me.

"They're gone now, Johnny," I told him. "They won't ever come back."

Downstairs, I taped a piece of cardboard over the window, washed the kitchen floor, dug in the carpet for pieces of glass.

Mr. and Mrs. Lugano came rushing into the house. He was first through the door, disheveled, wired, ready.

"Are you all right? What the hell happened? Are the kids . . . ?"

I tried to explain but before I could finish, their faces closed against me and they ran upstairs.

When they came down, their eyes were cold.

"We're calling the police," Mr. Lugano said. "And your parents."

I waited on the couch in the living room. Mrs. Lugano came out of the kitchen with a glass of milk.

"You will never set foot in this house again," she said as she carried the glass upstairs.

Out of nowhere, like some kind of space machine, a police car slid swiftly to the front of the house, jerked to a stop, went dark. Doors opened, slammed, a metallic crackling came from the sidewalk, and then two men in blue had their feet planted in the living room.

While the Luganos explained, the cops looked around the room, taking in the damage, their eyes always coming back to me. They had their notebooks out and were asking me for the boys' names when my father arrived.

He came in the door fast. The charge coming off of him was so strong even the cops caught it. They stood straighter, their cool cops' faces rippling into life.

My father could barely keep his attention on what they were telling him. He bent his head low, trying to concentrate on their voices. I could see his jaw clench. His lips were pressed so tightly together they'd almost disappeared. When he lifted his head, his hot blue eyes pinned me to the couch.

"Big-time," he said, coming across the room. "You've messed up big-time now." He shook his head slowly, still working his jaw and clamping down on his lips. This was personal; this was between him and me.

"What the hell were you thinking? *Were* you thinking? Do you have one thought for anyone but yourself? You had *one* responsibility here, *one* job to do, to watch over their children. That's what they hired you for, that's what they pay you for—*to protect their children.*" He paused before passing his final judgment. "You didn't even come close."

"She won't tell us the boys' names," Mr. Lugano said, and once again, all eyes were on me.

"You won't do *what?*" my father said.

"This isn't a game," one of the cops told me. "You've gotten yourself into some serious trouble here."

"So, you're going to protect the guys who did this," my father said, as if the cop hadn't even spoken. "You put two kids at risk, you didn't protect them, you didn't protect this house, but you're going to protect the guys who wrecked it. I bet you think you're being honorable. Tell me, is that what you think?" He was shouting now, his face shoved close to mine. "Huh, dummkopf? Is that what you think?"

"Do you know how Johnny feels now?" Mr. Lugano said. "Do you know what you've done to him?" This was worse than anger. These people hated me, hated me so much it made them hate my parents, too. Even years later, when the Luganos saw my mother and father at a party, they turned away, refusing to speak.

"Do you think we'll ever leave him alone again with any baby-sitter?" I knew they wouldn't—they were good parents, they loved those children to death.

"He's up there shaking, afraid to go to sleep," Mrs. Lugano cried out angrily. "Afraid they're going to come back."

"Just give us the names of the boys, and then we can talk with them," one of the cops said to me, and I knew he was saying: *Give us the names, for your sake, for ours.* With the boys' names, they could leave this family drama behind and get down to business, round up the boys, be their cop selves pitted against something surly out there in the street.

But I couldn't. Say the name Jimmy out loud and watch it being written into a cop's notebook? No, I couldn't. There wasn't even any choice about it. Every teenager knew you didn't rat on your friends, and every Dobie knew you never, ever gave in to pressure—standing alone against the crowd was the very definition of moral courage for my parents, especially my father.

The second cop had said nothing the whole time, just stood there watching. They seemed like bit players, the cops, dressed for a more major part.

"You *owe* them the names," my father said. "Have you given one thought, one tiny thought inside that thick skull of yours, to what could have happened here? They could've set this house on fire! They could've hurt those kids! This is *your* responsibility, *your* fault, your mess to clean up now. Crying? *You're* crying?"

Mr. Lugano started shouting then. "What the hell about my little boy crying in his bed upstairs?"

"This isn't about you," my father told me. "Nobody here cares about you anymore."

"We trusted you!"

But still I couldn't give their names.

The silent cop stepped forward then. "I might have a solution," he said.

First, he went into the kitchen with the Luganos to work it out with them. My father said nothing while they were out of the room, just stood there glaring at me, while the other cop shifted back and forth on his creaky shoes.

When the three of them returned, the cop explained the deal to me, one that the Luganos had agreed to reluctantly. He told me that if I convinced the boys to pay for the damage, then they would let the matter drop. No charges, no arrests, no more questioning.

"You tell the boys that either they come here this Saturday, meet with the Luganos, and make good for the damage, or you'll give us their names and they'll be arrested and charged. Okay?" His voice was stern, but there was no anger in his eyes. I held on to his gaze almost desperately.

I would have to make the boys believe I really would turn them in, he explained. "Even if you won't—"

"She will," my father interrupted.

"That's the only way this will work. Those boys wrecked this house. They owe the Luganos. You know that's only fair." He was appealing to my sense of justice, the only person in the room who seemed to believe that I might have one.

"The boys pay up and that will be that. No more questions. It's a good deal for them. Okay? You got it?" I nodded. "So you'll get them over here on Saturday?"

When I agreed, he told my father, "You can take her home now."

My father charged down the empty street, still not talking to me. He couldn't even bear to look at me. I watched our shoes. His were moving fast, mine made a pathetic ticktacking sound on the concrete as I tried to keep up. Occasionally I lost my footing and skittered over the icy sidewalk. I thought we might walk this way forever, my father's anger burning next to me like a furnace, the two of us rushing past snow-filled yards and low box hedges, our footfalls and our breath the only sounds.

He was a mast of moral fury, the worst kind, towering over me. I had no defense against him. If I trusted anyone on morality, it was my father.

My mother and father fought over what to do about me. My father wanted to straight-out forbid me to go to the Teen Center. He didn't know that I hardly went there anymore. My mother didn't think that was a smart idea. She was afraid of driving me away altogether.

My father ignored her. No more Teen Center, he told me. And worse—no more Jimmy.

"That's it. It's over. You meet with those guys tomorrow night and tell them to get themselves over to the Luganos' next Saturday, and then you can consider yourself permanently grounded."

I didn't know then that they'd argued over me. Didn't know what they had been saying about me since that night. But at fifteen, I told myself I didn't care what my parents thought. I certainly acted like I didn't—and wasn't that halfway there?

My father stopped speaking to me after that. For several days, maybe even a week, my dinners would be passed in a kind of exile: "Would you tell your sister to pass the peas."

I met with the boys and gave them the message. They couldn't believe I'd set them up.

"You fucked us over," they said, before turning their backs on me to discuss their next move. It was as though I had ceased to exist.

On Saturday, they went to the Luganos'. They went grudgingly, but with money in their pockets. The Luganos must have talked to the other families I baby-sat for, because I never had another call. I couldn't be trusted with children anymore.

The day my father began speaking to me again, I immediately wished he hadn't.

"Jimmy has an arrest record a mile long!" he roared. How had he found that out? I knew Jimmy was on probation when I first met him, though I'd never asked why. All of the boys got into trouble for the same things: drinking and driving, brawling in public, and then taking a swing at the cops when they arrived. They lived on probation like souls in limbo, neither good enough nor bad enough for a final judgment. To me, Jimmy's "probation" was just part of the package—his leather jacket, the James Cagney lips breaking into a Gladys Knight song, that rough callused hand gripping mine tightly as he slept. Tough, tender, hapless; in charge, in trouble; big man and little boy all wrapped into one. But my father knowing about the probation was a completely different thing. I felt like he'd reached into my secret nighttime world, yanked open the door to Jimmy's car, where we lay naked, and shone a flashlight in.

I waited until my parents were in bed that night and then snuck out the back door to meet Jimmy—the first of our secret rendezvous. Back then, I thought I was a clever little escape artist. Years later, my parents told me they used to hear me going out. Short of locking me in my room, however, they didn't know what to do.

I wasn't going to give Jimmy up. But holding on to him wasn't anything like those stories of star-crossed lovers in the books and movies I knew. I saw him only three or four times in the next two weeks, and each time we used our old meeting place, on the corner of Putnam and Clifford. He came without the boys those nights, so I figured they were still angry about the Luganos. And Jimmy himself had changed. There was nothing obvious; he wasn't hostile or mean. He just stopped reaching from the driver's seat to open the door for me, and no longer greeted me with the big, dancing grin I loved so much—simple omissions that had me scrambling to get back what I had lost.

Everyone was angry at me—my father, my mother, the neighborhood families I knew through baby-sitting, Ben, Timmy, Stevie, the girls at the Teen Center. Even Jimmy, it seemed. Except for my three Sacred Heart girlfriends—Sylvia, Linda, and Leslie—all the people in my life had turned against me. There were no eyes that brightened with love or pleasure when they saw me. The light had gone out and I couldn't figure out how to turn it on again.

That winter the weather was bitterly cold; the skies were steel gray. I imagine that I acted as if I were extraordinarily cheerful.

19

The Bottom of the Sea

THAT NIGHT BEGAN AS ALL OUR NIGHTS HAD ONCE BEGUN—JIMMY came for me with a carload of boys.

It was the middle of March, snow high and crusted over in the yards, Christmas lights long gone. The sidewalk, patched with ice, gleamed dully beneath the streetlamps. I hurried down Clifford, my hands, red and stinging, jammed into the pockets of my fake leather jacket, my chin buried in its fake fur collar. No one else was out. Between the tapping and skittering of my boots, I heard the soft thump of snow falling off the trees. Steam rose from my mouth. My eyeballs felt dry, my lips peeling; I bit at the little flags of flesh, then fumbled in my pocket for Chap Stick. I had the look of a thousand other suburban white kids, slatternly and a bit desperate.

When I got to Putnam Avenue, I leaned against a tree. Stamped my feet and waited. Twenty minutes? Thirty?

When Jimmy's car finally pulled up, it stopped several yards from me and then just idled, smoke pouring from the exhaust pipe, windows blank. I felt as if my whole body had paused to watch, to listen. Why was Jimmy doing that? Didn't he see me?

I walked over to the car and when I bent to look inside, I saw the boys had come. Then the passenger door swung open and flooded me in a wave of heat and smoke. Neal slipped out—"Hey, Kath"—and I slipped in. There behind the wheel was Jimmy. The smile was back on his face, his eyes were reddish, dancing. "Hey, babe," he said.

Ben was in the backseat with a man who occasionally appeared at the Teen Center, the one with the long blond hair I'd chased up the East Rock hill that night in September. His name was Scott, and he'd never come out with us before. He was a lot older than we were, in his thirties. Since the boys always owed him money, I assumed he was selling them drugs—he didn't have any job that I knew of.

Scott didn't know I'd tried to catch up to him as he climbed the hill the night I ran away. Only six months before, and it already seemed like years. He wore the same brown leather jacket he'd worn that night. His blond hair still hung to his waist. He had a hard face, a lean, mobile body. I was surprised he was out with us, tucked in the backseat like that. I didn't think cruising the streets with boys who still hid beer in their coat pockets would be very interesting to him. It was a compliment, I thought, his coming along with us.

In the backseat of the car there was a case of beer and a bottle of gin. Another couple of six-packs were stashed on the floorwell under Neal's feet.

Hey, hey, hey all around. Jimmy jerked the music loud, draped his arm over me, pulling me close, and we took off.

The road stretched ahead, then disappeared around a curve. Jimmy chased it down, sent it spinning under his wheels, only to see it unroll ahead of him again.

"It's cold as a motherfucker," Ben said from the back.

Neal asked me for a cigarette. His lips were the color of cherry candy.

"Whoa, your hands are like icicles," he said.

"They don't feel cold," I told him, trying to curl my fingers. "They feel like they're on fire."

Neal was always the smartest and quietest of the boys, middle class, college-bound. Unlike the others, he never got drunk, and he was always trying to get me to wear his gloves.

"I'll warm your hands up," Jimmy volunteered. He took my hands and pulled them inside his thighs, closing his legs around them. Then he spoke in my ear, "It's warm there."

The little pine tree hanging on the rearview mirror swung from side to side, smothering us softly with its scent. I felt like I had a reprieve. They weren't angry about the cops—not for tonight? Not ever? On Dixwell Avenue, Jimmy took a right and Ben grumbled, "Why you going this way?" It was just like old times, I thought, and I laughed aloud from a relief so pure, it felt like happiness.

We were across the street from the Dunkin' Donuts when Jimmy turned to reply to Ben and we veered off the road and crashed into something, throwing us back against our seats.

"Shit!" Jimmy yelled and got out of the car to see what we had hit. In the headlights, we watched him bend down. When he stood up again, he was grinning.

"A snowbank!" he shouted.

"A goddamn snowbank!" he laughed as he got back inside. He gunned the car backward while cars behind us honked angrily.

He screeched forward and we took off, the boys giving the other drivers the finger. If someone had started chasing us then, we might have been saved. But no one did. The boys laughed. "Fucking snowbank." "Sneaky motherfucker." "*Big* motherfucker." But the snowbank had jarred something loose. There was a heavy restlessness in the air.

"Don't open that beer, man. We get stopped, I'm fucked." The boys wanted to drink, but Jimmy wouldn't let them. He was on probation again.

They began to get irritable. "Man, shit, what did we get all this beer for?"

"Fucking pull over somewhere!"

Usually this was about the time Jimmy would choose to drop them off at the firehouse with some of the beer, but tonight he just kept driving.

"Jimmy, let's go somewhere we can smoke this joint," Scott said, and suddenly there was silence, like a dip into darkness. My neck prickled, but it was only Ben and Scott crouched back there.

"Maybe later," Jimmy said. "I want to cruise around some."

He asked me to light him a cigarette, and after I'd slipped it in his mouth, he pulled me closer to him. As I leaned against his chest, smelling his leather jacket, I felt like I'd been taken into a safe hiding place, and I could stay here and never, ever have to go home.

We cruised down Dixwell Avenue, by the strip mall with its barren parking lot, then under the railroad tracks, passing nothing but an office complex closed down for the night, a boxy building in a big square lot. Then some scraggly brush, buried in snow, and another darkened strip of stores. Traffic lights blinked on deserted corners. Grimy mountains of snow stuck to anything that stood still—lampposts, mailboxes.

The boys got quiet looking out. Their boredom began to weigh on me.

Greg Allman was singing about being tied to the whipping post; the bass held the song down and then turned slow and deliberate.

"Let's get the fuck out of here," Jimmy said, and he made a wide U-turn using all four lanes of Dixwell Avenue, letting the back of the car shiver a little. "Let's go up to East Rock."

We cut through the reservoir on that cement bridge, took the dark hill, up, up. . . .

How hard I'd chased Scott that night! Running, yelling, spurred on by that rope of yellow hair that swung from side to side. He'd vanished, right at the crest of the hill, at the entrance to East Rock. I guess you could say that tonight was the night I'd finally caught up with him.

We rolled into the park, our headlights revealing the black bodies of trees, their roots swamped in snow. The road had just begun to climb steeply when Jimmy veered to the left, plunged straight into the woods. The car churned, cleaved snow.

Jimmy cut the headlights. The snow glowed; shadows slipped wetly from trees. Scott lit a joint and when it was passed to Jimmy, he told me to open my mouth and he put his lips to mine and breathed the smoke in. I took off my jacket and a little hum went through the car.

"Kath, hand me one of those beers up front, they're colder," Scott said.

"Me, too," Ben mumbled and then repeated himself. "I want one, too, Kathy." I leaned over the backseat, propped myself there, and watched. Jimmy slid his hand up the back of my shirt.

I don't remember what we talked about: a concert they'd been to, pot deals they got burnt on, a fight, a cop, a father? I do know that they would have done most of the talking. I wasn't one for words back then, not in a car full of boys. And my recent brush with their anger, with so much anger inside and outside of my family, had made me cautious. The fear I had of losing Jimmy and the boys had gnawed a hole inside. I felt emptied of thoughts and feelings; a creature in waiting. So I sat there smoking, drinking, handing out beers, and taking the boys in through my skin, their harsh voices, their laughter, their thick-knuckled hands and tight jeans, the essence of them—that whole hard-ass, shaggy-dog, boys-to-men thing.

I drank my beer, pressed leg to leg against Jimmy. When I held the flame under his cigarette, he wrapped his hand around my wrist. They began to pass the bottle.

Neal leaned back against my right shoulder. His arm rested on the side of my breast. It seemed to have landed there by mistake; the car was that crowded. But then he noticed. I could feel him noticing. He didn't move.

Every time I took a breath, my breast swelled against his arm. The quiet between us was like an urgent, whispered conversation. My chest rose and fell. Neal turned his head stiffly to say something to Ben or Scott, keeping his body where it was. When he turned back around, he looked down at his hands. I held my breath for a few seconds, but that only made it come harder and faster. It was so obvious now, it was like my breast was petting him. Jimmy left the car to piss and that broke the spell. There was no reason to be crowded up against each other anymore. Once, by mistake, yes, that was the trick. Again and planned? No longer so enticing.

When Jimmy came back, he put his mouth to my ear. "I want you." He kissed me, filling my mouth with his tongue. It cleared the air, dissipated the heat, put me back on track.

"What did Chrissy do to you, Jimmy? Decide to fucking brand you?" Scott said roughly from the backseat.

Was it only then that I noticed the bruises on his neck? It was dark in the car and the collar of his jacket had hidden them but his jacket was open now and I could see them, big purplish red welts covering both sides of his neck. They were fearsome. She'd marked him with her teeth. That desire! That confidence! claiming him for all to see and he, yes, he letting her.

Unbidden, the image of Jimmy laughing as Chrissy dug her teeth in came to mind. Did her long hair fall across his face and did he lift it up, winding it around his fist? Did he almost burst with wanting to have her because he couldn't? He wore the bruises openly, I could see now—he wore them with pride.

"Ring around the collar," Ben smirked. They were laughing and that is the moment I began to change, not quick quick quick, like sweet Cinderella at the stroke of midnight, but slowly. Something was dissolving inside of me; the air itself seemed to shift, a dingy light coming up from the floorboards.

Jimmy put his arm around my neck. "You're mine, right, babe?" And pulling me close, he took my hand and put it on his crotch. "Feel that?" He wanted me now, he whispered again, and I was still thinking this was just a profession of desire, not a plan, still stumbling through the thicket of dark hair and long sharp teeth, when he said, "The boys can leave."

Leave? Go where?

"They'll wait outside if I tell them to." He turned to the backseat. "You guys can wait outside, right?"

"Outside? What the fuck . . . nah, man!"

"Fuck, I ain't freezing my balls off out there."

"Come on, don't be a bunch of pussies."

"It's cold out there, man."

But they grabbed their jackets anyway, grumbling and cursing, and opened the doors. A question stirred the air, a ripple of wonder and doubt, of expectation, of something very close to awe.

"Wait a minute, babe," Jimmy said and got out with them. I heard him yell, "Ben, close the fucking door! She'll freeze her ass off." And then I sat alone in the car, listening to the rise and fall of their voices outside, a stranger to myself, a "she" who could freeze her ass off.

Jimmy opened the door grinning rakishly, held out his hand. "Come on, babe, they said it was okay. Let's go in the back." It was a done deal.

"Come on," he cajoled. "They can't wait out there all night." I felt awkward getting out of the car in front of them and then crawling into the backseat with Jimmy.

"Jimmy, give us the bottle!"

"And my smokes!"

"And don't take all night, man."

They didn't say anything to me, though they were all watching. Their eyes had changed. They were regarding me with a cold, lively interest. There wasn't anything friendly about it.

Sex went fast with Jimmy, and everything felt wrong. My shirt stayed on and being half bare didn't feel seductive, it felt babyish and obscene, more like I'd forgotten to put my pants on. My body was cold and dumb. Heavy luggage being moved about. My feet looked white as fish.

Outside, I could hear them stamping their boots on the snow, spitting, talking, laughing. The windows had steamed and then frosted over, curtaining us in ice.

When Jimmy was done, he was full of gratitude—"Oh, babe, that was good," he said, nuzzling my neck—but it wasn't the same. There was something false in his manner, something slick and keening.

I pulled on my pants, thinking of the boys freezing outside.

"Wait a minute, babe," Jimmy said, and leaning close, wrapping his arms around my shoulders so I could feel the soft cotton of his T-shirt, the hardness of his chest, he asked, "why don't you let the boys have a taste?"

Does it matter what was said next?

He pressed his case with his usual charm and some schoolboy

logic, only he wasn't Jimmy anymore and I wasn't Kathy, wasn't
Jimmy's girl, wasn't any girl I recognized. But there she was in his
eyes: a girl who would fuck four boys.

"Come on, babe, do it for me," he said. "I want them to see how
good you are." His smile then was the smile of a man who knows how
charming his smile can be. "It's no big deal. You do it with me." The
boys were hollering to come in out of the cold.

"Jimmy, hurry up, fucker!" And then someone said "Fuck *her*," and
I heard them laugh.

"They're freezing their balls off out there, babe. What do you say?"

"But . . . I don't want to."

"Why not? You like them, don't you? They like you. They're out
there freezing their asses off for us. Come on, Kathy."

"Hey, Jimmy, here comes Chrissy!" With her name came a flash of
the day-lit world, all that was public and acknowledged, and another
flash, not a thought at all, though I write it down here as one: They
had decided to put me in my place, to, in a sense, finish me off. From
now on, this is where I would always belong, in a car parked in the
woods, late, late at night, here and nowhere else, like a dirty secret.

After that everything seemed to come at me through a haze, like I
was hearing the echo and not the original sound.

"Hey, fuck it, we're coming in!" Jimmy opened the door, yelled,
"One second!" and as he closed it, the boys were coming toward us.

"What do you say, babe?" he asked. "Okay? For me."

They stood at the car doors, darkening the frost on the windows.

"Babe, you got to. I told them you would."

He'd told them? I guess certain elements tumbled into place then,
Scott's presence, the ill-tempered restlessness, Jimmy's rush, the slick
sweetness afterward—they must've thought it out beforehand, discussed it with one another. But all I really remember is a great rushing
and clashing in my brain. The dream, worn and frazzled already, held
together only by my desire to have it so, disintegrated and I woke, as
my parents and teachers always warned I would.

Another girl might have . . . But what does that matter? I wasn't
another girl. "I"—that mysterious concoction of desires and history,

relationships and inclinations, hope, fear, pleasure—was nothing but a raggedy coat wrapped around the thing they wanted.

Fists banged on the car roof.

"Okay, babe?"

I know I whispered it, but I said it. "Okay."

Scott must've gone first. He was so much older than the other two and not at all nervous. I guess Ben and Neal crowded into the front seat, though maybe they took turns waiting outside, I'm not sure. But I know Jimmy was there because I remember what he did. When Scott got on top of me and pushed himself in, and I started crying, Jimmy reached over the seat, took my hand, and said (for the first time), "Kathy, I love you." He kept hold of my hand.

When he was done, Scott decided I should suck him. He pushed me down on him, but I gagged and threw up. He leapt out of the car, cursing, "Stupid bitch," while somebody in the front seat laughed. "Hey, hey!" Jimmy said. "Go easy, man."

When Neal got into the back, he looked angry. I kept my face turned into the seat.

Ben was soft and had to use his fingers to push himself inside. He was so heavy, he was pressing the air out of me.

"I can't breathe," I told Jimmy.

But Ben kept going, his breath huffing in my hair. Panic swept through me and I started screaming.

"I can't breathe! I can't breathe!" And then he stopped.

More beers were cracked open. I dressed. Bent down into the backseat, into the darkness near the floor, I pulled my panty hose up over each foot, then up over my legs, thinking how ugly they were, the color, a pale pasty hue called "nude," the white crotch at the top, so modest and sanitary, poked through with little breathing holes. Above me, the boys talked loudly, laughed, passed the bottle.

Jimmy put the car in drive. No one suggested I move up front. Neal slid into the backseat with Ben and me. On the drive home, I hugged the door, staring silently out the window, seeing nothing until the gray house came into view, its porch lights on.

As I got out of the car, one of the boys said, "Kath, don't tell anybody and we won't." I headed up the driveway toward the back door and the kitchen light, tripped, and fell over a snowbank.

(In the years to come, that would be the image I would fix on, not anything that came before, but that stumble and then my face in the snow. Each time I conjured up that moment, I made myself taste the rough dirty ice, feel again the cold moisture seeping through my jeans. It was as if I wanted to punish that girl, push her face into the snow for what she had done.)

I fell once more just trying to get into the house and up to bed. My mother had been washing the kitchen floor, so she'd moved all the chairs over by the back door. I walked into that blinding kitchen light, my panty hose sticking to my skin—they were strangling me! I had to get them off!—and my foot hooked onto a chair leg so that I went crashing to the floor. As soon as I landed, I burst into tears.

"Honey! Are you all right? Did you hurt yourself?" My mother hurried over to me and all I could think was *Uh-oh, she's gonna know I'm drunk.* No one but a baby would cry at this fall. I had to invent something fast.

"Jimmy and I broke up," I told her, climbing to my feet.

"Oh, I'm sorry, honey," she crooned, helping me up from the floor. Not a word was said about the fact that I wasn't supposed to be seeing Jimmy; that hadn't been her idea anyway. There were just the two of us alone in the kitchen, and the only thing that mattered to her was that her daughter was crying, her stubborn, difficult daughter. "What happened, honey?"

I backed away from her so she couldn't smell my breath.

"He was mad about something and we had a fight."

"Well, maybe you two could work it out, talk about it when he's cooled down some." Gently, she brushed the hair back from my face. I kept my mouth closed, my head down, and breathed through my nose. I knew she was grateful for this mother-daughter moment, for—finally!—this child's confidence. She would have liked it to continue, for me to need her, be close to her again, but suddenly a great wave of sleep was arching over me. I could feel its cool darkness all the way down to my bones.

"I'm really tired," I told her. "I think I need to go to bed."

"Okay, honey, go get some sleep. Things will seem better in the morning," she said. "And, Kathy, even if you two can't work it out, someone else will come along that you'll care about just as much, maybe even more. I know it doesn't seem that way now but it will happen." Her face was very close to mine.

"All right?" She was nodding, hooking me with her bright eyes. "Okay?"

The rope was thrown. I had to at least look like I was reaching for it, though my spirit was sinking down into that hole in the bottom of the sea; hooks and lures couldn't catch it.

"All right, Mom."

20

Commander and Foot Soldier

THE SKIES WERE LEADEN THAT SUNDAY, THE SNOW SOOTY, BUT ST. RITA'S Church was lit up as bright as a banquet hall. Father Sheridan took his place at the altar, giant Father Sheridan in purple Lenten vestments, raising his large white hands. Everyone stood, and then everyone knelt, bones crackling and popping, and then, in one voice, everyone prayed: "In the name of the Father, the Son, the Holy Ghost . . ."

My family took up a whole pew. Beth Ann knelt on one side of me, my mother knelt on the other, her face lifted expectantly toward the altar, refreshed and hopeful. The light streaming down from the ceiling had flattened the stained-glass windows that lined the church, turning the saints into opaque blocks of blue and red. They seemed to be trapped inside the glass, looking out at us with their dark, tragic eyes.

Father Sheridan's blond hair was shorn close to his head, and he wore thick black-framed glasses like the kind they issue to grunts in the Army. He was a young priest, more drawn to the hope of Jesus' resurrection than his great suffering.

"This is the blood of Christ," he intoned, as he lifted the gold chalice high. He always spoke as if he'd never said Mass before, as if he was infusing each word with its own essence. This made the older people twitchy and my parents swoon. Father Sheridan was good friends with my mother and father, good enough, and worldly and compassionate enough, to have told my mother she could start using birth control. After six children and two miscarriages, the doctors were worried about her surviving another pregnancy, and Father Sheridan said it was more important that she be around to be a mother to the children she had than to give birth to any more.

At the Kiss of Peace, I turned as I was supposed to and shook the hand of the man behind me, avoiding his eyes. I'd always felt more in tune with the old people in the parish, who preferred to take the Mass in a solitary fashion, not forced to touch their neighbors or be sociable, but never more so than now. "Peace be with you," I heard the man say. "And with you, too," I replied as we shook hands, relieved to have gotten that over with.

When Father Sheridan took his place behind the lectern, he paused before starting the homily, his gaze moving over the faces of his congregation. Then he began talking gently, softly, meaningfully, about the Virgin Mary, and a black curtain fell across my brain.

As soon as we returned home from church, I pulled on my jeans and boots and went out the door, heading up Clifford toward the Teen Center.

For two days after the night in the car, I'd stayed huddled in bed, telling my mother I couldn't go out, couldn't go to school, because I was sick. And I was, of course, lying there hour after hour in dumb misery, stripped of thought, feeling, motivation. Why get up and dress? Why wash? Why eat? I felt as if I were on a high bridge suspended in fog, unable to see the land I'd left behind or the one I was heading into. I didn't know what had happened that night, only that it was big and awful. I hadn't seen it coming, had no idea what to do next.

But on Sunday, the third day, I had risen from my bed, as if my Catholic upbringing demanded that of me. As I dressed for Mass that morning, I felt as if I'd been erased from existence, like someone pummeled and then left on the ground—to survive, or not. I suddenly decided that I had to go back to the Teen Center and walk in there *with my head held high*, as I put it to myself, because I needed to show them that I was still alive, that I existed on the other side of that night in the car. And, just like that, with "head held high," I had a plan of action. Instead of hiding away in my bed, I would face the Teen Center crowd—and that night in the car—head-on.

Mountains of frozen, dirty snow filled every yard I passed. Winter still had Hamden in its teeth. When I reached Putnam Avenue, my father's words began to circle in my head: *Time to face the music, kiddo.*

My father's belief that you should never run and hide or shift the blame or take the easy way out was rooted deep in my bones. He'd made it clear in the stories about his own life that the finest form of bravery was to stand alone against the crowd, and that he expected his children to be forthright and brave, too, to do the right thing even when it wasn't easy. Of course, the challenges he would have imagined us facing were those of a child—owning up to undone homework, or defending an unpopular opinion in the classroom. My own situation was one he could never have dreamed of.

If my father had known what happened, what would he have done? Gone to the cops? The boys' parents? Or hunted the four of them down? And what would he have wanted me to do? All I know for sure is that he never would have wanted me to act alone. But as I walked toward the Teen Center that afternoon, I thought my father's morality was a perfect fit for my circumstance, and I heard his words as marching orders. *Time to face the music.* Only one and a half more blocks to go; I could do it. I had to.

When I stepped inside the firehouse, all hell broke loose. "Look who's fucking here!"

"That douche bag coming in like . . ."

"Gang bang!" Their astonishment and delight couldn't have been keener. A group of girls who were sitting on the floor, knees tucked up against their chests, began to open and close their legs. Some of them held up four fingers. Boys crowded in from the poolroom in back.

My vision refracted, and as bizarre as the scene already was, it became more so with faces split in two, revolving around and around one another, a circle of mouths, twin tongues wagging, half a leer, a startled eye. And below the kaleidoscope of faces, down on the concrete floor, the crowd of girls kept spreading their legs and clapping them shut like singing clams in some hyperactive cartoon.

Alan, the new director, came racing into the front room and ordered me into his office. Once we were inside, he slammed the door shut behind us and told me I had to go home.

"They've spent the last two days talking about beating you up," he said. He would drive me home, but I had to go *now*.

"I don't know why you had to come back here," he said irritably. He told me to follow him out, and to stay close behind. We cut through a throng of kids. The girls were off the floor now, their faces rubbery with rage.

"Fucking sleazebag!"

Boys grabbed their crotches when I went by. "What about me, Kathy? Gag on this."

They followed us out and amassed by the entrance. *(So long, rebels, so long, outlaws.)* Alan's car was in the driveway. He ran around to the driver's side, yanked open the door, and hopped in, leaving me standing on the sidewalk, waiting for him to unlock the door on my side. Instead he turned the ignition over several times, trying to start the engine in the bitter cold. The girls began to scream, "Fuck her up!" and all I could think about was how much I wanted to be in that car. But then a snowball hit my back. Suddenly all the Westerns I'd watched with Sylvia, all the boys' adventure books I'd read, merged with my father's tales of heroism. I turned to face the mob.

Whap! A snowball hit my chest and sprayed up into my face. "Fuckwad!" they yelled, a brand-new word to me. Snowballs flew by my head, a stick hurtled through the air, whirling like a boomerang, a crumpled soda can bounced off the car, and then, finally, the door opened, and I ducked inside.

Alan dropped me off at my house with advice I no longer needed—not to return.

I went through the kitchen—"Hi, honey!"—and straight upstairs.

Halfway to the attic, a thought stopped me dead in my tracks: *Life will never be the same.* The life I'd thought of as my creation from that day when I had stepped onto my parents' lawn wearing a candy-striped halter top—that life was mine no longer. Before I could bear even to think about what had happened that night, they'd named it. Before the shock had even lifted, they'd begun to spread the word of a gang bang and the disgusting girl who had let it happen. As narrators of my story, the kids at the Teen Center weren't compassionate or insightful or even very imaginative, but the tale they told was remarkably convincing; it had the ring of hard truth, for what kind of girl would let four boys do what those boys had done to me?

To be honest, I don't remember much of that March. I must have moved through it like a sleepwalker. I was shaken awake in April—not by a kiss, but an errand run. Usually my mother sent Beth Ann, but she wasn't home that day and there was a prescription that needed to be picked up at the pharmacy.

I stepped out of the house cautiously. In less than one month, without my having noticed, the world had been transformed. Winter was gone, not one gritty trace of it left behind. The trees were suddenly sprinkled with tight green buds. Across the street, big black birds filled the old people's lawns. They moved across the grass with their heads bent down, eyes intent on the ground, more herd of cows than any winged thing. It was time for short-sleeve shirts and nylon windbreakers. Spring again.

I set off down Treadwell on my errand, avoiding the route I would usually take, because I didn't want to go past the firehouse. But immediately the sidewalk began dragging at my feet. Was I really going to let fear control me now? Less than a month had passed since the night in the car, but I told myself that they'd thrown me out, they'd had the final say, what more could they want? I turned around and made myself head up Clifford toward Putnam Avenue.

When I reached Putnam, I was a block and a half from the firehouse, two blocks from the Country Club Pharmacy. I kept up a steady chant: *Go on, get going, you can't run all your life.* I was commander and foot soldier, ordering myself along, grim in all that birdsong.

At Tom's Market, I saw a group of kids gathered outside the Teen Center. I could cross over to the other side of the street, but they'd still see me. They would have to yell. Everyone would hear.

As I drew closer, I didn't recognize any of them, but then again I was blind with panic. My ears were roaring. Three houses, two, one— *What can they do to you? What's the worst thing? Don't be a chicken-shit*—they were coming down the firehouse drive, blocking the sidewalk in front of me.

Then a group of boys walled me in, but I could only concentrate on the face right in front of mine. It was large and beet red with pleasure and loathing. I stared at it as if mesmerized. Everything else was a blur.

He wet his lips. I could smell the inside of his mouth. He laughed, leaning close.

"Remember me?"

I shook my head.

"Yes, you do," he said loudly. "I fucked you."

This beet-red boy?

"But I don't even know who you are," I protested.

He thrust his face into mine. "Then how the fuck do I know you?" I forced myself to move, pushing past him and through the crowd. As I headed toward the corner, I heard their machine gun laughter at my back.

I never walked by the firehouse again. Not that it made much of a difference. A few days later, when I was heading down Whitney Avenue on my way to buy groceries for my mother, a car screeched to a halt in front of me, and a group of girls jumped out, yelling obscenities and then surrounding me. They wanted to beat me up, but, as I was beginning to learn, it isn't all that easy to throw the first punch. They needed some sort of trigger—my yelling back, or trying to run— but I froze and my fear saved me, that and the fact that the driver of

THE ONLY GIRL IN THE CAR   173

the car started honking for them to get back inside. They were block-ing traffic.

My name had a life of its own now, just as I had wanted, just as Roscoe and Craig had warned me it would. Boys said whatever they wanted about me. Suddenly everyone had had sex with me. My de-nials sounded pathetic, so after a while, I stopped. I'd become the route by which timid boys lost their virginity without losing their timidity. It was too valuable a route for them ever to surrender.

My house seemed much too bright and loud that spring. Windows crashed open, people banged up and down stairs, shouting, Sebastian barked sharply, chopping the air into bits. At the dinner table every-one ate and talked at breakneck speed. My mother's face, as normal as could be—those hazel eyes and full lips, the small furrow running along the tip of her nose—now seemed to belong to a stranger.

I hadn't told anyone, not even Sylvia. Not about the night in the car, not about my reputation, not about what was happening now on the streets. Of course I hadn't. Wouldn't, couldn't, never, ever.

My secret was the reverse of most secrets, which, if you tell, you tell only to your closest friends. That girl in the backseat was hidden from my friends and family but well-known, unforgettable even, to an ever-growing number of people. Without her, I was an imposter. But I wanted to be that imposter, and was willing to do whatever it took to keep her alive. So I knew I'd have to be careful not to go any-where outside of school with either Linda or Leslie. That way I'd avoid having them see a carload of girls shrieking names at me or guys sprouting from the sidewalk insisting that they, too, had had sex with me. That way I wouldn't lose them as friends, for I was sure that was what would happen if Linda and Leslie knew. I wasn't as nervous about Sylvia. Her mother kept her on a tight leash, so we spent most of our time inside her house or mine. She floated in her own dream-world anyway. She could easily miss what was going on. Or not un-derstand it even if she saw it.

I began riding my bike on errands, a blue bike I hadn't been on since I was twelve. I went fast, telling myself that if I could run over that leaf up there on the road, right over the center of it with my front tire, I could win a fight with half a dozen girls. Gliding silently downhill, I scanned the street, every nerve in my body alive and sharp. I could hear a footstep in a thunderstorm. I could brake on a dime. I had eyes in the back of my head. My fingers itched at the brake levers, not touching them but ready to draw. So I tried to imagine myself: gunslinger at high noon.

But no matter how fast I bicycled or what stories I told myself about cowboys and gunslingers, all it took was one blast of a car horn and imagination fled. I was Kathy Dobie, that slut, pedaling fast and looking stupid on a girl's blue bicycle.

21

Sister, Sister

I WAS READING JIM CARROLL'S MEMOIR, *THE BASKETBALL DIARIES*, MY schoolbooks stacked around me on the kitchen table like fortress walls. Musician, poet, high school basketball star and onetime junkie, Carroll told the story of his early teenage years in the deadpan voice of a city boy who flinched at nothing. From the opening line—"Today was my first Biddy League game and . . ."—I felt like Carroll had taken me into his confidence.

I'd read my first memoirs that spring when Leslie gave me Nicky Cruz's *Run Baby Run* and Piri Thomas's *Down These Mean Streets.* Like Carroll, Cruz and Thomas had grown up in New York City, and as young boys all three of them had known the life of the streets—the cops, the gangs, the sad old alcoholic men and sexy neighborhood girls, the local junkies and preachers—as well as any homeless person did. Carroll seemed to get by on wit and bravado alone. Whether boosting clothes from a department store or diving from high cliffs into the dirty Harlem River, he displayed a great disregard for rules— and an equally great desire to plunge right into whatever action he could find. I loved him for that. And for all the mistakes he made, the way his life just seemed to spin out of his control. Carroll became a junkie before he turned fifteen, while he was on a search for something entirely different, something he called "purity." No one I knew would speak as honestly about his or her life as Carroll did. And so I read *The Basketball Diaries* with the kind of ravenous hunger I'd once thought was reserved for food.

As I sat there lost in my book, I was surrounded by my mother's relentlessly upbeat posters, hung one above the other all the way to the ceiling and bearing messages like "This Is the First Day of the Rest of Your Life." Jim Carroll would find that sentiment as depressing as I did, I was sure. But the bond between Carroll and myself was to be short-lived, for when I arrived at one of the diary entries from the summer of '64, there was a description of a sexual encounter that instantly jarred me out of my easy alliance with him. Enter Winkie and Blinkie, blond twins identical down to their leather-trimmed underwear. Carroll had sex with one sister, his friend with the other, and it didn't matter which was which, for they were both exactly the same—two big-breasted, dim-witted, enthusiastic girls who would have sex with any boy who asked. Here, in a book that anyone could read, thirteen-year-old Winkie was described as "a Bronx poodle walking slut." And this by the same writer who wrote of "the stars breathing down" and just wanting to be "pure." I loved this writer, but he felt the same way about girls-who-fuck as the boys of Hamden did. That's how all men felt, I concluded. Even the poets. It was as if my case had been presented to a higher court, and I'd been convicted. I'd never find a better place than Hamden.

Summer was approaching. School, which had unexpectedly become my safe haven, would end. Though Joan and her Sacred Heart friends were bubbling over with malice toward me, excited by the turn my life had taken that night in East Rock Park, they were held in check by Linda's presence at my side. They were afraid of her, so all they would dare were gleeful, hostile glances in my direction, and gossip among themselves, loud enough for me to hear but not so loud as to attract Linda's attention. No screaming, no threats; no being taken by surprise. I could live with that. Never knowing what would happen or when, which face at the mall or on a crowded street corner might suddenly light up in recognition—that was the hard part. The faces always looked the same, disgusted and alive; *douche bag* and *fuckwad* were their favorite words.

Thinking about the summer, I realized that once our vacation started, there would be no safe place for me outside the house. For three long months, no one jollying me along or petting my head and calling me "munchkin" or "Scooby Dooby Doo" or any of the dozens of tender, ridiculous nicknames Leslie and Linda had for me. I had no defense against that future, against thought or dreaded memory, not even the book in front of me. Especially not the book in front of me. I put *The Basketball Diaries* facedown on the kitchen table and headed upstairs to disappear into sleep.

I couldn't think about that night, but I felt as if it was always thinking about me, a stalker without respect for civility, for daylight, or privacy. I might be eating a bowl of Cheerios or taking notes during class or climbing the attic stairs, when suddenly it would leap out at me, not in a whole, coherent memory, but in a stream of filth: shock, shame, guilt. I would try to duck and flee, but a black swarm would explode, swoop, cackle in my head—Scott's furious face when I threw up on him; my naked legs; the girls' mouths dropped open, appalled; Chrissy's neat, shiny ponytail, and Big Ben, soft as a worm, using his hand to grimly tuck himself inside . . .

The afternoon of Winkie and Blinkie I dreamed of little men in yellow cowboy hats and twirling mustaches chasing me down. I kept trying to fly away from them—I knew I could fly, I'd done it in other dreams—but I could only rise a foot or two from the sidewalk, and as my feet furiously pedaled the air, I kept descending, inch by awful inch. I could feel their hands pulling at my shirt. I sobbed in fear and frustration—why couldn't I make this dream come out right?

In May, Michael graduated from Notre Dame High School, Cindy from St. Rita's. I was at the end of my sophomore year. At Sacred Heart we gathered in the back garden to offer prayers to Mary the Queen of Heaven on the month of her Ascension. Instead of studying for my final exams, I took long afternoon naps and then read unassigned books late into the night. For the first time in my life, I received barely passing grades in all my courses. My religion exam was marked with a large D and a note from Sister Mary Margaret in the margin that said *If you need to talk, I'm here.*

And then suddenly it was summer. I planned to spend all three months of it in my room.

That's where I was the day my mother drove Cindy into New Haven for her back brace. Earlier that spring our family doctor had discovered a curvature in Cindy's spine. The only cure was a brace she would have to wear for the rest of her teenage years. The fittings had been done with measuring tape and plaster, so Cindy had no idea what the brace would actually look like. None of us did. *Though by now, Cindy knows,* I thought as I lay there on the bed waiting. And I found myself staring at the door, willing her to walk through it.

Then the doorknob turned and there she was, fluid, tomboy Cindy with her narrow face and rakish widow's peak, strapped into a bulky contraption and walking into the room like a zombie. A rod with a cup attached had been placed under her chin, forcing it up. In order to look at me she had to turn her whole torso sideways, and as soon as she did, she burst into tears. Instantly our mother came up from behind and put her arms around Cindy, desperate to offer comfort. Just as fast, Cindy's tears dried up, her eyes snapping open so wide that I could see the angry red veins at the edges: She was fourteen and caught twice; embraced when she most wanted to fly free.

"It's what's inside a person that counts, Cindy," our mother was saying. Marriage and motherhood must have made her simple, I decided.

After one or two more unsuccessful attempts to find something consoling to say, our mother left the room, and Cindy slid her pants down to show me what had been done to her. She had to wear an elastic waistband now, because of the thick armor of plaster encasing her hips. When she opened her shirt, there was a metal bar that went from the plaster girdle up to her chin and stood stiffly between her breasts. Two more bars went up her back, their ends poking from her shirt collar and through her thin blond hair as if she were a parcel ready to be hooked and carted through the air.

"All the kids in school are going to be looking at me—that girl in the brace!" she cried. "How can I go anywhere in this ugly piece of . . . this stupid, horrible, this dumb, disgusting . . . ?" She couldn't find an adjective scathing enough. But she was looking at me. As she sat straight-backed on the edge of my bed, her hands at her side to balance her, she was asking a real question—how could she be seen in that brace?—and she was expecting me to provide an answer. She assumed I could, that I was wise enough, that I cared enough—I was her sister Kathy, after all, fellow adventurer and ally since she and I were three and four years old. I'd forgotten that person, but she hadn't.

"Let's go outside and walk around the block and see what happens," I suggested. "It might not be that bad. But the longer you wait, the harder it's gonna be."

Cindy protested at first, but soon we were heading down the driveway, Cindy staring straight in front of her with her head held unnaturally high. Halfway around the block we ran into a friend of hers, an excitable girl named Grace. Cindy froze as Grace ran toward us, ready for her shock or pity.

"Hey! What are you doing? Where are you two going?" Grace asked. And then she noticed the brace. "What's that?"

Cindy gritted her teeth. "I've got a curve in my spine," she explained bitterly. "I have to wear this until it straightens out."

"What a bummer," Grace said, cocking her head in sympathy. But then her face brightened, "Jennifer's having a pool party! Are you going? She wanted to borrow one of my bathing suits—as if it would fit her!" Then she started talking about how tall and skinny and flat-chested Jennifer was, and which neighborhood boys would be at her party.

When Grace's mother called her inside, she took off, shouting over her shoulder, "See you later! Don't forget the party!" Three thuds up the stairs, one bound across the porch, and she was gone.

"She didn't even care," Cindy said into the silence, sounding stunned.

"She hardly noticed."

We walked on, past the house where Patrick Cahoon lived, Patrick the Teen Center King who'd taught me the meaning of "69," past

Timmy and Lucy's house, too, where any one of the Teen Center gang could have been visiting. But the fear that had become my constant companion had somehow receded. I'd thrown my lot in with Cindy that afternoon. This was an emergency. At that moment, her life seemed more real than my own.

When Cindy and I returned to the house, we poured ourselves two glasses of Kool-Aid, and went to the living room to discuss her situation. As we sank to the floor, folding our legs Indian-style, Cindy, who wasn't yet used to the brace, toppled over backward.

Shock blanched her face and she looked at me accusingly. Then she burst out laughing. After I pulled her upright I squatted there on my heels, doubled over. Tears ran down our cheeks, our laughter so helplessly out of control that Cindy had to get to her knees or it would have knocked her over again.

Once, when we were younger, Cindy had made me laugh so hard that I'd almost died, but then she'd saved my life. We'd gone snorkeling in a pond on Cape Cod, where our family was camping. We were far from shore, paddling around facedown in the water with our flippers, masks, and tubes. When she turned her face to me, she looked so strange—somber and goggle-eyed, lips distended like a monkey's—that without thinking I laughed. The breathing tube popped out of my mouth, and my next breath in was all water. Gasping and coughing, my mouth working the air like a beached fish, I was unable to draw a clean breath. I began to panic.

"Turn over," Cindy commanded. She put her arm around my chest and began swimming me in. We'd both taken lifesaving courses at summer camp. We knew the drill. When we reached the shallows, I leaned over while she thumped my back, knocking the water out of me. As soon as I could breathe, I tried to tell her why I had laughed in the first place, but she wasn't amused.

"You could've drowned out there," she said severely.

The truth of this was suddenly real. I could have died; she had saved my life. We thought that's what being sisters meant. We went over the event again and again, exhilarated by the close call and by our achievement, hers as well as mine—I didn't struggle, did I? I felt like a model drowning person.

We were enormously proud of our relationship. Who knew what else we would be called upon to do, what battles we would fight to the death, what people we would save if only given the chance? And hadn't we promised each other that if either of us became a "vegetable" the other would sneak into the hospital and pull the plug?

So there we sat on the living room floor, trying to plot the future. Cindy was allowed to take the brace off for one hour a day. One hour of freedom. How to use it? Or as Cindy said, "What can we do with one lousy fucking hour?" The brace was already teaching her how to swear. We were as close as we'd been for the last year. And now I had a chance, through her, to have some kind of summer, after all.

We would bicycle to New Haven. That was my idea. I, too, wanted to be free—free of Hamden. I convinced Cindy to wait until ten o'clock at night, steering us to an hour when the streets would be empty. That evening we took our bicycles out of the garage and set them up in the driveway, ready for takeoff. At exactly ten, Cindy unstrapped the brace, cracking it open as if she was breaking the back of a chicken, and spreading it flat. Then she set the brace on the floor next to the bed, where it stood upright, all hanging leather straps and buckles, thick white pads and gleaming metal.

Cindy slipped into her shorts, a gauzy Indian shirt, and buffalo sandals, and then we ran down the stairs. Our watches were fixed to our wrists.

"Good-bye, girls!" our father called, his face suffused with pride. Much later, when we were all adults, gathered together for a Thanksgiving dinner, he said to my mother, "Our children are friends. At least we did that right."

"One hour now, Kathy!" Our mother made it clear that I was in charge. If anything went wrong, I would be responsible. Before I could even ask myself the question that had begun to plague me—why didn't she and my father ever see any vulnerability in *me*?—we flew out of the house.

Cindy and I hopped on our waiting bikes, pushed off with our feet, and rolled down the driveway onto the street, not a car in sight. Our tires hissed on the pavement, and the wide black river of Tread-well flowed before us. We passed by our neighbors' houses so swiftly that they seemed to be blowing away, then took the turn onto Whit-ney in a big, sweeping curve, our bodies leaning to the right, letting the slope power us around the corner. Cindy sped past, taking the lead. She stood up on the pedals, her short hair waving like a flag, turning now to grin at me.

Past the fruit and vegetable market, faster and faster. All I wanted was to get away from here, away from the pizza place, the Country Club Pharmacy, the beauty parlor, the movie theater, the Texaco gas station.

And then, the beginning of freedom. We left the town center be-hind, and Whitney Avenue swooped down and curved to the left. We were entering a tunnel lined with windy trees. Tall wild grasses and Queen Anne's lace had sprung up between the narrow sidewalk and the avenue; they swayed toward the street like river weeds. I could hear the sound of the waterfall to my left, coming down hard, a sheet of noisy glass, a man-made waterfall pouring over a concrete wall, overflow from the reservoir.

"You Are Entering NEW HAVEN." We shot by the white sign and Cindy checked her watch. She whooped. "Six minutes!" The city had closed for the night but wrought-iron lamps shone on empty side-walks and apartment doorways. A soft, skyward-pointing beam of light traced a Gothic church spire. Back alleys, spidery fire escapes, even empty lots were illuminated by hidden spotlights, and suddenly the whole scene appeared to me as if it were a stage waiting for some-one—Dylan Thomas? Eugene O'Neill? Marlon Brando?—to step out and say something grand and transforming.

Cindy and I rode on, reaching the green in the center of New Haven in twenty minutes. We bought two Cokes at the McDonald's, then sat down on the grass. We had the green to ourselves; our Cokes, which we were forbidden to drink at home; and another thirteen minutes. We discussed clothes—was there a way to look sexy in a brace, or at least hide the rod at her neck?—and tried to find a solution to two of her more immediate problems: the difficulty of sleeping in the brace, and the way the plaster girdle made her sweat and then itch. We decided baby powder was worth a try, but as far as sleeping went, I could only come up with the lame reassurance that, though she had to sleep flat on her back without a pillow, the metal rods digging into her back and the chin cup holding her head rigidly in place, she'd probably get used to it.

On the way back, we left ourselves some extra time and rode slowly, taking the downhill stretches without pedaling, gliding side by side. As we hit the curve in the road that takes you from New Haven into Hamden, I heard the waterfall again but couldn't see it. At that moment, the night seemed to be making a promise to me.

I'd sailed up and down this street, around this curve, in cars packed with cursing, laughing boys, happier than I'd ever been in my life. I rode it now on my bicycle, not happy exactly, but aware of something unalterable in the world, its richness and its beauty. No matter what happened, and regardless of whether I was happy or not, the world would go right on being beautiful. It would always be there, waiting.

22

The Bridge Back

I HAD TO SEE JIMMY AGAIN. FIVE MONTHS HAD PASSED SINCE THE NIGHT in the car. It had taken that long for the numbness to wear off, and when it did, what emerged from the fog was the image of Jimmy. The apparition was so vivid, it was almost a physical presence.

There had been four boys with me in the car in East Rock Park. What happened that night tied me to them in an awful intimacy that had only deepened as each month went by and I hid the truth from all the people closest to me. I couldn't have explained why I needed to see Jimmy's face, the face that had hovered over the front seat watching the whole time, but it's obvious to me now that I was looking for some acknowledgment of what I'd gone through and was hoping to find it in his eyes. Jimmy would have to see that night as something terrible that had been done to *me*—a girl he knew well, whose hand he had clutched while he slept. I needed someone to see it that way. It would inject some sense, some tenderness, back into my universe.

They say people return to the scene of the accident to try to absorb what happened there. Jimmy's face was my accident scene.

One Friday night in August, I went to stay at Sylvia's house for the weekend. The gas station where Jimmy worked was only a few blocks away. I told Sylvia I wanted to see him the next morning and asked her to go with me. Unlike my return to the Teen Center, I was going to take this trip with a friend at my side.

Sylvia knew that I'd had a boyfriend, that after our freshman year at Sacred Heart I'd found a life that was separate from hers. But she'd never seen Jimmy, and had caught only glimpses of that life from the clothes I wore, the pack of Marlboros in my pocket, and the way I sometimes arrived at her house not in my parents' car but on foot or dropped off by a stranger I'd hitched a ride from, coming up the front walk surefooted and happy, almost swaggering. Since I hadn't spent much time with her that year, she assumed my other life was more enthralling than the one she and I shared. She didn't know it had ended.

We woke that Saturday to a bright, steamy morning. The light outside the window was the yellow of pollen and bees. As soon as we dressed, we headed out her back door and down the two cement tracks of her driveway. Sylvia was singing, "In the summertime, when the weather is hot, you can swish right up . . ." She was so rarely let out of the house, it was like we were setting off on an adventure.

Sylvia's street, Park Road, was lined on one side with trim white houses that had small front yards, and backyards crisscrossed with laundry lines attached to porches by pulleys. No one ever sat out on their front steps, and all the little sunporches were curtained. I thought old people must live in all the houses; it was that careful a neighborhood.

My street, by comparison, was filled with kids on bicycles, hopscotch squares drawn in pink chalk on the sidewalk, and older brothers noisily mowing the lawns. My family's power lingered in my mind—I still thought they lived in the center of things.

Even the name of Sylvia's street, *Park*, seemed dull. I thought it showed a lack of imagination. Unlike Treadwell. These days, when I looked at our street sign, I thought it was solemnly nodding to me. "Tread well," it said, offering encouragement and warning, both at once.

We walked along under big shade trees across the street from a city-run nursery, where rows upon rows of red, yellow, pink, and white roses bloomed and baked in the sun. Between the insects and the hot, glancing light, I had the general impression of an unpleasant busyness over there. After four short blocks, Park Road curved gently to the left and ended abruptly, rudely almost, after all those billowy trees, and there we were at State Street. The gas station was right on the corner.

There was a man at the pumps, a rag stuck in his back pocket. I asked him if Jimmy was working that day.

"Jimmy, there's a coupla young ladies here to see you!" he shouted.

Jimmy came out of the garage. His face looked thicker than I'd remembered, and his jaw, scraped clean, was pale. No wolfish shadow there. I'd never seen him this early in the day, so soon after he'd shaved. I had no plan in place, no words rehearsed.

"Uh, Kathy," he said, looking surprised and then, I couldn't deny it, uncomfortable.

He glanced behind him, as if his work was waiting for him in the garage and waiting precariously, a car barely balanced on a lift, perhaps.

Jimmy, it's me! I wanted to cry out.

"This is my friend Sylvia," I said instead. Sylvia looked as if she had just taken a bath. Her cut-off jeans were perfectly trimmed, each thread the same length, making a fluffy fringe of white on her olive thighs. Her shirt was pressed. She never sweated. It suddenly seemed important for Jimmy to know that I had a girlfriend, and a girlfriend who was this clean and cute, so obviously girlish, so obviously good.

Before I could say anything further, a carload of girls screeched into the station like an unfunny cartoon. The two Chrissys, Joan Connolly, and Georgie. It seemed unbelievable, this bad luck, as if they'd been waiting five months for their cue.

"What the fuck are you doing here?"

"You fucking slut—you show up here!"

They were tripping over one another in their indignation. They couldn't believe I'd popped up again, here of all places, on their turf, and more important, on their time. From their point of view, my life had stopped that night in the car, never to go forward. They could move on—graduate from high school, make new friends, fall in love, get married—but my life story had already been written.

"You don't fucking take a hint, do you?"

"Fuck her up and she'll take a hint," Georgie said, looking like an enraged dwarf next to beautiful, long-haired, red-lipped, white-toothed Chrissy—she who was so obviously the right girl for Jimmy.

"What's going on here?" I heard the man ask.

"Yeah, I'll fucking break her nose," Joan said, ignoring him and rubbing her clenched fist like a lucky stone. Violence became her. Her blue eyes were electric. Those big, rawboned hands made admirable fists. The girls made a circle, closing us inside.

"Who do you think you are, douche bag, coming around here?"

Chrissy stepped in close, her face a breath away from mine. "This is *our* turf—" Joan cracked her knuckles while Chrissy shouted, "Don't you know what you are? You're nothing but a dirtbag. Dirt-bags don't belong here."

"Jimmy, I think you should take these two girls home," the man said.

"You're gonna drive that douche bag home?" the girls wailed.

"Break it up now," he told them. "Time for you all to leave. Jimmy, you two girls, get in the car." And while he stood watch, we made our escape.

"You better not come around anymore," Jimmy said to me as we drove off. "They come over to the station a lot." He might as well have been the mousy director of the Teen Center driving me home that March afternoon, put out by all the trouble I was causing him.

"Well, it was nice to meet you," Sylvia said as he pulled up in front of her house. She thought Jimmy had saved us.

"Uh, nice to meet you, too," Jimmy replied.

"Be cool," he said to me. Be cool?

I almost said *okay*. The word jolted me.

Do it for me, Kathy. I told them you would.

Okay.

I plunged from the car.

"Bye, Kath," he added, my name on his lips like a knife. But it meant nothing to him; he hadn't even intended to wield it.

Once inside Sylvia's house, I didn't offer any explanation and she didn't ask. To Sylvia, what had just happened made perfect movie sense: We'd been surrounded by a violent mob and told to get out of town by sundown.

"I believe they was in a hanging mood," she said gaily, rubbing her neck. She zipped around the kitchen, from stove to refrigerator to cabinet, getting things ready for the family dinner that night, while I sat at the kitchen table watching her.

I'd taken off my earrings, delicate silver loops with three blue stones strung on each wire. As Sylvia sang and chatted, sliced and chopped, I twirled the earrings around on the tabletop with my finger, then stuffed them in my pocket. I wouldn't wear them anymore. They were very pretty. They reminded me of girls I knew, slim girls with willowy hair who burned incense in their rooms and smelled faintly of patchouli.

I no longer remember what we did the rest of the day. But around ten or eleven that night, after we'd eaten and Mr. DeAngelis had gone up to bed, we heard a car horn blasting outside. Sylvia and I had been watching TV, with Mrs. DeAngelis and Albie asleep on the couch behind us.

"Hey, fuckin'—" Boys' voices. A carload of them, parked across the street. "Come on out! We know you're in there!"

Mrs. DeAngelis woke with a start. "What's that yelling? Who's out there?"

"Come on out!"

"What are those boys yelling? They yelling for you?" she said, looking at me. She went straight to the window and drew the curtains. Now they were leaning on the horn and all yelling at once, but nothing was coming through clearly except my name.

Mrs. DeAngelis jerked open the front door and yelled, "You get out of here now or I'll call the police! You hear me? Get out of here!"

She didn't look like some lady who was going to call the cops. She looked like someone who would grab the thing nearest to her—a pot, a leg of lamb, a meat cleaver—and take care of the problem herself. Her black eyebrows had shot straight up to the roots of her hair like dangerous birds ready to swoop down. She had God, the sleeping houses, the leafy trees, and every white lacy curtain in every kitchen window on the block on her side. That's why the boys fled, I think—someone else had grabbed the moral high ground.

When she came back in, slamming the door shut, Albie was pacing the floor like an animal whose cage had been rattled. His eyes were wide and he was breathing hard. It had a kind of ha-ha-ha sound—was he going to start giggling?

"You get out, too," Mrs. D. told me. "I want you out of this house now."

"Ma! It's not her fault!" Sylvia protested, but her mother had gotten hold of the movie script and it wasn't a Western anymore.

"I'm not having any trouble here. We never had anything like this here. This is a quiet neighborhood! There's old people sleeping right next door! I'm not having it. She goes. Now."

"But, Ma, how's she gonna get home?"

"She can call her father. She can call him and tell him we've got a store to run in the morning, we work hard around here, and I'm not having carloads of boys coming around here howling for her all hours of the night, we don't live like that—"

"Ma, she doesn't live like that, either," Sylvia said, laughing nervously.

But Mrs. DeAngelis had always had her doubts about me. "She's years ahead of you," she had warned Sylvia. "And you're too much of a follower." Now she'd been proven right.

"Albie! Go up to bed! And you, too, Sylvia." She turned to me. "Call your father and then you can go wait for him outside."

"Ma! Outside!"

But Mrs. DeAngelis was past arguing.

My father answered the phone right away, so I knew he was up late.

"Mrs. DeAngelis doesn't want me to stay overnight" was all I said.

I walked out the back door and crouched down on my heels, hiding in the shadows against the side of the house, in case the boys returned. I lit a cigarette, pulling on it hard. It flared for a moment and then settled into a steady burn. It seemed alive to me, quiet and alert, as loyal as a dog.

I listened for cars—dangerous cars and my father's car. My ears were like eyes as I followed the road past the shuttered greenhouses of the city nursery, around the curve and uphill toward the entrance to East Rock Park.

Above me, a window screen scratched open.

"Psssst . . ."

I stood up. Sylvia, hanging out of her bedroom window. "Kath, I'll call you tomorrow," and she was gone, the screen sliding back into place with a snap.

I settled down on my heels again, and pictured my father sitting in his armchair in the living room, going over the papers he often brought home from Yale, Muzak playing softly, a drink on the lamp table next to him, ice cubes melted into slivers, the rest of the house sleeping. I thought of him on the road now, gliding smoothly toward me.

And then there he was, pulling into the driveway. He leaned over to open the door for me.

"Mrs. DeAngelis changed her mind, huh?" he asked as I climbed inside.

"Yeah, she's got to get up early tomorrow," I said. He didn't seem to require any further elaboration.

The patter of voices on the talk radio station eased us into a comfortable silence. At the entrance to East Rock Park, the road veered downhill and he drove as if he were cutting that road himself, through the dark trees, past the plush lawns of the big white houses, straight across the reservoir. How powerful and swift the big station wagon seemed in his hands!

Sitting there watching the streets fly by, I felt newly calm, the way a child feels after a long cry. Exhausted, yes, but also opened up, no defense against the truth and no desire for that defense, either. It had dawned on me that there was only one way those boys could have found me at Sylvia's house: Jimmy had told them. In fact, Jimmy must have brought them there. He was in that car. I wasn't going to pretend that wasn't so.

The second betrayal drove home the first. Somehow Jimmy had managed to deny any connection to me—and to the night in East Rock Park. The burden was mine alone to carry.

As my father drove me home, I sensed how much strength I would need to hold on to my own vision, my own truth, and I became even more protective of my memory of that night, more distrustful of other people's interpretation. Everyone must be kept away. It was like keeping a crime scene intact until the big boys, the experts, got there to examine it.

Only in this case *I* would be the expert—who else could say what that night meant to me? And so I would store the experience away, keep it guarded for years.

23

Metamorphosis

"THE EXPENSE OF SPIRIT IN A WASTE OF SHAME . . ." MRS. COLASANTO sat at her desk reading one of Shakespeare's sonnets aloud while we followed along in our textbooks. Junior English with Mrs. C. was the only class in which Linda, Leslie, and I chose to sit up front, though at the moment Linda was resting her head on her open book. Shakespeare always affected Linda this way. From the first "how oft" or "thine outward thus," Linda's eyelids would droop, and her body would slump in her chair. But the line had jolted me. The classroom walls seemed to melt away at those words, as did the parking lot, visible through the windows, the statue of Jesus, the green and well-groomed grounds. Nothing existed but the voice of this long-dead writer shooting straight across the centuries, speaking directly to me. I refused to believe Shakespeare was talking about sex, though Mrs. Colasanto said that was so. He seemed to be describing my life exactly and warning me against it, but not unkindly, for he was warning himself, too.

Mrs. Colasanto was short and plump with a small, pug-nosed face, nut-brown hair, and slightly protruding eyes that were dark and lively and moist. She reminded me of a fairy tale frog—a noble prince resided within. She was my favorite teacher. She thought we were perfectly capable of being moved by Shakespeare and Chaucer and Emily Dickinson. The only lay teacher I had at Sacred Heart, she was married and the mother of college-age daughters. I envied those girls and liked to imagine them studying for careers in math or science, as engineers perhaps, or lab technicians, anything that didn't require a passion for reading and writing. For that, their mother would have to come to us.

One day that fall, I paper-clipped a poem I'd written to the last page of my regular homework, and handed both poem and homework to Mrs. Colasanto at the end of class. The poem's opening lines were an obvious imitation of Shakespeare: "Darkness unrelieved holds no curse / But in the shadow of the sun some hearts are born . . ." Unfortunately every time I'd read those lines back to myself, the Beatles broke into song in my head—*Here comes the sun, dah-dah-dah-dah*—and I had to continually wrest myself away from that rhythm to make my poem sing a different tune. It had taken me almost a month to write five verses. But when I'd finished, I was sure I'd created an astonishing piece of work to show Mrs. Colasanto.

The next day I took my place in class, too nervous even to look at her; I told myself she probably hadn't had time to read my poem, which now seemed unmistakably awful—how could I have showed it to her? As she moved up and down the aisles, returning yesterday's assignment to each student, I pretended to be reading my textbook. When at last she drew near my desk, all I saw of her was the pleated skirt that covered her knees and her square-heeled brown shoes.

"Kathy, your poem is wonderful," she said. Her voice was warm and serious. I fixed on that seriousness, and the matter-of-fact way in which she'd spoken. Perhaps she meant it. I'd begun to think that the only image I would ever project would be the slut, and that anything good inside me, anything valuable, was going to remain hidden. "If you have anything else you'd like to show me, I'd love to see it," she continued, handing me my poem and my homework. She made no mention of the assigned essay at all. Maybe she'd decided that I was above such banal requirements. If I could write poetry, then homework was mere child's play. It was very easy for me to swing from self-loathing to self-glorification in those days, slug to genius and back again.

Not long after that, Mrs. C. stopped me as I was leaving class. "You must keep writing," she said. She wanted me to write more—today and tomorrow and the next; she meant for me to make myself into a writer.

Every day after I got home from school, I would put on a pot of coffee and slip into my jeans and a black sweatshirt—which seemed to me a serious, writerly sort of outfit. I'd set out my pens and note-books, push up my sleeves, and get to work. On the stories and poems that I began to hand to Mrs. C. regularly, as if she had given me an as-signment, she wrote comments like, *Beautiful description!* and *The per-fect metaphor!* I lived for those compliments, became greedy for them, noting the presence of every exclamation point—and also mourning their absence. If she wrote *Beautiful!* I felt blazingly happy. *Nice* made me scour the writing for what was wrong. And a blank margin meant that my writing was so bad it had embarrassed her into silence. But I had a reader—and what a reader! Mrs. Colasanto loved language, as I did, and for the first time I had the feeling of being unique and valu-able to an adult. When I gave her a short story or a poem that she liked, I felt I had served her something delicious to eat.

I wrote to please Mrs. Colasanto, and I wrote to fill the hours. There was nothing else for me to do, no place for me to go at night or on weekends, not even Sylvia's. After the night when the boys had showed up at her house, Mrs. DeAngelis wouldn't allow her to see me. And since Sylvia had switched to Hamden High that year, our only contact now was over the phone. But one afternoon that fall, when her mother had refused once again to drive her to my house, Sylvia took a stand: "Fine," she said, "I'll *walk* there," and marched out the front door. Her parents, always so protective that they had never allowed her to walk the mile and a half between our homes, followed her in the car, driving slowly alongside, her mother yelling to her fa-ther, "Grab her!" and her gentle, mild-mannered father absolutely re-fusing. "It's not right, Norma," he told her, shaking his head gravely. Her mother relented—halfway.

From then on, Sylvia was allowed to come to my house, but I was still banned from the DeAngelises'. So except for school, I was almost always home.

Most evenings, I worked at the kitchen table while my father worked in the living room. He had his papers and coffee and I had mine. We both worked late. The house would go quiet and dark on the upstairs floors, with everyone else tucked away for the night, except Bill, who was always out. When I wasn't writing, I was reading— poems, novels, plays—memorizing lines that moved me or were playful or simply contained a catchy rhyme.

I felt I had company, secret company, wise to the ways of the world and not at all shocked by my situation. If someone were to recognize me at the back-to-school sale at Sears, I wasn't alone. I had T. S. Eliot with me, whispering in my ear: *In the room the women come and go / Talking of Michelangelo.* He enjoyed a place like Sears, I was sure; it was grist for his mill. And as I waited in the long line at the cash register, surrounded by a sea of overflowing shopping carts and hoping not to see anyone I knew, it was Robert Louis Stevenson who observed: *The world is so full of a number of things / I'm sure we should all be as happy as kings.*

All my early stories were cheats. I simply wrote down the bad dreams I was having at night as if they were the inventions of my conscious mind. Our class was reading Kafka that fall, and if a grown man could wake up as a cockroach, why couldn't a girl discover a doorway cut into her bedroom wall? And when she stepped through that door, why couldn't she find herself in a gloomy mansion, moonlight streaming through one window, illuminating piles of white sheets huddled against the walls, each sheet covering the body of a dead woman?

After she read that story, Mrs. Colasanto sent me to the school counselor. Until then I hadn't even known that we had one. Though she was obviously trying to help, it was the only time that Mrs. C. disappointed me. I had thought she of all people would understand that there was no subject, no thought or feeling, forbidden to a writer.

When I told the school counselor, a young nun, that the story of the murdered women was just a dream I'd had one night, she said, "Oh, that's all right, then, we thought you made it up," and I was free to leave. After that, I stopped giving my creepier stories to Mrs. Colasanto, but I began to conjure up an audience for them nonetheless. The readers I imagined had hearts and minds that were large and tolerant, of course, and unafraid of anything dark or strange; in fact, they had a passion for it. My audience was simply the distilled spirit of every writer I'd ever read—Dickinson, Poe, Thomas Hardy, and Victor Hugo; Sylvia Plath, Carson McCullers, and Graham Greene; Madeleine L'Engle and Lorraine Hansberry; Robert Louis Stevenson, Bernard Malamud, and Mario Puzo; Xaviera Hollander, Saul Bellow, Eugene O'Neill, Jim Carroll—and Lewis Carroll, too.

With my notebook and my pen, I could amuse myself for hours, even as my long-held fear that the world was passing me by became real—the world of dates and dances, rock concerts and Friday nights at the beach or the local pizza parlor, surrounded by a group of friends. In fact, this was the world that Cindy had now entered. Every time she sailed out the door in one of her gauzy Indian blouses and silver jewelry, I bent deeper into "my work." I sensed another world, invisible but immense, one to which I was hooking my fate through the act of writing.

That fall I set about remaking myself. It's a process I've watched many teenagers go through in the years since I became a journalist— one that is both reactionary and immensely creative, and never fails to fill me with admiration. There was the seventeen-year-old black girl from Newark, New Jersey, who, in the middle of a tumultuous adolescence filled with too many boys, too much heartbreak, a pregnancy, and an abortion, decided to become a Muslim. She found peace, and some breathing room, by veiling herself and praying to Allah five times a day.

There were the squatter kids, more drifters than runaways, who gave themselves names like Pain Dog and Peasant Rose, Chronus and Dirtbag Mike, pierced their tongues with bolts, and wore dirt-

encrusted clothes like suits of armor. They turned abandoned build-
ings on the Lower East Side into the homes they'd never had.

And there were the white girls in California, who were so envious
of the black and Mexican kids who made up the majority in their
schools that they decided to become skinheads, donning Doc Martens
and shaving their heads, trying to make their white skin into a tribal
flag, a symbol of belonging.

My own self-transformation wasn't as colorful as many I've wit-
nessed, but it, too, had to have a physical manifestation. So that fall I
asked Sylvia to cut my hair. She used pinking shears and chopped it
off at my chin. Then we renamed ourselves—Maxwell for her (inspired by the coffee can in my mother's kitchen), and Winchester for
me. Winchester sounded intriguing, but it was also the name of a gun.

I started digging through my mother's classical records, and her
collection of Gershwin recordings, listening to them in the privacy of
my bedroom. Rock belonged to the Teen Center, to the boys in the
car, the two Chrissys, the strangers cornering me on the street. I was
determined to carve a new space for myself, one without a trace of
teenage culture. But Chopin was too dry, Beethoven too big and certain; only Rachmaninoff, Tchaikovsky, and Gershwin's *Rhapsody in
Blue* were romantic enough for my fifteen-year-old heart.

Once I even borrowed a recording of the opera *La Traviata* from
the school library, but as soon as the soprano's voice came soaring out
of the tiny speakers of my bedroom turntable, setting all the dirty coffee cups on my desk a-tremble—I'd never heard anything like it in
suburbia—I jumped up in alarm and turned it off. What would Bill
and Cindy and their friends think? Bill's friends already made jokes
about me as the grim and bookish sister. In trying to escape one label,
I'd never considered that I'd be stuck with another.

Sometimes I despaired that everything worthwhile had been
taken, leaving me only the scraps. From the opening bars of the
Rolling Stones' "Paint It Black," my skin prickled. Why should this be
their song? *Fuck it, I don't care.* And so I learned to let go of songs,
clothes, streets, whole seasons. Good-bye, spring and summer; that
was *their* time, warm days when *they* would be outside. I only liked

nighttime now, late at night when Hamden was so quiet it seemed as if everyone had died, and I liked the rain and I liked the cold because *they* didn't.

The next project was my half of the bedroom. One Friday evening when Cindy was out, I took the bells I'd been collecting for years, the exotically costumed dolls, the big chunky candles, put them into cardboard boxes, and shoved the boxes into the crawl space that ran behind our bedrooms. I said good-bye to my jewelry, all of it too delicate for the person I was becoming. Bye to the music boxes, the incense and perfumes, the children's books that still sat on my shelves. Good-bye to the angel bookends.

I even dismantled my private chapel—the plaster saints and dried rose petals and shells I'd arranged in the bottom drawer of my dresser. There was no God, I'd decided (though I still talked to Him incessantly). Since I'd already announced my atheism to my parents and stopped taking Communion at Sunday Mass, disposing of my chapel felt like I was finally making a clean sweep of the last remnants of my old life.

I had just finished putting a conch shell, a beeswax candle, and St. Teresa in a box when my mother knocked on the bedroom door. She came in carrying a load of clean laundry. "What did you do with everything?" she asked, stunned by the sudden emptiness. When I told her I had packed up all my belongings, she said, "Don't those things mean anything to you?" Her voice was angry, but she was peering into my face like she might see right through it and into my mind—what was going on in there?

"They just don't fit me anymore," I told her.

"Some of those things were presents from people who care about you."

"Well, that doesn't mean I have to hold on to them forever."

"So you're just going to throw them away?"

"No, I *put* them away. They're right there in the crawl space."

Her eyes were glued on mine, and after a long moment of silence, a silence that I found acutely uncomfortable, she said, "I don't even know who you are anymore."

I couldn't tell my mother that I was no longer a girl who would collect angel bells and china hearts and that I didn't want to live a lie—or more of a lie than I was already living. So I simply shut her out, ignoring both the despair and anger I heard in her voice. The trouble with having a family was that we were all tangled up with one another. It was like living in a crowded room—every time I moved I knocked something over.

My clothes were now as stripped down as my bedroom—black sweatshirts and threadbare T-shirts that said I had more important things on my mind than appearances; straight-legged jeans and scruffy, low-heeled boots. With the boots on my feet, I felt strong and swift and determined. I didn't want people to see me as a girl—too risky. I suppose I wanted them to see only a brain or a soul. I began to think of my hidden self as winged, and one day I would fly out of Hamden for good.

24

The Christmas Gift

ON CHRISTMAS DAY, I WOKE TO THE SOUND OF A BELL RINGING AND my parents' voices on the floor below as they moved from bedroom to bedroom waking us. At the window, the darkness had just lightened into a blue-gray and the horizon was a ribbon of pale white. The clock said seven A.M. Now the sound of the ringing bell was heard on the stairs, the door was swinging open, and my parents, Beth Ann, and Stephen, all of them in their pajamas, were piling into the room, calling, "Merry Christmas!" Every year it was the same, our Christmas ritual. My parents' faces were doughy and pale from lack of sleep; their breath smelled of coffee when I kissed them.

Downstairs, the fire was lit, the stockings my grandmother had knitted for each of us when we were born stuffed to overflowing, packages heaped in gleaming mountains around the tree. We always opened our presents in our pajamas, though this Christmas Bill was wearing his jeans and a T-shirt and he was sprawled on the couch, yawning vigorously. Had he just come home? I didn't know. Michael sat in one of the armchairs, grinning and rubbing his hands. "Let the games begin!" he proclaimed. He was completely unabashed in his appetite, his confidence, his enjoyment of us all. When he'd returned from his first semester at college a few days earlier, we saw that he'd grown his hair long, but it was so curly that instead of falling down his back it rose in a halo around his head, a bushy orange afro. He had even grown a beard.

I sat down on the floor with Beth Ann, Cindy, and Stephen; there we bobbed back and forth like shuttles on a loom. It would take the entire morning and half the afternoon to get to all the presents. We opened them one at a time, taking turns while everyone else watched.

When we were little, we made all our gifts. One Christmas, Beth Ann made my father sandpaper by gluing salt and sugar onto sheets of brown construction paper. Sometimes there were joke presents, like the year that someone—was it Bill or Michael?—gave a gift-wrapped turnip to Stephen. The first joke this year was in Michael's stocking, a rolled-up poster of a gorilla with the caption "When I Want Your Opinion I'll Beat It Out Of You," which was something Michael always used to say. "That's perfect, just perfect," Bill called out from the couch, laughing along with the rest of us. It was like Michael had never left for college, Bill had never run away, I'd never tripped out into the world in my halter top and hip-hugger jeans. We'd always teased and celebrated Michael's self-confidence; it was part of us, like a family pet.

"Well, I think this package has your name on it, kiddo," my father said, placing a large, square-shaped box wrapped in green and gold on the floor in front of me. From the look on my parents' faces I knew this was the big present, something special. Every year there was one for each of us. When Cindy and I were six and seven it was two black kittens wearing red bows and hidden away in the laundry basket in the basement; when I was nine it was a blue bicycle.

I was nervous opening my present while everyone watched. What if it were something awful? Something girlish that would've been right for me a year ago but no longer. Or worse, what if it was something practical and grim? Family surprises were treacherous; if my parents had misread me it would cut to the bone. I knew I spent all my time at home now, reading and writing and arguing politics with my father, but I couldn't bear it if they gave me the complete works of some radical nun.

When I tore the paper across the front of the box, I could hardly believe my eyes—was this a joke? Was it only a typewriter *box* with something else tucked inside? I looked up at my mother and father. "A typewriter?" I said carefully.

They were beaming and nodding. A typewriter! The first one in our house. A writer's present, and just in case I didn't understand that they understood, my mother said, "That's for all that writing you're doing now."

I leapt up to thank both of them, happy to be carried toward my parents on a genuine wave of enthusiasm, for I was rarely affectionate with them anymore—in fact, whenever they reached to touch me, without thinking, I cringed. The two of them felt like large furry bears when I hugged them; my father's flannel robe was warm from the fire. I knew they were relieved.

As everyone continued opening presents around me, I sat on the floor in front of the typewriter, rolled a piece of paper into the carriage, and began to hit the keys.

Silver spider legs high-stepped onto the page, leaving wet black footprints behind. Tiny, precise; I'd never seen a prettier *a*. I felt like I was playing the piano, clack clack clack clack clack, a bell dinged, I hit the carriage, and zing!

For a long time my mother kept smiling at me, trying to catch my eye. I was completely happy with the present but unable to meet her expectant gaze. Random letters gave way to words, *georgia, lipstick, alley, shadow*, which gave way to sentences, then rhymes, *merry merry christmas bells. merry merry christmas hell.*

"What are you typing there, honey?"

"Now I know my ABCs," Bill recited in a simpleton's voice. "Tell me what you think of me."

"Nothing, just playing around," I told her, ignoring him and typing, *a tisket, a tasket, a green and yellow casket*. I was thrilled with the present, and deeply, stubbornly unhappy with my life.

That wasn't the only big present from my parents that year—they also gave Cindy and me tickets to a Sunday matinee of *Grease* on Broadway. And on this, our very first trip to New York, we'd be going alone. Two train tickets to Grand Central were inside the package, money for cab fare, the theater tickets, and a handmade certificate announcing that we were having dinner at Sardi's, already paid for. At the end of the evening, my parents would pick us up outside the restaurant.

With a typewriter and train tickets to New York, my parents had given me the wings I would need to fly away from them—did they know?

Late that night, I sat on Michael's bed looking out the window at the empty intersection of Clifford and Treadwell. Ever since he had left for college in August, that window had become my eye on the world, this room my refuge, and my jail. Bill kept vampire hours, coming in just before dawn, so I always had the room to myself. When I wrote up here, I leaned my notebook on the windowsill so that I could watch the streets below. By keeping the world that I'd lost in view, I felt a little less cut off.

I watched the flashing traffic light swinging on its wires, dreaming of New York City, only two hours distant and yet impossibly far. That is where I would move as soon as I graduated from high school. Where else would you go if you were leaving a small town to become a writer? But there was only one acceptable route away from my family—college. Since my freshman year at Sacred Heart, everyone—my parents, my relatives, my friends and teachers—assumed I'd be going, and because of them, I did, too. I'd decided to apply to New York University, knowing nothing about it except the most important thing, right there in the name.

Though I'd not yet actually been to the city, I'd always felt its presence. It was there in my books and my music, in the old movies I watched with Sylvia, on the silky labels inside Grandma Callahan's furs, on TV every Thanksgiving when we went to Great-aunt Bert's house to eat jelly doughnuts and watch the Macy's parade. Sometimes New York appeared to me only in black and white, the city as seen from a distance at night, a dark island shooting up immense towers of pearly light. Other times, I imagined the city as a great jumble of people, characters, really, from those books and movies, burly cops and wisecracking newsboys, jazzmen and businessmen, dockworkers who coulda been contenders, desperate gang kids turning to Jesus, beautiful women in sequined dresses smoking, drinking, never thinking about tomorrow, a junkman singing right before dawn. Everyone was hungry—for money, for love, for fame or purpose; survival wasn't a given. I knew I'd fit right in.

I fantasized about my future in New York City with the same fervor a prisoner serving a life sentence might bring to his thoughts of heaven. But my sentence was not interminable. As I sat there on Michael's bed that night, my eyes glued to the flashing traffic light, I told myself, *Less than two years and you'll be free.*

25

Seaward on the Waves

THAT NIGHT IN THE CAR HAD THE UNFORESEEN EFFECT OF OPENING UP a Pandora's box of ugly feeling in me—emotions I never wanted to feel and couldn't remember ever feeling before: jealousy, bitterness, rage, self-pity, self-disgust, despair.

I fought with everyone that spring, driving a wedge between me and my family that would last more than a decade. I pushed my mother into fits of exasperation, made Cindy cry.

"You care too much about what other people think of you. I don't care," I told her one evening, in what might have been the most astonishing lie of my life. "Most people aren't worth thinking about." All Cindy was doing at that moment was choosing a shirt to wear, as I lay in bed with a book watching her. Whenever she went out now, she put clothes on under the brace, ducked into the alley that ran behind our garage, slipped out of the brace, and left it there until she came back home. She was like a fairy tale princess who escaped her father's castle each night after he'd fallen asleep and danced until dawn, only to sneak back into bed before the king awoke.

She stood in her white bra, her dungaree shorts, a beaded strand of leather around her neck, examining two blouses, both white, both pretty and faintly crumpled, so no matter which one she wore, she would look wonderful, and also like she didn't care how she looked. She had a large crowd of friends, boys and girls in equal numbers.

She told me I was a snob. "That's not exactly an insult," I replied evenly.

"I hate you!" she shouted, her eyes brimming with tears. "Sometimes I wish you weren't my sister."

"Well, just pretend I'm not." I cracked open my book.

We were supposed to be above such ugliness in my family. Was I a sinner? No, a sinner confesses and then she's free: "Go forth and sin no more." But I had no way of banishing these feelings, my anger at my parents, my envy of Cindy, my wariness around Bill and his friends. I couldn't rid myself of the sense that mine was the black heart buried and boiling inside my loving family.

My mother and father would have had to work hard to reach me during this time. It would have taken a sustained effort, and a willingness to rise above rebuffs and failures and keep coming back for more. But they had five other children, as well as aging parents, aunts, and uncles to take care of. My grandmother had suffered a massive heart attack earlier that year and undergone a quadruple bypass. My mother was worried about her, and as I found out years later, secretly fighting a depression of her own. My father had been promoted to director of operations at Yale, reporting only to the provost and the Yale board, and was facing enormous pressure himself. He loved working with people, and now he was working with budgets.

And I? I was playing the part of a tough girl. I wanted my parents to see through that act; they swallowed it hook, line, and sinker.

I could have turned to religion or drugs or some cult where you shave your head, marry a stranger, and play tambourines all day, but instead I discovered Ayn Rand—Rand and her superheroes, Rand and all her contempt for flawed humanity. As soon as I began reading her, I was completely in her thrall. I began to fashion myself after an Ayn Rand hero, and after reading *The Virtue of Selfishness*, my third Rand book, I passed it on to Sylvia with a note: *Sylvia, I know it's hard at first but if you stick with it, it will become clearer and clearer. If you have any questions, I'm always here.* Now the disciple had a disciple.

An Ayn Rand hero invariably has high cheekbones and a contemptuous mouth. His eyes are cold and clear. And except in Rand's first book, *We the Living*, the hero is always a man. He might be an architect, a composer, a sculptor, an entrepreneur, but whatever he is, he loves his work, loves it so much that the world will try to destroy him for it. He is pure, he never compromises, never says what people need him to say.

According to Rand, the vast majority of people smile too much. They try too hard to get along. They flatter and simper and cringe. One time Sylvia reduced the entire Ayn Rand philosophy to the pithy phrase "The masses are asses." And, of course, she and I weren't. We began to ration our smiles, curb our enthusiasm, disdain emotion, softness, shoppers in the mall. I learned another walk—neither male nor female—a swift, long-legged stride. Gone was the girl who sashayed down the street swinging her hips and licking her lips. But not because I was ashamed, no, not that—I was an Ayn Rand hero.

My pariah status suddenly acquired nobility. I wasn't sitting home alone every night because I was scared of people; I simply didn't need them. I wasn't bewildered by the world, unsure of how to enter it again; there was nothing and no one worth my time in Hamden. And, so, the girl they called a *douche bag* began to tell herself she was actually superior to most of the human race.

My mother could hardly stand to be around me. One day as she was driving me home from school, I announced that I didn't need anything from her. I'd missed the school bus and had to call her for a ride home. She and I were crammed together in the Pinto, our bucket seats close to the floor.

"I don't do things because I *need* to. I do them because I *want* to," I proclaimed, this distinction being very important to me at that time in my life.

"Well, what about other people? What about their needs?" she asked.

"That's not my responsibility. If I do something for someone else, it's because I want to, not because I'm being selfless."

"Well, you're my responsibility. I'm not picking you up from school just because it gives me pleasure. I still have to get dinner fixed and—"

"Well, you shouldn't have come, then."

"Kathy, sometimes you have to make sacrifices for other people!"

"Well, you shouldn't."

"So, I should've left you here at school? Let you find your own way home?"

"Yeah, if you didn't want to pick me up."

"Agh!" my mother yelled, gripping the steering wheel.

We argued all the way home. But when we arrived, my mother suddenly calmed down. Or so it seemed to me then. Now I think she was fighting back.

"You know what?" she said casually. "If you and I weren't related to each other, if we just met on the street, I don't think we'd even like each other."

I stomped up the stairs and into my room, slamming the door behind me. *My own mother!* I kept exclaiming to myself, trying to work up an outrage or pump out some tears. But neither came. I was stunned, but I knew I'd driven her to it. Besides, I thought she was right. It surprised me that my mother had shown herself to be just as capable of the hard truth as I thought I was. It was as if a wish had been fulfilled, a painful wish, one of those they tell you to be careful of. And now that the truth had been revealed, the guilt removed, our ties could be cut. I was free to leave her, and my whole family, behind.

But within the hour, my mother came upstairs to take it all back. She sat next to me on the bed, asking for a hug to show that, underneath it all, we really did love each other. In her embrace I felt my insides kick and struggle.

It was only my father who accepted my challenge to duel. Everyone else wanted me to be nicer, more agreeable, or at least apologize at the end. But my father and I were like two men fighting, fighting hard, no punches pulled, no tears, either. He never even winced, never seemed to take our arguments personally. How I enjoyed fighting with him.

One night I used my smoking as a bait. If I was old enough to drive, I was old enough to smoke, I announced. It was a Saturday night when Cindy and Bill had taken off with their friends, a spring night with the scent of lilacs drifting in through the open kitchen window.

"You *do* know smoking causes cancer," he said to me, as we faced off from opposite ends of the kitchen table.

"There's no proof of that," I replied rashly, and he looked at me like I'd landed from Mars. Sometimes I argued with my father about serious things, like the death penalty or the meaning of patriotism, sometimes about ridiculous things, like this argument right now. It hardly mattered to me what we fought about. I had only one guiding principle: Whatever my father said, I took the opposite view. I was angry; I needed his company. Engaging his attention was surprisingly easy.

"What do you mean, there's no proof?" he said, almost shouting in frustration. "That's all there is."

"I'm talking scientific proof, studies and things."

"What do you think *I'm* talking about?" I took a swig of my coffee, he took one of his. Our cups hit the table with a clank-clank. His blue eyes were flaring. I stared right back at him. It seemed unbelievable that I'd ever been afraid of him.

I thought my father enjoyed our sparring matches—a worthy opponent at last!—but when I asked him recently what I was like during that last year and a half at home, he answered steadily, without any hesitation at all, "Aggressive. Defensive. And offensive."

That spring, when Sylvia and I decided to make a movie that would display our Ayn Randian selves to the world, we couldn't come up with a narrative for a heroine whose main attributes were disdain and pride. She would be deeply passionate, of course, while also being unmoved by most human beings, for they hardly deserved her attention. But what would a woman like that *do*? We decided our protagonist was dying and we would show her last day on earth, filled with extravagant, romantic gestures.

I was to play the heroine and Sylvia would do the filming, since she was taking a television broadcasting course at Hamden High and she knew how. She borrowed the 16-millimeter camera from her class. The camera had no sound, so the script was easy. Just think: wild, aching, doomed.

We decided the heroine would go to the ocean and . . . what? Swim naked? Walk restlessly? No! Scratch the ocean. She would down a glass of champagne in one thirsty swallow and then hurl it against a wall. "Could you catch the falling glass in slow motion?" I asked Sylvia.

And she would ride a horse, very fast, tearing her hair on branches of low-hanging trees. I didn't know how to ride a horse, but how hard could it be?

In the yellow pages, Sylvia and I found a stable in the nearby town of Milford where we could take out horses by the hour. As soon as we arrived, the three men who worked there took a lively interest in us: our camera, our movie script, my long skirt and lack of horsemanship.

"You've never been on a horse before? I think I better give you lessons," the youngest of them said to me, smiling broadly. His yellow-blond hair was pulled back into a ponytail; he had pointy satyr's ears, devilishly pretty and pale white.

"I'm sure I can figure it out," I said, "if you'll just show me the horse." The men laughed.

"You planning on riding sidesaddle in that skirt?"

I didn't know what he was talking about.

"If she ain't riding sidesaddle, *I'll* give her lessons."

"Who do we pay?" I asked, not even glancing over at Sylvia but sure that her face was as disapproving as mine.

"You can pay me," the ponytailed man said. "And John will saddle you a horse, but I'd hate to see you thrown to the ground—that's not supposed to be in the movie, is it?"

"Where's John?" I asked.

They pointed out a man by the fenced-in area where they kept the horses.

"You sure you don't want some help getting up on that horse?" Ponytail was smiling at me in a friendly and interested way; his blue eyes were so clear I could see feathery gold flecks in his irises. But I knew I couldn't respond. If I opened myself to Hamden again, to any part of its day-to-day, prosaic life, I was sure I would be swallowed up for good.

I lifted my chin in the air and turned swiftly away, grabbing the back of my skirt as I turned because it was a wraparound and there was a bit of wind that day—wind I would ride on my horse, I thought, like Eliot's mermaids "riding seaward on the waves."

Heads held high, Sylvia and I went striding off. We heard hooting and hollering behind us. Was that applause?

Out of the corner of her mouth, Sylvia hissed, "You're holding your skirt *open*."

I blushed straight to the roots of my hair, got up on that horse, and rode it not through low-hanging branches and whipping leaves but a tangle of embarrassment.

The horse and I never got into any kind of rhythm. We rolled along like two weary workmen—I could feel his huge chest and inside it, his slab of a heart. He seemed to be laboring. Whenever he tried to break into a trot, I bounced up and down in the saddle, smacking it with my rear end—but who was spanking whom? It wasn't at all like I'd imagined it would be.

A year and three months left, all of it stuck inside this stiff and cheerless Ayn Rand persona. I couldn't figure out how I was going to last that long.

26

As Happy As Kings

THE SUMMER AFTER MY JUNIOR YEAR, I FINALLY MANAGED TO REENTER the world—as a union-dues-paying pot washer wearing a blue work shirt with a bulldog on the breast pocket, thick work pants, and heavy, rubber-soled shoes. In June, I began to work in the Yale kitchens. It was my first job, not counting a two-week stint providing service with a smile at McDonald's.

My official title was "general service assistant" and I was part of a small crew that swept and mopped the floors, washed the heavy kettles, made sure the chefs had everything they needed, and kept the storerooms stocked, unloading fifty-pound bags of potatoes and onions and rice from delivery trucks. New Haven seemed miles and miles away from Hamden, and the hard work released me from my head. Five days a week I had somewhere to go, a job to do. And I had company. I'd become a citizen of the democracy that I'd been hearing my father describe at our dinner table for years.

There were black, brown, and white faces, male and female, young, middle-aged, gray-haired. We worked in the din of pots and pans clattering on stoves, water running, meat frying, voices hollering, "Hand me that towel there, love!" and "Where the hell is that boy with those potatoes?" Clouds of steam rolled off the stoves, and behind those clouds the cooks labored. In their white chef's jackets and pillowy hats, they looked like sturdy angels.

Whenever I picture that summer, I see myself striding happily down a long concrete basement corridor, pushing a metal trolley filled with cans of tomatoes that jiggle and rattle against one another. Every time I turn the light on in one of the basement storerooms, there's a sudden scurrying motion on the floor. These are the first cockroaches I've ever seen—leggy, three-inch-long creatures with a lacquered reddish shine to their shells. But I'm not afraid of the water bugs, or the long, empty corridors that wind and turn, or even the windowless storerooms, though I'm claustrophobic. I'm completely at home here.

Riding the freight elevator up from the basement, I feel a jerk as it lands, opening on to a high-ceilinged, white-tiled kitchen with a shiny island of stoves as big as a banquet table. On weekdays, Geraldine runs the kitchen. A short, wide, chocolate-brown woman buttoned into her chef's whites, she has forearms as bulky as a dockworker's, the skin darkened in patches from burns. "Honey, open those cans for me," Geraldine says. Here everyone is called *love, honey, sweetheart,* and even—especially if the woman being addressed is older and married—*baby cakes.* This is exactly the kind of easygoing atmosphere that suits me right now in my life, for if I open my mouth to try to say something serious, all I can do is spout Ayn Rand, make declarations. I've built a self to present to the world, but it is all a construct, hollow and artificial. In the bustling kitchen, with a job to do and a place on the team, I can just *be.*

My uniform suits me, too. It's a badge of membership. There is hard work to be done and it has to be done right, so if I have to wear a hair net or a blue and white paper hat when I work the serving line, I just wear it. A paper hat is a laughably small price to pay for belonging. The people I work with like me, and I like them. Life is suddenly very simple.

Every dining hall has a first, second, and third chef. Besides Geraldine, our first chef, we have Freddy, who is very round and very white, his hands like soft dinner rolls, and grouchy Julius, a big-bellied gray-haired man with a crumpled face who lumbers around the kitchen like a bear, leaving dirty pots and pans, egg splatters, puddles of pancake batter, and charred towels in his wake. Julius is close to retirement, slowing down, and sometimes a whiff of panic comes off him as he throws pots onto the stove and jerks smoking pans out of the oven. Ilsa, our desk clerk, who checks the students in at each meal, is a grandmother, a Polish woman whose blond hair is piled on her head in swirls like a pastry. I always take my fifteen-minute breaks with her, the two of us smoking and drinking coffee out of juice glasses with such camaraderie you would have thought we were two confirmed drinkers meeting in a bar. We also have a couple of Yale work-study students who come in at mealtimes to help me on the serving line and at the dishwasher: wisecracking Jason, a cute, curly-haired Jewish boy from Manhattan; and Ruben Gonzalez, a slight-boned, big-afroed, sweet, cynical, strong-willed Brooklyn boy, both of them reaffirming my belief that New York City is the place for me.

As I wash the kettles in the deep steel sinks, Julius and Freddy argue behind me. "Move your big black ass," Freddy calls out airily. When Julius calls Freddy a fat white cracker, Freddy challenges him to a duel. "Choose your weapon!" he cries, and I turn to see Freddy raising a spatula, his legs set apart like a fencer's. The insults, the shouts, even the water running into the sink seem joyful. A burden has been lifted, and whenever the chefs send me downstairs for eggs or onions or potatoes, I feel light on my feet, quick and strong.

At the end of that summer, the head of our GSA crew asked me out. Carl must have been in his mid- to late twenties. His full name was Lawrence Carlson, but only management called him Lawrence. He was a man of few words, quietly dependable, and handsome. Though Carl and I worked side by side, and I worked just as hard as he did, he treated me with a gentleness that was close to courtly. When the two of us worked alone together in the storerooms, he talked even less than usual, and in the silence that grew as we dragged boxes across the floor, cut them open, and filled the shelves, the air became moist and charged. His skin appeared to shimmer.

After I finished my last day of work, Carl and I left together. It was a warm breezy night, I remember it well. We were sitting in Carl's Pontiac with the windows rolled down, outside a red and yellow neon-lit bar in the black part of New Haven. He'd gone in and bought us two beers and we drank them in the car, listening to the music spilling out of the open doors. The tar on the street shone like water, and the leaves on the trees were a silvery green. As we sat there nursing our beers, Carl told me the manager of our dining hall had called him into the office early on in the summer and had warned him away from me. "He told me you're Mr. Dobie's daughter and you're off-limits." Carl looked pained as he said this, as if what the manager had really meant was that he, Carl, wasn't good enough for the daughter of the boss. Wasn't good enough because he was a black, working-class man. And perhaps that is what the manager meant.

"He did that on his own!" I told him, surprised. "My father never would've told him to say that!" I don't remember anything else that we talked about, just the look of humiliation on Carl's face and my view of the summer shifting to include Carl's restraint, his frustration, the threat of losing his job hanging over his head, the way he, a grown man, had been talked to like a bad little boy, and how admirable he seemed to me now. After we finished our beer, Carl drove me home, parking on the Clifford Street side of the house where the tall hedges hid us from view.

"Well, good night, thanks for the beer," I said, hesitating, for I knew I'd never see him again. School was starting in another week and I was being moved to another dining hall where I'd work only on weekends. How does one say good-bye? And for no other reason than that you're young, and life is taking you somewhere new? Carl didn't bother with words. He leaned over, his face suddenly large, the skin glowing and . . . His lips moved over mine with the utmost attention and tenderness, sending my breath into a hard run. I held the side of his face; it was larger than my hand.

Who thought of this? I wanted to cry. *Who could live without it?* With the air buzzing and my body as charged as a racehorse at the gate, I said good night to Carl again. I just *couldn't* have sex with him, or any man.

At fourteen, my body had still been a child's. I didn't feel much sexually but I didn't care, because I didn't know what I was missing. At fifteen, I ached to be free of my body and go flying down some lonesome (but poetically moonlit) highway. At sixteen, well after I'd learned sexual shame, my body woke up. The timing seemed designed by someone with a not-very-funny sense of humor.

That fall, the beginning of my last year in high school, the sun felt almost holy, swinging in the sky like Father Sheridan's censer, showering light down on emerald lawns and yellow trees. The air was sharpening; it gave a glint to everything as it honed itself into the cold knife tip that would one day drive in winter.

Senior year, and at the very moment when the class queens had reached the apex of their lives, they began to lose their stranglehold, so that everything felt slightly disarranged. Nine months later, this world would dissolve. The days seemed to pick up pace as if time itself was tunneling toward that change. No one seemed to be what they once were. Even the shy, awkward girls, the ones who had faded into their uniforms like freshly shaved recruits in boot camp, suddenly had a brightness in their faces, an almost feverish look.

Sylvia and I had sent in our applications to NYU. She was nervous about being rejected because it was the only college we'd tried to get into, but I was so certain of my future in New York City that the application process seemed almost a formality. Of course they'd let us in.

I was beginning to feel happy, and less cautious. So when I went into the senior lounge one afternoon to get my chocolate milk, having abandoned my usual practice of checking to see who was there before entering, I found myself surrounded by the class queens.

"The Teen Center? Is that on Putnam Avenue?" Louisa asked Joan loudly. They so rarely got a chance at me alone, they had to jump at it when they did. I put my money in the vending machine. I didn't even think about responding. What was I supposed to say to them—that I wasn't the grotesque cartoon they'd reduced me to?

"That's right, at Putnam and Whitney."

"Oh, I heard some story about that place." They started laughing, and the shrill sound drove a timid freshman out of the lounge before she even got to the vending machine. They *owned* the senior lounge; they'd come into their inheritance. The rest of us were looking ahead. The future was ours—it always belongs to those who are unhappy in the present.

Just then Linda came gliding into the room. When she saw the cluster of girls, she tossed her head, making a show of it, like she was flipping back her hair, though her close-cropped afro didn't even stir. Leslie was right behind her, wearing a faded blue, silver-studded dungaree jacket over her uniform. While Leslie stopped to talk to the girls, Linda went straight to the soda machine. She made a great pretense of studying her choices. "Eanie, meanie, minie, mo," she said, enunciating each word. Her silver bracelets slid down her arm as she dropped the coins into the machine slot.

"Ohhhh, Leslie, you're so cute!" Louisa cried.

"She's like a little puppy dog."

"Can I feel it?"

They were petting Leslie's afro.

"It's like a bush, it's all springy."

"It's soft!"

"What happens when you wash it? Does it stay up like this?"

"Isn't she adorable?"

Leslie was soaking it up, cocking her head and batting her long lashes at them. A lover, not a fighter; she just couldn't help herself.

Linda looked sideways at me and then slid behind Louisa, cobra-like. She reached for Louisa with her right arm in slow motion . . . and then she brought her hand down on Louisa's head and began petting her.

"Ohhhhh," Linda cooed. Louisa jumped. I could see her skin flinch, eyes flash furiously. But whatever word was on the tip of her tongue, she bit it down.

"I just wanted to feel it," Linda said sweetly, but her eyes were dead cold. "It's like a . . . a . . . pancake! It's so smooth and flat."

The girls shot looks of pure hatred at Linda. Leslie was giggling. "A pancake!"

Linda put her arm around Leslie's shoulders, squeezing her close, and said haughtily, "Come on, buddy-o'-mine, let's go." Then: "Ta ta, girls! See you around the quad!" She turned once to see that I was following, gave her beauty queen wave, fingers closed, hand shifting, back and forth like a metronome. "See you later, alligators!"

Leslie was doubled over in laughter, but there was a breathlessness to the sound, a note of shame.

When we got close to our table, Leslie ducked out from under Linda's arm, whirled around on one foot, came to a stop, one hand raised, and sang, "Stop! In the name of love . . ." She did Diana Ross *and* the Supremes. Gladys Knight *and* the Pips.

"You're gonna make me pee in my pants!" Linda hollered, clutching her stomach.

The bell for class was ringing.

Leslie turned to me. "Okay, Dorothy, ready?" Sometimes she called me Dorothy, sometimes Chief.

"Ready when you are," I said, meaning exactly that, for I had no idea what she was going to do next.

She put her arm out for me to grab, sounded the first note, and we went skipping out of the cafeteria, singing, "We're off to see the wizard!"

Linda caught up to us in the crowded hallway, her skip a giant's version of ours. She floated right by us, all swinging arms and legs and lifted chin, completely straight-faced. Girls scattered and giggled helplessly. Was there anyone luckier in friendship?

27

After All

THE BOYS OF HAMDEN HAD ONE LAST MESSAGE FOR ME.

The summer was coming to a close and my new life was about to begin. In one week I would be leaving for New York. Today was my last day as a Yale food service employee. To celebrate, Sylvia and I were taking ourselves out to dinner at Sam's Pizzeria.

When I finished up work at four, I shed my GSA uniform and put on the black sundress and the ankle-laced, wedge-heeled shoes I'd long ago moved to the back of my closet but never quite forgotten. Three summers had passed since I had dressed up and played the part of a beautiful girl. Only now did I feel free to do so again, for I was on my way out of town—and I was in New Haven, not Hamden, after all. I had a few hours to kill before meeting Sylvia, so I decided to stroll down to the green, where I could listen to one of the city-sponsored jazz concerts that were put on almost every Friday evening in the summer.

Stan Kenton and his band were playing, and the New Haven green was filled with picnicking couples and families. Sitting down on one of the benches at the edge of the green, I watched as fathers struggled to open bottles of wine and wandering children were coaxed back to their blankets with bribes of fruit and cookies. Here and there, a solitary Yale student sat on the grass reading. The sound of jazz trumpets swirled over us, like a canopy. The beep of a car horn seemed tinny and festive. A breeze pulled at my hair and sent an occasional napkin or paper plate flying.

I saw them coming from far away. My heart started hammering, even as I doubted my eyes.

Don't be stupid. It can't be, I told myself. This was the city, it belonged to strangers, hundreds and thousands of them, *they* wouldn't be here. Besides, the boys were on the opposite side of the green. They couldn't possibly have spotted me from that far away.

There were eight of them, and they seemed to be heading straight toward me, stepping around picnic blankets, dodging the small children in their path, never looking down. I kept thinking: Any minute now they're going to veer right or left, find the person they're looking for, call out a name, and turn into somebody's harmless friends, sons, or carousing brothers.

Their steamroller progress began to attract attention. People who had glanced up from their blankets only because those feet were so close to their sandwiches now became riveted; *What was going on?* Unbelievable and yet inevitable. While my body objected and my thoughts froze, two and a half years dropped away. And then the boys were assembled in front of me. Leering. Their leader had a wide-nosed, fleshy face that I recognized but couldn't place.

(And wouldn't until fifteen years later, when out of the blue it came to me and suddenly, I knew his name: Paul DiRusso. He was one of my brother Michael's friends, someone who went on family picnics with us when we were kids and once had almost drowned me in a lake, holding me down between his legs in a game that went on too long; a Notre Dame boy.)

"Are you Mike Dobie's sister?" he asked, the grin never leaving his face. Michael? Notre Dame? They'd known about me in a private Catholic high school in West Haven? I shook my head rapidly. "No."

That made him laugh out loud. "So you're not Bill Dobie's sister either?"

"I don't know who you're talking about," I said, and the thought of

Peter's betrayal, three denials, the cock crowing, flitted through my head.

They were all laughing now, except for the ringleader, whose sweaty face suddenly shone with hatred.

"Come on! We know who you are." He dug into the pocket of his jeans. The jeans were tight, so it took him a while to extract what he was looking for—a fistful of change. As he held it out to me, his palm opening slowly, I froze. I had no idea what was going to happen next.

"There are only eight of us," he said. "This should be enough."

I got up and walked away fast.

"Fucking dirtbag!"

"Go back to Howe Street where you belong, you cunt!" they shouted. Howe Street: That was where the prostitutes trolled in New Haven.

And then the coins came flying at me, some of them hitting my bare back. On the green, people stared and, I thought, clutched their children to them.

The boys didn't know me, of course, but I knew them, knew they were still virgins, and because I had gone (again and again) to the place they hadn't yet been, they hated me, even as they envied the boys I'd had sex with. I knew, too, that it gave them as much pleasure to hurt a girl, to poke her and see her twitch, as it would to make love to her. Either way, they would feel more like men when they were done.

I got to Chapel Street, took a right. But where could I go? There was no safe place.

Just keep walking, I told myself, and suddenly I pictured myself walking straight through time—out of that day, into the next, through five more, until I got to New York City. It still feels like I arrived here on foot.

I only lasted one semester at NYU, dropping out after I was put on academic probation. I hadn't considered how difficult it would be for me to live in a dorm with a couple of hundred boys and girls my age. The past wasn't to be banished so easily. But failing at NYU didn't really matter—the city, not college, had been my dreamed-of destination.

From where I sit writing this, on the fourth floor of a house I rent in Brooklyn, I can see tarred rooftops, wooden water towers, flocks of birds, a small silver plane crossing a huge expanse of milk-striped blue.

This row house used to be a boardinghouse for sailors passing through (the docks are only seven blocks from here), and it still is, in a way. Not that the three people I live with are transients, but they are currently without spouses or children, healthy bank accounts, or predictable futures. In the morning, I can hear the adjunct professor of philosophy singing in the shower.

In the more than twenty years I've been in New York, I've never lived alone, never wanted to. But I've never lived with a boyfriend, either. I need more freedom, and solitude, than I could manage if I lived as part of a couple. I once saw a photograph of Diego Rivera's and Frida Kahlo's home in Mexico City: two houses built side by side, connected by a second-story walkway that went from her bedroom to his. This seemed the perfect living arrangement to me then, and my boyfriend and I now have our own version—with the Brooklyn Bridge as the walkway between us.

Loose domesticity suits me. As long as I have a place I can retreat to, a hideaway—this top floor, my attic room—I enjoy being surrounded by other people. While I work, I like hearing the sounds of whistling or laughter coming from the floors below or the clunk-clunk-clunk of Tim's sneakers in the dryer; like knowing that Ed is reading Kant at the kitchen table downstairs or Chris is fixing his bike in the living room. Sometimes Chris, a New Orleans boy, stops at a phone booth on his way home from work and asks if I want some Popeye's chicken, biscuits, rice and beans; sometimes I cook dinner for all of us. Their girlfriends spend the night, leaving their French shampoos and herbal facial scrubs on the shelf in the shower; Ed's friends from his university days in Germany use this house as their New York City hostel; Tim holds a Fourth of July barbecue, attended entirely by musicians, and late in the evening guitars, accordions, and horns are pulled out and a chaotic babel of sound gradually finds its way into a tune they all recognize. I know each of my housemates and both of my cats, Fate and Will, by their footfall, much as I once knew my brothers and sisters by theirs. Chris's feet make a snapping sound as he comes upstairs in his hard-soled office shoes at the end of a workday. He flies down them on weekends, though. Tim's footstep is the most solid, and I can imagine him as the small Indiana farmboy he once was, whose first words were the proud declaration "I carry." And when Will comes thumping down the stairs, you'd think he was a grown man, not a fourteen-pound cat. In short, I live much as I did growing up—amid the sensual, comforting ruckus of a large family.

From my attic perch, I can see my neighbor Daphne sitting on her stoop across the street waiting to greet the bus drivers, the garbagemen, the UPS, FedEx, and postal workers, all old friends. Daphne's a large, baby-faced woman who suffers from diabetes and various heart ailments. She was born in Trinidad but raised in that redbrick house, and she took care of her mother and father there until they passed away. She's always dreamed of visiting Venice, where she'll meet the love of her life—an opera singer with a robust appetite. Whenever a bus driver honks on this block, I know Daphne's on the stoop.

Every neighborhood needs their Greek chorus, and ours is sitting on orange milk crates outside the El Beriyah deli right across the street: three older black men from the projects one block away. There's kind, no-nonsense Cyril with his spotted dog, slender Cooper, the retired cop, and Bear, who has only one tooth. When I need a break from writing I join them on the milk crates and trade stories, especially with Cooper; I have a few of my own to tell now.

When I was a teenager, I thought I'd write fiction and poetry, but real-life stories turned out to be a better fit. I start each one hungry for contact, and filled with trepidation. Will they trust me—the Navajo gangmembers or the skinhead girls, the death-row prisoner, the mother whose daughter was murdered? Will we connect? Will I be taken in? The stakes feel very high. Most of the people I write about would be considered outsiders, and what I listen for in every interview are the stories they tell themselves about their own lives. What narrative has this person fashioned to help him or her survive?

Once, when I was interviewing runaway teens at a local shelter, I came across a girl whose face was like a shuttered house. Even her voice was a monotone. She was sixteen but big-breasted and big-boned. Between that and her sullen face, she could easily be mistaken for someone in her mid-twenties, an unpleasant someone, and my hunch was that it had been a long time since anyone had treated her as a young person—if ever.

She gave only two answers to most of my questions: "yeah" and "uh-uh." The interview wasn't going well, or so it seemed. Then she asked if I wanted to hear something she wrote, and pulled a crumpled sheet of notepaper from her jeans pocket, something she'd obviously been carrying for a long time. The title of her poem was "To Someone Who Was Always There." She read: *When I was hungry you fed me / You held me when I cried / You gave me your coat when I was freezing in the cold* . . . When she had finished, I asked who it was written for. "Nobody," she said.

What could I possibly do to honor that moment? Bear witness by writing about it.

Last year I met a Harlem street minister named Reverend Betty Neal, a seventy-five-year-old woman with a poodle haircut and Bette Davis eyes. Reverend Betty used to minister to the prostitutes in Times Square, anointing them with holy water on the sidewalk in front of a porn theater while their pimps, who were sure the girls would make more money after receiving the reverend's blessing, stood by and watched. When she told me this, Reverend Betty hollered with laughter. She had a great sense of fun and a natural-born affinity for the street; she loved hookers, pimps, homeless people, EMS workers, firemen, and especially cops. Her storefront office was decorated with toy police cars. When cops were in a jam—and there's no trouble quite like a-cop-in-trouble—they came to Reverend Betty for advice and counseling.

When the police commissioner retired, Reverend Betty brought him a singing fish, Billy the Big Mouth Bass, as a going-away gift. "Billy" was mounted on a plaque, with a motion detector hidden inside. All morning as the reverend and I waited outside the commissioner's office, I watched the fish turn its head, open its mouth, and start singing, "Just call me angel of the morning" to every big, burly, dark-suited detective who walked in the door. And every time the song started up again, the seventy-five-year-old reverend, as skinny as a fence post, danced across the oriental carpet with her head thrown back and her fists pumping the air. The detectives, those with a good sense of humor, anyway, sang along with the fish. The commissioner didn't seem to enjoy it that much when we were finally let into the office and the reverend made her presentation, but the rest of us had a good time. I took the Brooklyn Bridge home that day, laughing all the way across, so that anyone passing me would have thought I was mad. I kept repeating to myself, *Someone* pays *me to do this?* So I have found a way to enter in, after all.

There is a quote that hangs on my computer—I no longer know where I got it, or who it's from, but it reads: "No interesting project can be embarked on without fear. I shall be scared to death half the time." The wisdom and encouragement I draw from that quote seems to me to come straight out of what happened to me during my teenage years.

As I blindly circled the New Haven green that day, I told myself to keep walking—walking out of that town, into the future. What I didn't know then, but surely know now, is that my future had already begun. I'd stepped straight into it one night in March, an ice-cold night when I was fifteen.

Acknowledgments

I always knew I would write this story someday, but without the prodding and encouragement from Sandy Close and Richard Rodriguez of Pacific News Service that someday may have been many years from now. Thanks to both of them and Mark Schurmann for their wise friendship throughout my writing life.

I must thank *Harper's Magazine* for publishing the article that was the genesis for this book; to Colin Harrison for taking me into *Harper's*, Lewis Lapham for his gallant support, and my editor, the tough-minded and loyal Ellen Rosenbush, most of all. A special thanks to my former editors at *The Village Voice*, Ellen Willis, Amy Virshup, and John Larsen, for opening the door to writing for me, and then letting me run loose. They knew how to support a writer's obsessions but never her flaws. And to *Vibe* magazine for their continued support.

To my fellow writers, all of them, but specifically in this case to Donna Gaines and Ruben Martinez—thanks for many late-night conversations about the pitfalls and joys of the writing life; i.e., the tricks of the trade. And my thanks to James McGoon, Lee Gershuny, Sylvia DeAngelis, Peter Burnett, Joe Rodriguez, and Barbara O'Dair, who have helped me feel less alone and made me a braver person. Lt. Joseph Heffernan and Mauricio Mule have each in their own way helped me to remember the past more precisely, and more joyfully.

To my sister Beth Ann Dobie and my friend Marisa

Steffers, my undying gratitude and deep respect for their close, thoughtful reading of the manuscript.

My love and thanks go out to my aunt, Barbara Dobie, and my father and mother, for digging through many old photographs and supporting a project that I can only imagine must be the cause of some pain.

To my siblings, Michael, Bill, Cindy, Beth, and Stephen—you are my first tribe, and writing about our early years was a great joy. Their children, my nieces and nephew, Cara, Tracy, Jamie, Corissa, Alana, Nicholas, and Julia have renewed my sense of family. As three-year-old Alana once put it, proudly, "These are my people." They are. And so are my "street godchildren," especially Ahmalh Mendelsohn.

I can hardly offer enough praise to the three women who made this book happen. My agent, Kris Dahl, who stuck by me through thick and thin, who knew when "I wasn't waving / I was drowning," to quote Stevie Smith, and dove in to save me. And she made it all look easy. Simply put, this book would not have seen the light of day if it weren't for her. Susan Kamil has made me feel truly lucky; she possesses editorial brilliance and plain old human caring in equal measure. Thank you for taking this book under your wing, and making me a better writer. And to my co-pilot on this journey, Beth Rashbaum, the deepest respect and love. It's a rare editor who can honor and protect the writer's voice while also remaining a reader who requires clarity and honesty from that writer. Beth's acuity and sensitivity and hard work have made this a far better book than it would've been if I'd been left to my own devices. And, never was the editing process more memorable or fun. This time around, I was hardly the only girl in the car.

And a great big kiss and hug to the three people who have lived with this book more thoroughly (and patiently and lovingly) than anyone else—my sister Cindy, my dearest friend Chris Waters and, of course, James Hamilton.

About the Author

KATHY DOBIE has written for *Harper's, The Village Voice, Vibe, Salon, Pacific News Service,* and a number of other publications. She lives in Brooklyn, New York.